Visitors to the Inner Earth

Visitors to the Inner Earth

by Professor Solomon

Illustrated by Steve Solomon

Top Hat Press
BALTIMORE

Copyright © 2011 by Top Hat Press

All rights reserved

ISBN 978-0-912509-10-5

http://www.professorsolomon.com

Top Hat Press
Baltimore, Maryland

CONTENTS

1. Enkidu 1
2. Orpheus 5
3. Æneas 13
4. Apollonius of Tyana. 25
5. King Herla 39
6. Cuchulain. 44
7. Elidore 49
8. Sir Owen. 53
9. Thomas the Rhymer 59
10. Paiute Chief 65
11. Robert Kirk 70
12. Hans Dietrich. 77
13. Reuben 84
14. Captain Seaborn 91
15. Saint-Yves d'Alveydre. 123
16. Olaf Jansen. 135
17. Morgan 141
18. Doreal 156
19. Guy Ballard. 162
20. Richard Shaver. 188
21. Margaret Rogers 227
22. Lobsang Rampa. 237
23. Walter Siegmeister 253
24. Dianne Robbins 265
25. Rodney Cluff 272
    Appendix 1: How to Visit the Inner Earth. . . 277
    Appendix 2: Reactions to *Etidorhpa* 285
    Appendix 3: Found Manuscripts 288

The Inner Earth—Has It Been Visited?

Works of fiction that describe visits to the Inner Earth are familiar to readers: Dante's *Inferno*; Jules Verne's *Journey to the Center of the Earth*; Lewis Carroll's *Alice in Wonderland*; Abraham Merritt's *The Moon Pool*; the Pellucidar novels of Edgar Rice Burroughs (*Tarzan at the Earth's Core*, etc.). Less familiar (though no less readable) are the alleged FACTUAL ACCOUNTS of such visits.

This book is about individuals who actually visited the Inner Earth—or so it was claimed. Their stories are taken from a variety of sources: ancient poems, medieval chronicles, New Age pamphlets, pulp magazines, folklore studies, self-published accounts.

Did they in fact make these visits to the Earth's interior, either physically (entering at a cave, or a fairy hill, or the North Polar opening), or else spiritually (a journey of the soul)? So we are told. Read on, and judge for yourself.

1.
Enkidu

THE EARLIEST REPORT OF A VISIT TO THE INNER EARTH is found in the *Epic of Gilgamesh*. This ancient poem, lost for centuries, was recovered in the ruins of Nineveh. It is perhaps the oldest literary work in existence.*

The *Epic of Gilgamesh* is the story of a historical figure: Gilgamesh, son of Lugalbanda. This Sumerian ruled the city of Uruk around 2500 B.C. The fifth king of Uruk, Gilgamesh built the formidable walls that surrounded the city. He also built the Temple of Ishtar, a ziggurat that towered over the mud-brick houses and narrow lanes of Uruk.

Neither walls nor temple would endure as a monument to the king. His fame was preserved, however, by the *Epic of Gilgamesh*. The poem tells of Gilgamesh's friendship with a wild man. And it includes an account of that friend's visit to the Netherworld.

---

* In 1853 Hormuzd Rassam—an archaeologist digging in Nineveh—unearthed the library of King Ashurbanipal. It consisted of tens of thousands of inscribed clay tablets. The tablets were shipped to London and deposited in the British Museum.

Twenty years later, George Smith—an assistant curator sifting through the tablets—came upon the Gilgamesh poem. He deciphered the cuneiform inscriptions and published a translation.

The inscriptions were the work of an Assyrian scribe. But the poem itself had been composed half a millennium earlier, by a Babylonian priest named Sin-liqe-unninni. (His name meant "O moon god, hear my prayer!") Sin-liqe-unninni had based his work on an earlier Babylonian poem, which in turn had been based on a series of Sumerian tales.

And whence those tales? Were they based on fact? Quite possibly. For according to the poem, King Gilgamesh had composed an account of his life; inscribed it on a tablet of lapis lazuli; and incorporated the tablet into the city wall, to commemorate his rule.

The wild man was Enkidu (IN-ka-doo), a rough, unruly fellow who had been raised by gazelles. Enkidu was generally to be found in their company, roaming the grasslands or drinking at water holes. But one afternoon he showed up in Uruk; wrestled with Gilgamesh; and became the king's close friend and sidekick. Together, they embarked upon a series of adventures (most notably, the slaying of the ogre who guarded the Cedar Forest).

One day, in the main square of Uruk, they were competing in a ball game—a croquetlike sport that was played piggyback. Gilgamesh was mounted on Enkidu's back, wielding the mallet. The pair lurched about as the game grew heated. Suddenly the ball, along with their mallet, fell into a hole and plummeted into the Netherworld—the Land of No Return—*the abode of the dead.*

Gilgamesh wept at the loss. For the ball and mallet had been carved from a special tree: one that belonged to the goddess Ishtar. Moved by his tears, Enkidu offered to descend into the Netherworld and retrieve the fallen items.

Enkidu prepared for his descent into that gloomy place. And Gilgamesh warned him about the Netherworld. As a visitor, he must be respectful to its inhabitants, the shades of the dead. He must maintain a grave demeanor. And he must not attract attention to himself, by either his actions or appearance. *The shades must not be alerted to the fact that he was alive.* Should he fail to heed these warnings, Enkidu would be seized by the shades and permanently detained.

Enkidu promised to heed the warnings. And he lowered himself into the hole and descended into the Netherworld.

Arriving there and searching for the ball and mallet, he passed among the shades of the dead. But Enkidu ignored the warnings and acted foolishly—talking with the shades, laughing loudly, and neglecting to don a shroud. Recognized as an intruder, he was taken captive.

His cries of distress rose to the surface. Gilgamesh became aware of Enkidu's predicament. And he appealed to the gods for help. He pointed out that his friend had not died, and therefore did not belong among the dead. The

sun god agreed, and helped Enkidu to free himself from the shades.

It was with a cry of relief that Enkidu emerged from the hole. With copious tears he embraced Gilgamesh. And Gilgamesh chided him for ignoring the warnings.

"At least I learned an important lesson," said Enkidu.

"What was that?"

"Never visit a place known as the Land of No Return!"

Gilgamesh questioned him about the Netherworld. How did different individuals fare in the afterlife? Were conditions the same for everyone? Did a king maintain his privileged status?

Enkidu thought back to his conversations with the shades. And he replied that a man fared according to his past behavior—*and according to the funerary rites of his sons.*

"Their remembrance offerings of food and water are critical," said Enkidu. "The more offerings in your behalf, the more agreeable your existence in the Netherworld. A shade who receives daily offerings from his sons? He will sit in the company of the gods, dine well, and listen to soothing music."

"And a shade who receives no daily offerings?"

"He eats scraps and crumbs that are tossed to him."

Gilgamesh thought about his late father, Lugalbanda, who had preceded him on the throne. And he resolved to be diligent in making offerings—that the shade of his father might thrive in the Netherworld.*

---

* Gilgamesh's resolution was not wholly altruistic. It was believed that the good fortune of the living was dependent upon the well-being of their ancestors in the afterlife—a well-being that arose from dutiful veneration.

2.
Orpheus

THERE FLOURISHED IN THE GRÆCO-ROMAN WORLD AN assortment of cults known as the Mystery Religions. Among them were the Eleusinian Mysteries, the Dionysian Mysteries, and the Mithraic Mysteries. Their doctrines and rites were secret, revealed only to initiates. And the most secret of these cults? The Orphic Mysteries, or Orphism.

Due to its secrecy, our knowledge of Orphism is limited. We know that its devotees led an ascetic life, and sought personal salvation. We know that their prime goal involved the afterlife: by embracing Orphism, they hoped to escape the cycle of reincarnation and achieve communion with the gods. And we know that they worshipped the chthonian, or subterranean, gods—deities whose home was Hades rather than Mount Olympus.

In addition, we have some knowledge of the founder of the cult: a musician named Orpheus. His descent into Hades, of course, is a familiar tale in Greek mythology, retold by both Virgil (in the *Georgics*) and Ovid (in the *Metamorphoses*). But what more is known of the life of Orpheus? And what is the real story of his descent into Hades?

Orpheus was born in Thrace (according to a brief biography by Diodorus Siculus, the first century B.C. historian); his father was King Oeagrus. From an early age he showed a gift for music and poetry. With his lyre he roamed the hills of Thrace, singing of things divine. His music was said to charm men and beasts alike. (Even trees, it was claimed, swayed to his music!) And at some point he traveled to Egypt. There he acquired the mystic knowledge that would form the basis of his own teachings.*

---

* It has been alleged (by Aristotle and others) that accounts of his life are fictional, and that Orpheus was purely a mythological

Such was his renown as a musician that Orpheus was asked to join the Argonauts—the Greek heroes who sailed in search of the Golden Fleece. (For this chapter in his life, our source is the *Argonautica* of Apollonius of Rhodes.) He sang the dedication hymn at the launching of the *Argo*. And as its *keleustes*, he set the rowing tempo, spurring his shipmates on with his melodious voice. But the magic of his song proved useful in other ways. With music he calmed the sea; settled a quarrel; stilled the Clashing Rocks; drowned out the song of the Sirens; and lulled into sleep the dragon that guarded the Golden Fleece. Thanks to Orpheus and his lyre, the Argonauts were successful in their quest.

But upon his return to Thrace, the musician was dealt a cruel blow by the gods. He fell in love with a nymph named Eurydice. But on their wedding day, Eurydice—dancing in the grass with her bridesmaids—was bit by a snake and died.

Grief-stricken, Orpheus languished on a lonely beach, singing dirges to the waves. But finally he decided to visit a necromancer.*

---

figure. (One encyclopedia refers to him as "the personification of a tendency.") But W. K. C. Guthrie, the leading scholar of Orphism, has argued otherwise. "In favour of his historical existence," says Guthrie, "is his individuality." And Jane Harrison, in her *Prolegomena to the Study of Greek Religion,* deems him to have been "an actual person," who won fame as "a mighty singer, a prophet and a teacher, bringing with him a new religion."

It has also been alleged that the Orphic cult had its beginnings in the sixth century B.C.—long after Orpheus was supposed to have lived—and could not therefore have been founded by him. In any case, Orpheus (assuming that he existed) either originated the cult or else inspired it.

* Necromancers were found throughout the ancient world. (For example, there was the Witch of Endor, whom King Saul hired to conjure up the ghost of the prophet Samuel.) Their job was to consult with the spirits of the dead, for divination and other purposes. Usually, they did this by summoning the spirit into the realm of the living. But sometimes a necromancer would descend

The necromancer lived in a cave near the town of Ephyra. Orpheus went to her and begged to be reunited with his bride. The necromancer agreed to assist him, for a fee. Seating him in the rear of the cave, she performed a sacrifice; gave him a potion to drink; and chanted spells. Her voice echoed from the stone walls; her eyes glinted in the torchlight.

Finally, she pointed to a portal. "That is the entrance to the Underworld," she said. "Descend to Hades, seek out Eurydice, and bring her back with you!"

The potion had induced in Orpheus a sleeplike trance. Now he felt himself separating from his body. It slumped to the ground. And leaving it behind, he stepped through the portal.

Before him was a stairway, steep and luminescent. Orpheus started down it. And he descended into the depths of the earth.

●

At the bottom of the stairway Orpheus passed through another portal. He emerged into a wasteland—a desolate landscape of strewn rocks and stunted trees. Before him flowed the river Acheron. All was dark, silent, and devoid of life.

He approached a boat that was moored on the river. On the boat sat Charon, the ferryman of the dead.*

---

into Hades and do his consulting there (a practice the Greeks called *katabasis*).

Practitioners of necromancy are still to be found: old-fashioned shamans in tribal societies, and newfangled channelers in our own. The channeler may set up shop in a dimly-lit parlor instead of a cave; murmur New Age platitudes instead of spells; and employ a Ouija board. But the goal is the same: consultation with the departed.

* Charon (KAIR-on) is a psychopomp—an otherworldly figure who conducts souls into the afterlife. *The Book of King Solomon* (purportedly an ancient chronicle) offers a glimpse into the work-

Charon looked at Orpheus and shook his head. The living, he said, were not permitted to cross over into Hades. But then Orpheus sang; and his music charmed the ferryman. Waving him aboard, Charon transported him to the opposite bank.

There waited Cerberus, the watchdog of Hades. His three heads barked furiously at the visitor. But again Orpheus sang and was allowed to pass. And still singing, he drew near to the palace of Hades.*

The singing could be heard throughout the Underworld. Such was its power that Sisyphus—about to roll his rock up the mountain—instead sat down on it and listened. Tantalus—reaching for the grapes that kept retreating—shifted his attention to the music. And drawn by the music were the shades of the dead. Hundreds of them flitted about Orpheus, murmuring eerily.†

Entering the palace, Orpheus approached Pluto and Persephone on their ebony thrones. The rulers of Hades

---

day of one such figure: the Angel of Death. Taking a break from his grim rounds, the Angel of Death has stopped in a tavern for a beer. One of the regulars sidles up to him and asks how many souls he gathers in a typical day.

"'A hundred or so.'

"'How far do you range? Do you operate outside Israel?'

"'Presently, no, I gather only Israelites. Other nations have their own psychopomps.'

"'Psychopomps?'

"'That's what we call ourselves. Skilled professionals who conduct souls to a realm of the dead. The Greeks, for example, have Charon the Ferryman. Good friend of mine, by the way.'"

(My translation of *The Book of King Solomon* is available from Top Hat Press.)

* His frequent singing made Orpheus the perfect subject for one of the earliest operas: Monteverdi's *L'Orfeo* (1607).

† Virgil describes them as *"quam multa in foliis avium se milia condunt"*—"like a multitude of birds gathering in the foliage of a tree."

glowered at him. Undaunted, he greeted them.*

Pluto asked him what he wanted. And Orpheus begged that Eurydice's fate be reversed. Let her return to the land of the living, he pleaded.

At first the rulers of Hades refused his request. But then Orpheus sang; and their hearts were softened. It was agreed that Eurydice could return with him—on one condition. She was to follow behind Orpheus. And he must refrain from looking back at her until they reached the upper world. If he did look back, her reprieve would be annulled.

Eurydice was summoned. The situation was explained to her. And she followed Orpheus—his gaze fixed straight ahead—out of the palace.

The reunited couple approached the river. Charon was dozing on his boat and had to be roused. His eyes widened in astonishment at the sight of Eurydice—a resident of Hades, allowed to leave! But he ferried them across.

And the two lovers, in single file, climbed the stairway toward the land of the living. Their faces were bright with joy; but their eyes could not yet meet—their lips could not yet touch. Above them a dim light appeared; and they quickened their pace on the stairs.

Orpheus reached the portal and stepped through it. He was back the cave. With a cry of exultation, he turned and looked at his beloved.

And Eurydice began to fade away. For she had yet to reach the portal—and Orpheus had violated the condition of her release.

"Farewell," said Eurydice. And with a heartbroken cry, she vanished.

Orpheus darted forward, grasped at empty air, and realized what had happened.

---

* According to Ovid, he tactfully began: *"O positi sub terra numina mundi, in quem reccidimus, quicquid mortale creamur"*— "O gods of the Underworld, to whom all mortals must eventually come."

Now twice bereft, he returned to his body. And slumped on the floor of the cave, he sobbed.

•

Why, it may be wondered, did Orpheus look back? Why did he violate the prohibition, thus losing Eurydice for a second time? Various explanations have been offered:

1. In his exultation he forgot about the condition that

had been imposed.

2. Having himself reached the upper world, he assumed he was free to look at her.
3. He was assailed by a sudden doubt—that she was no longer behind him.
4. He feared that she might falter at the last moment and need his help.
5. The action was instinctive—he looked back before he could stop himself.

Any of the above might explain his blunder. But did that blunder really undo their reunion? Or had reunion been a false hope from the start?

According to Phædrus (quoted by Plato in the *Symposium*), the latter was the case. Phædrus argues that Eurydice was a mere shade—a ghost whom the gods had no intention of restoring to life. They were offering a false hope to Orpheus, to chastise him for his lack of courage. He wished to rejoin his beloved? He should have done so in the only way possible—*by dying as she had.*

And Phædrus has a point. For if Eurydice was a shade, she *had* to return to Hades—whether Orpheus looked back or not. Their reunion, in the land of the living, was never a possibility.

●

Orpheus still had years of life before him. It was during those years that he apparently founded Orphism—a cult based on his descent into Hades, and on the knowledge he had acquired in Egypt. But he also wandered about Thrace, singing mournful songs.*

---

* Orpheus is still remembered in his homeland. According to the classicist J. G. Frazer:
"In the popular songs of the modern Bulgarians there is said to be a musician named Orfen, who sings and plays so sweetly that the birds and ravenous beasts come from the mountains to hear

And the death of Orpheus?

In the second century A.D., a Greek named Pausanias traveled about the country, taking notes for a guidebook he planned to write. In the course of his travels, he visited the town of Dium. There he was shown a monument: a pillar surmounted with an urn. The urn, he was informed by locals, contained the bones of Orpheus.

And Pausanias was told two versions of the musician's death. In one, Orpheus was slain by a group of angry women, whose husbands had left them to join his cult. In the other, he was struck by lightning—punishment from the gods for revealing their secrets.

But the death of Orpheus, whatever its circumstances, does not conclude his tale. Ovid describes what happened next:

> *Umbra subit terras, et quae loca viderat ante,*
> *cuncta recognoscit quaerensque per arva piorum*
> *invenit Eurydicen cupidisque amplectitur ulnis;*
> *hic modo coniunctis spatiantur passibus ambo,*
> *nunc praecedentem sequitur, nunc praevius anteit*
> *Eurydicenque suam, iam tuto, respicit Orpheus.*

> The singer's soul beneath the earth did speed
> And recognized where once he'd come to plead.
> But now straight to Elysium he raced
> And found Eurydice. The two embraced.
> There now they stroll, fond lovers side by side,
> The sweet-tongued poet and his patient bride.
> Or sometimes she walks first, or sometimes he—
> Who may look back now at fair Eurydice!

---

him. Hence it has been conjectured that this Orfen is Orpheus, and it is held by some that the present Bulgarian inhabitants of the Rhodope mountains are descendants of the ancient Thracians, who, though they have been affected by Slavonic influence, have preserved the poetical traditions, mythology, and religious customs of their ancestors."

3.
Æneas

A FEW MILES FROM NAPLES, THE DARK WATERS OF LAKE Avernus—Lago d'Averno—draw a modest number of tourists. The lake's claim to fame? The ancient Romans deemed it to be an entrance to the Underworld. Thomas Bulfinch, in *The Age of Fable,* describes it thus:

> The region where Virgil locates the entrance to this abode [the abode of the dead] is perhaps the most strikingly adapted to excite ideas of the terrific and preternatural of any on the face of the earth. It is the volcanic region near Vesuvius, where the whole country is cleft with chasms, from which sulphurous flames rise, while the ground is shaken with pent-up vapours, and mysterious sounds issue from the bowels of the earth. The lake Avernus is supposed to fill the crater of an extinct volcano. It is circular, half a mile wide, and very deep, surrounded by high banks, which in Virgil's time were covered with a gloomy forest. Mephitic vapours rise from its waters, so that no life is found on its banks, and no birds fly over it. Here, according to the poet, was the cave which afforded access to the infernal regions, and here Æneas offered sacrifices to the infernal deities, Proserpine, Hecate, and the Furies.*

Tourists may stroll along the lake and take in its ambience. And they may visit that cave that led to the Underworld. (It is located about 200 meters to the left of the parking area.) A caretaker gives informal tours of the cave, identifying it as the "Grotta della Sibilla"—the Grotto

---

* Lake Avernus (from *aornos* or "birdless") is one of dozens of inactive volcanos in the region. At another, the Solfatara, clouds of steam bellow from the earth, mud boils, and a sulfurous odor fills the air; and it is to that infernal landscape that most tourists go, rather than to the serene, if mildly spectral, Avernus.

of the Sibyl. For it was here, he explains, that dwelt the Cumæn Sibyl.

And who was the Cumæn Sibyl? She was the soothsayer—the chief prophetess—of the Romans. Over the course of a millennium, a succession of women occupied the position. Their qualification for the job? The ability to enter into a trance, receive inspiration from Apollo, and utter prophecies.

The caretaker does not wish to confuse his listeners. So he does not mention the other Grotto of the Sibyl, about a mile away. But it too is worth visiting. The second cave is man-made—carved into a hillside near the ruins of Cumæ—and impressive. A long passageway, trapezoidal in shape, leads to an Inner Sanctum. It was there that the Sibyl, seated on a throne and flanked by a pair of hounds, chanted her oracles. (The dog-ties are still visible in the wall.) This improved Grotto was her home from the fourth century B.C. onward. Before that, according to the historian Strabo, she dwelt in the cave by the lake.

But the Sibyl was not only a prophetess. She was also a necromancer—a medium who communicated with the dead. And it was a desire for such communication that brought, to her doorstep one morning, Æneas, prince of Troy.

•

The Trojan War had ended, with the defeat of the Trojans and the burning of Troy. But one of their chief warriors had managed to escape: Æneas, a cousin of King Priam. As a reward for his piety, the gods had allowed him to survive; and Æneas—along with hundreds of his countrymen, including his elderly father, Anchises, whom he had carried on his back—had fled the burning city.

These Trojans fled to the port of Antandros; assembled a fleet of ships; and, with Æneas as their leader, sailed off. During the next few years they made attempts to settle elsewhere: in Thrace, and on the islands of Delos and Crete. But the attempts failed; and the refugees kept moving on.

ÆNEAS

They stopped briefly at Buthrotum; and its king uttered a prophecy: "You will settle in Italy—such is the will of the gods. There you will found a city that will achieve greatness. And the descendants of Æneas will rule this city."

Perhaps the king simply hoped to keep them moving. But heedful of his prophecy, the Trojans headed for Italy. Their route took them through the strait of Messia, with its deadly whirlpool. And they made a stopover on Sicily (where they spotted a Cyclops). During the stopover Anchises died; and Æneas buried his father on the island.

But then came an abrupt change of course. As the Trojans were leaving Sicily, a storm arose. (Had they offended Neptune in some way?) Their ships were driven across the sea, and blown ashore near Carthage.

The queen of Carthage was a young and attractive widow named Dido. She welcomed the Trojans to her city, and held a banquet in honor of Æneas. By the end of the meal, she had fallen in love with him. But Dido struggled with these feelings. For she had vowed to remain faithful to the memory of her late husband.

Soon after the banquet, Æneas and Dido went hunting together. It began to rain; and the pair took shelter in a cave. Stranded there for hours, they wound up making love.

For several months they lived together as lovers. Finally, Dido made a proposal to Æneas. His people would settle in Carthage, alongside hers. And he and she would rule jointly.

Æneas seriously considered the proposal. For he had become enamored with the queen; and his countrymen needed a home. But as he slept one night, he was visited by Mercury. The messenger of the gods reminded him of his destiny. Æneas was to found a city in Italy—a city that would achieve greatness. "O Trojan, sail on!" urged Mercury.

Æneas agonized—and decided to sail on. As much as he wished to remain with her, he would have to leave Dido. Destiny and the gods were calling. Yet he could not bring himself to inform her of his decision. So in secret, he readied the Trojan ships for departure.

Dido discovered his plan, and berated him—cajoled him—pleaded with him. But Æneas insisted that he had no choice. And with his countrymen, he departed.

As they sailed away, Æneas looked back to the shore and saw the smoke from a funeral pyre. He feared the worst; and his fears (as he later learned) were justified. For Dido—devastated by his departure—had taken her own life.

With his fleet of ships, Æneas sailed towards Italy. On the way he stopped at Sicily, to perform funeral rites in memory of his father. And the ghost of his father appeared to him in a dream.

"Come visit me in the land of the dead," said Anchises.

"But how shall I get there?" asked Æneas.

"Seek out the Sibyl at Lake Avernus. She will conduct you to the Underworld."

Æneas left Sicily with his fleet, and sailed along the west coast of Italy. He was looking for a place to settle—and for Lake Avernus.

•

Æneas stood outside the cave. His sword and helmet glinted in the sun. "Hello?" he called out.

A local had given him directions. And he had hiked up from the beach and followed a path through the woods. At the lake he had turned left, as instructed, and walked along the shore. And there it was—the cave of the Sibyl.

His greeting was answered with silence. The place seemed deserted. There was not a sound—not even the singing of birds nor the humming of insects.

Then an elderly woman emerged from the cave. The Sibyl was a crone—bent, wizened, and disheveled. She stared at him and cackled.*

---

* How elderly was the Sibyl? During their return from Hades, she would tell Æneas the following story:

As a young neophyte, Deiphobe (her given name) had caught the eye of Apollo; and the god had sought to seduce her. To ingratiate himself, he had offered her any gift she desired. Deiphobe

ÆNEAS

Æneas started to introduce himself. But the Sibyl cut him short—his identity was known to her. And she began to prophesy. The Trojans, she said, would encounter hardships as they sought to establish a new home. They would have to fight for possession of the land. And Æneas would be called upon to be brave and stalwart.

Æneas thanked the Sibyl for her prophecies (obvious though they were). And he explained his purpose in seeking her out. He wished to visit his father in Hades. Would she take him there?

To his surprise, the Sibyl readily agreed—with two conditions. First, he was to return to his ship and sacrifice to Persephone. For the queen of Hades must be acknowledged with an offering. Secondly, he was to acquire the Golden Bough. It would serve as his passport to the Underworld.*

---

had pointed to a small heap of sand and said: "I wish to live for as many years as there are grains of sand in that heap." Apollo had granted her wish—a thousand years of life! But alas, she had neglected to ask that they be years of *youth*. Thus, as the years passed, she became increasingly cronish in appearance. She was now 700 years old.

"Who, seeing me today," she would lament to Æneas, "would think that a god once found me lovely?"

* Here's Virgil on the Golden Bough:

> *latet arbore opaca*
> *aureus et foliis et lento vimine ramus,*
> *Iunoni infernae dictus sacer; hunc tegit omnis*
> *lucus et obscuris claudunt convallibus umbrae.*
> *sed non ante datur telluris operta subire,*
> *auricomos quam qui decerpserit arbore fetus.*
> *hoc sibi pulchra suum ferri Proserpina munus*
> *instituit*

Amidst the branches of a shady tree
There grows a bough that's hidden, hard to see,
With leaves and stem of gold. This Golden Bough
The queen of Hades with holiness did endow,
But did conceal it in a forest deep

Æneas returned to his ship and performed the sacrifice. Then, rejoining the Sibyl, he followed her into the forest. "You're supposed to find it yourself," she said. "But I'll take you to it."

The Sibyl led him to the Golden Bough, which was growing on an oak, and told him to break it off. But only if he was worthy, she said, would he be able to do so.

Æneas grasped the Golden Bough and broke it off. The Sibyl purred with satisfaction and led him back to the cave. There she sat him down on a stool; lit the contents of a tripod; and instructed him to inhale the fumes. Æneas did so (as did the Sibyl) and fell into a trance.

"Follow me," she said. "The gate to the land of the dead is always open. And getting to that land is easy. What's not so easy is getting back—but we'll worry about that later."

She hobbled to the rear of the cave. Æneas rose from the stool—and from his inert body—and followed after her. They passed through a portal, stepped onto a stairway, and descended into the earth.

•

The river Acheron lay before them. The Sibyl hobbled towards it, with Æneas close behind her. His head was still spinning—from the monstrous forms they had encountered upon emerging into the Underworld. Gorgons and harpies had swirled about them, along with the specters of such ills as War and Famine and Disease. Trembling with terror, Æneas had reached for his sword. But the Sibyl had stayed his hand. She had assured him that these were but illusions—apparitions that greeted new arrivals. "Ignore them. And let's get moving—your time with your father

---

That shadows might its gleam a secret keep.
And whosoe'er would to that realm descend
That lies within the earth, at Life's dark end,
Must find this branch and pluck it from the tree
And bring as gift unto Persephone.

will be limited."

Charon was loading some shades into his boat. As the two visitors approached, he shook his head and waved them off. "The living may not cross over into Hades," he said. "Read the sign."

"This is Æneas, prince of Troy," said the Sibyl. "He has come at the behest of his late father. And take a look at this." She held up the Golden Bough.

The ferryman's mouth fell open. And he allowed them into the boat.

He punted the boat across the river. No sooner had it reached the opposite bank than the shades disembarked and passed into Hades—on their way to rewards or punishments.

But Cerberus was barking at Æneas and the Sibyl. The Sibyl tossed him a morsel; and the three heads fought for it. One gobbled it down; and the watchdog sank into a stupor.

"Drugged," said the Sibyl with a wink. And she led Æneas into Hades.

They passed through a forest that bordered the river. The forest was the dwelling place, said the Sibyl, of innocent souls who had died prematurely. Among them were children, she said—"Flowers plucked from life before they could bud!" Here too were men executed for crimes they had not committed.

And the Sibyl pointed out a grove of myrtle trees. It was known as the Grove of Grief, she told Æneas. Disappointed lovers roamed its paths—unhappy souls who had died from the pangs of unrequited love. Yet not even death could alleviate their grief. "These unfortunates water the grove with their tears," said the Sibyl.

Suddenly Æneas stopped and stared. Walking in the grove was a young woman in royal garb.

"Dido!" he cried.

Indeed it was she. For the queen of Carthage halted at the sound of her name.

"Dido!"

But she would not acknowledge him. Dido bowed her head and gazed at the ground.

"Alas," said Æneas, tears welling in his eyes. "It was true then—that funeral pyre was yours. Was I the cause of your death? Forgive me, my love! I parted from you unwillingly—I had no choice! The gods had decreed that I sail on to Italy. Did I dare oppose the will of the gods? Shirk my duty? Argue with my destiny? Yet had I known that your grief would be so profound—O Dido, Dido, my love!"

As he addressed her, Dido had remained silent and expressionless. She had looked down at the ground, refusing to

acknowledge his presence. Now she turned and began to walk away.

"Stay, don't flee," he pleaded. "I beg of you, *forgive me!*"

But Dido disappeared into the grove. Æneas sank to his knees and wept.

The Sibyl reminded him that their time was limited. With a moan of sorrow, Æneas stood up. And the two resumed their journey.

Emerging from the forest, they came to a fork in the road. One way led to Tartarus, indicated a signpost; the other, to Elysium. The fortress of Tartarus could be seen in the distance. It was surrounded by high walls and a river of lava. From within arose a terrible din—the cracking of whips, the clanging of chains, cries and groans. The wicked were receiving their due, said the Sibyl. And she named the crimes for which they were being punished.

"Your father, thankfully, is in Elysium—the home of the blest."

They set off in that direction. Along the way they stopped at the entrance to the palace of Hades, and left the Golden Bough there—as a gift for Persephone. And continuing on, they entered Elysium.

They found Anchises in a meadow. Æneas ran up to his father and sought to embrace him. But they passed through one another. (Living souls and shades are of different densities.) So instead of embracing, they exchanged looks of joy. "You've come at last," said Anchises. "I knew you would."

He led his son on a tour of Elysium. They strolled through fragrant fields and leafy groves. Everywhere were shades. Clad in white robes, the shades were picnicking, tossing balls, reciting poetry, singing and dancing. An appreciative crowd had gathered around Orpheus, who was playing his lyre. And on every brow was a white headband—the badge of the blest.

A number of shades were lined up at a river. Æneas asked why.

"That is Lethe, the river of forgetfulness," said Anchises. "If you need to reincarnate, you drink of its waters—to erase your memories."

Anchises led his son to a bocce-ball court. A game was in progress; and a group of shades—some in armor, others in togas—had gathered to watch.

"This is why I asked you to visit," said Anchises. "I wanted you to behold these men."

"Are they my ancestors?"

"No, your descendants! For you shall engender a noble line. And they shall establish a city—a city that shall achieve greatness and bring order to the world. *The city of Rome!*

"You see that fellow with the spear? That's Romulus, the founder of the city. Beside him is Tullus, an early king. And he with the plume on his helmet? That's Fabius Maximus, the general who will outwit Hannibal. Those two fellows sipping on nectar? The Gracchi brothers, civic reformers. And Cato and Pompey and Scipio Africanus. And over there by the refreshment stand—Julius Cæsar, conqueror of Gaul. And Augustus Cæsar, the emperor who will preside over Rome's most glorious era.

"These are the heroes who will distinguish your lineage. *And who will honor you as the founder of their nation. For such is your destiny.*

"Go now, my son—beach your ships in Italy and find a home for our people. Carry an olive branch, yet gird yourself for war. And may the gods bestir themselves in your behalf."

"I shall do so, father," said Æneas. "That *your* lineage may be distinguished."

The Sibyl tapped him on the shoulder. "Our time here is nearly up," she said.

Father and son sought to embrace; but again they passed through one another. So they parted instead with salutes of farewell.

"Let us return to the land of the living," said the Sibyl. And she added with a cackle: "If we can find our way back!"*

---

* Our main sources for the life of Æneas are the poets Virgil and Ovid. Virgil, of course, is the author of the *Æneid*—the epic that recounts his travels and tribulations. And Virgil's own sources? The *Iliad*; the historical writings of Hellanicus; and the chronicles of Nævius and Ennius. So the *Æneid* may possess a degree of historical accuracy.

To be sure, Virgil commits a number of anachronisms. For instance, he has Æneas consult the Sibyl in the man-made grotto at Cumæ—not built until centuries later—rather than in the cave at Lake Avernus. And his Trojans conduct themselves like Romans. But Virgil's aim was to inspire, not inform. The *Æneid* is a patriotic epic. It seeks to glorify Rome, in the person of a heroic ancestor.

Central to the *Æneid* is the Roman virtue of *pietas*, of which Æneas is the embodiment. *Pietas* may be translated as "devotion to duty"—duty to family, to homeland, and to the gods. Thus, his leaving Dido, in order to pursue his destiny, is seen as praiseworthy. Æneas is acting dutifully. (When he tries to explain this to Dido, she walks away in stony silence. Who can blame her?)

The *Æneid* is the national epic of Rome—the expression of her fundamental values, such as valor and patriotism. Yet its most poignant scenes take place in Hades. Life attains its fullest meaning, Virgil may be saying, only when it confronts the realities of death.

4.
Apollonius of Tyana

APOLLONIUS OF TYANA IS VIRTUALLY UNKNOWN TODAY. Yet according to G. R. S. Mead, his biographer, "Apollonius of Tyana was the most famous philosopher of the Græco-Roman world of the first century." During a busy and influential lifetime, Apollonius was a traveler (ranging as far as India); an advisor to emperors; a sage with disciples; an author (none of whose works have survived); a healer; and a reformer who, says Mead, "devoted the major part of his long life to the purification of the many cults of the Empire and to the instruction of the ministers and priests of its religions."*

He was also a visitor to the Inner Earth. For while in India, Apollonius descended to the Abode of the Wise Men and studied there.

Apollonius was born to a wealthy family in Tyana, a town in Cappadocia (a Greek-speaking region of Asia Minor, in what is now central Turkey). A precocious child, he was educated initially by learned tutors. Then, at the age of fourteen, he was sent to study in nearby Tarsus. (Saul of Tarsus—the future Saint Paul—may have been around at the time.) But a year later Apollonius moved on to Ægeæ, a seaport in Cilicia, to study at the local temple of Asclepius.†

---

* G. R. S. Mead—private secretary to Madame Blavatsky and editor of *The Theosophical Review*—was the author of *Apollonius of Tyana: The Philosopher-Reformer of the First Century A.D.* (1901).

† Scattered throughout the Græco-Roman world, the temples of Asclepius (known as *asclepieia*) were the hospitals of their day. An afflicted person would make a pilgrimage to one of these temples. There he would pray and sacrifice to Asclepius, the god of healing. He would then spend a night in the temple—sleeping in its

The priests at the temple adhered to various philosophies. But it was to a Pythagorean that young Apollonius was drawn. And he was soon adopting the philosophy and lifestyle of Pythagoras.*

As part of that lifestyle, Apollonius became a vegetarian, dressed plainly in white linen, wore his hair long and went barefoot, remained chaste, meditated, and gave away his property. But most notably, he took the Pythagorean oath of silence (the *echemythia*), vowing not to utter a single word for five years. And Apollonius kept his oath, allowing

---

enkoimitiria, or slumber hall. As he slept, Asclepius would visit him in a dream and reveal a treatment. The temple priests would subsequently administer the treatment.

The main temple of Asclepius was located at Epidaurus, the birthplace of the god. A son of Apollo, Asclepius was raised by Chiron the centaur, who taught him medicine. He met his end when Zeus—upset that Asclepius was restoring the dead to life and thus disturbing the natural order—struck him dead with a thunderbolt.

Asclepius is remembered today for figuring in the last words of Socrates. As he lay dying, Socrates reminded his friend Crito to perform a sacrifice that he, Socrates, owed to Asclepius.

And physicians may recognize his name. For the original Hippocratic Oath was sworn to Asclepius and his daughters Hygieia and Panacea.

* Pythagoras was a philosopher for whom the essence of the universe was numbers. He taught that mathematics, music, and astronomy were interrelated; that they were fundamental to an understanding of the natural order; and that their study would lead to a harmonious way of life. He also taught that honey cakes, frankincense, and hymns of praise were more welcome to the gods than animal sacrifices. And he was a physician, writing treatises on such subjects as the medicinal qualities of the sea onion, and recommending certain verses of the Iliad for their curative properties.

Pythagoras also founded an ascetic brotherhood—a secret society whose members were instructed in such mysteries as the transmigration of souls and the music of the spheres. Among their rituals was rumored to be a descent into the Underworld.

himself not even a murmur.*

What were the benefits of Pythagoreanism? Later in life, Apollonius would send this letter to a rival philosopher:

> To Euphrates: If someone associates with a true Pythagorean, what will he get from him, and in what quantity? I would say: statesmanship, geometry, astronomy, arithmetic, harmonics, music, medicine, complete and god-given prophecy, and also the higher rewards—greatness of mind, of soul, and of manner, steadiness, piety, knowledge of the gods and not just supposition, familiarity with blessed spirits and not just faith, friendship with both gods and spirits, self-sufficiency, persistence, frugality, reduction of essential needs, ease of perception, of movement, and of breath, good color, health, cheerfulness, and immortality. But what do those who see you come away with, Euphrates? (Translated by Christopher P. Jones)

And his daily prayer became: "O ye gods, grant that I have little and need nothing."

After five years of study and silence, Apollonius had completed the probationary period. He was now a full-fledged Pythagorean. And resuming the use of his voice, he became an eloquent spokesman for the philosophy. Acclaimed for his learning, he began to teach at the temple of Asclepius; lecture at other shrines; and acquire disciples.

During this period his father died; and Apollonius came into a sizable inheritance. But deeming the possession of wealth to be unbefitting a Pythagorean, he gave most of it away to relatives. He did, however, retain a portion—to finance the travels upon which he was soon to embark.

There followed years of teaching throughout Asia Minor. And then he decided to journey to India. For like Pythagoras before him, he wished to visit the legendary Abode of

---

* Permitted, however, were movements of the hand, eye, or head. Apollonius is said to have quelled a grain riot in the nearby town of Aspendus, using only gestures and a writing tablet.

the Wise Men and partake of their wisdom.*

Apollonius began his journey in Antioch, accompanied by two servants. (One was a stenographer; the other, a calligrapher. Among their duties was to record his thoughts as he traveled.) His seven disciples had declined to accompany Apollonius, and had tried to dissuade him from making so arduous a journey. To which he had replied: "Since you are faint-hearted, I bid you farewell. As for myself, I must go where wisdom and my guardian spirit may lead me. The gods are my advisors and I can but rely on their counsels."

But while passing through Hierapolis in Syria, he acquired another companion: a young man named Damis. "Let us go together—you will follow God, and I shall follow you!" said Damis, who would become his chief disciple and his Boswell.†

---

* Pythagoras is known to have visited Egypt. But according to Maurice Magre, author of *Magicians, Seers, and Mystics* (1932), he also visited India. Magre relates a tale in which Apollonius stayed overnight at a semi-ruined temple. In the morning the caretaker of the temple gave Apollonius a map, engraved on sheets of copper, that had been passed down in his family. It showed the route that Pythagoras had taken to India, and to the Abode of the Wise Men.

† Damis kept a diary of his years of travel with Apollonius. After his death, the diary was preserved.

A century later, Philostratus—a sophist in the court of Empress Julia—was commissioned to write a biography of Apollonius. He set to work, using as sources two previous biographies (by Maximus of Ægeæ and Moeragenes of Athens); a collection of Apollonius's letters; and, for "more detailed information," the diary of Damis. The result was his *Life of Apollonius of Tyana*—a masterful work that reads like a novel (and which has been accused of being one). Of Philostratus, Professor Basil Gildersleeve has written:

"He was to be to Apollonius what Plato was to Socrates...[a] transfiguring genius. His powers were not to be hedged in by a prim array of authorities. He was to write a romance which should admit every species of prose composition; he was to produce a work which should fascinate the reader by the variety of its contents and the liveliness of its style; at once a biography and a volume of travels; a fairy tale and a history; a treatise of zoölogy

Apollonius continued eastward, with Damis serving as guide and translator. They soon arrived at the Euphrates river—the border between the Roman and Parthian empires. A customs official asked if Apollonius had anything to declare.

"Moderation, Justice, Virtue, Temperance, Courage, and Endurance," he replied.*

"You must register these servants," said the official, mistaking the feminine nouns for the names of slaves.

"That I cannot do," said Apollonius, "since these are not my servants that I bring across the border, but my masters."

Apollonius, Damis, and the two servants crossed the river and continued on to Babylon. They wound up staying there for eighteen months. During that time Apollonius studied with the Magi and was initiated into their mysteries. He also became a confident of the king, to whom he explained the Pythagorean lifestyle; offered advice on ruling; and talked about the nature of the soul—talks so enlightening that the king ceased to fear death.

Finally it was time to resume their journey. The king gave Apollonius camels, provisions, and a guide. And he asked what gift the philosopher would bring back to him from India.

"A fine gift, O king," said Apollonius. "For if my meeting with those men makes me wiser, so will I return to you a better man than I am now."

---

and a manual of morals; a picture-gallery of human characters and a showcase of natural curiosities." (*Essays and Studies,* 1890)

Most of what is known about Apollonius comes from the *Life of Apollonius of Tyana*—for of Philostratus's sources, only that collection of letters has survived.

And Damis's diary, it should be noted, is known to have existed solely by dint of Philostratus's references to it. Could it have been nothing more than an invention? A literary device in what is, conceivably, more a historical novel than a biography?

* One is reminded of Oscar Wilde's response to the same question, as he entered the U.S.: "Only my genius."

"Just return to me," said the king, tearfully embracing him. "That will be a fine gift."

And Apollonius departed from Babylon. He had camels now, and—displayed on the lead camel—the protective insignia of a king.

His route took him and his companions through the Caucasus. There they passed the mountain where Prometheus had been chained. (Locals showed them the remains of the chains.) And one moonlit night, they were set upon by an *empusa*, or vampire. (Apollonius repelled it with a rebuke.) But for the most part, the journey through Central Asia was uneventful; and Apollonius and Damis passed the time by engaging in philosophical discussions.*

Then one day they began to see men riding on elephants, and realized they had reached India. Crossing the Indus river, they arrived in the capital city of Taxila. And there, for three days, they were the guests of King Phraotes.

Despite his wealth, Phraotes lived a life of moderation and restraint. A devotee of philosophy, he was honored to host a philosopher; and during one of their talks he asked Apollonius: "In Greece would you deign to accept me as a guest?"

"What do you mean?" said Apollonius.

"Because I consider you far superior to myself; wisdom is greater than royal rank."

On the morning of Apollonius's departure, Phraotes provided him with a new guide. He also gave him a letter of introduction—to Iarchas, head of the Abode of the Wise Men. The letter began:

> King Phraotes greets Iarchas and his company of sages.
> Apollonius, a very wise men, considers you wiser than himself, and comes to learn from you. Dismiss him not, therefore, without a knowledge of that which you know. Thus shall your wisdom not be lost, for no one speaks better or remembers better than he.

Setting out from Taxila, Apollonius and his companions crossed the Hyphasis river. (A monument on the bank marked the spot where Alexander and his army had turned back.) They pressed on, prodding their camels through marshland (home to a species of unicorn, Philostratus tells us)—across

---

* Philostratus provides transcriptions of several of these discussions—copied presumably from Damis's diary.

a mountain (where monkeys were used to harvest pepper-trees)—through rich farmland (irrigated by canals that brought water from the Ganges).

Then their guide began to shake with fear. For they were nearing the Abode of the Wise Men; and its residents were viewed by the Indians with awe and trepidation.

Suddenly a young man came running toward them. He carried a golden rod: the emblem of a messenger. Approaching the travelers, he greeted them in Greek. And he announced that Apollonius, unaccompanied by the others, was to come with him.

"For *they themselves* have invited you."

Leaving his servants and Damis behind, Apollonius followed the messenger. And though practiced, as a Pythagorean, in the control of his emotions, he was visibly excited.

The messenger took him to a hill that was enveloped by a cloud—a thick mist that hid all but the summit. He led Apollonius into the cloud and through a gate.

And they descended into the Abode of the Wise Men.*

---

* Philostratus is unclear as to whether they ascended or descended. (Probably his source—Damis's diary—was similarly unclear.) But the Abode must have been reached by going down into the earth. Though Philostratus does not explicitly say so, there are several indications.

To begin with, he quotes Apollonius as saying: "I saw the Indian sages who inhabit the earth, yet who do not live on it—who are protected on all sides." If not *on* the earth, where else but within it?

And in speaking of their location, Philostratus states that "the sages dwelt within, visible or invisible as they please." That gate was the entrance to their subterranean monastery.

Finally, the Abode of the Wise Men bears a striking resemblance to Agharta. (For more on Agharta, see chapter 15.) Like Agharta, the Abode is the underground home of sages. It has a mysterious entrance. And it is an eighteen-day march from the Ganges, reports Philostratus—the same distance that is said to lie between Agharta and that river.

Jean-Claude Frère, in his study of secret societies, and others have concluded that both Pythagoras and Apollonius visited Agharta.

They made their way through a series of dim tunnels. Along the way was a well that glowed with a bluish light...a fiery crater (the Fire of Forgiveness)...the Jar of Rains and the Jar of Winds (used by the Wise Men to influence the weather)...a variety of idols (representing Indian, Egyptian, and Greek gods). Despite having a guide to follow, Apollonius tread warily, like someone navigating the corridors of a fun house.

And he was led into the main hall of the Abode.

The Wise Men—eighteen of them—were seated in a circle. They were elderly men with turbans and beards. They wore tunics that left one arm and shoulder bare. Each was holding a staff. Several of the sages rose as Apollonius entered, and came forward to embrace him.

The head Wise Man, Iarchas, was seated on a throne. He greeted Apollonius in Greek, and asked to see the letter of introduction. (Clairvoyant, he was aware of its existence, though apparently not of its contents.) Apollonius passed the letter to him.

Iarchas read it, nodded approvingly, and asked the reason for his coming. Apollonius gave a satisfactory answer. Whereupon, Iarchas smiled and invited him to attend their daily rites.

"Well now," said Apollonius, "I should certainly be wronging the Caucasus and the Indus, which I crossed to get here, if I did not witness your rites."

The Wise Men rose and made their way to a purification chamber. Apollonius followed after them. In the chamber they bathed, decked themselves with garlands, and chanted.

Still chanting, they filed into a temple. A fire was burning on the altar. They assembled before it and began to pound the floor with their staffs.

And like a troupe of magical acrobats, *the Wise Men rose several feet into the air.*

Apollonius watched in amazement, as they levitated and sang hymns of praise to the gods.

Then they returned to the hall and settled into their seats. And Iarchas offered to answer any questions that

Apollonius might have. "Ask away," he said, "as you have come among Masters who have knowledge of all things."

"Do you have *self*-knowledge?" asked Apollonius.

"Of course!" replied Iarchas. "We are able to know all things because we *began* by knowing ourselves. Otherwise, we would not have dared to embark upon the quest for philosophical knowledge."

A lengthy conversation ensued, touching on such topics as virtue, the nature of the soul, and Homer. Afterwards a banquet was held.*

Apollonius spent four months with the Wise Men. During that time he learned their doctrines and absorbed their wisdom. Eventually, Damis too was allowed to attend the philosophical discourses and the rites in the temple. Witnessing the levitation of the Wise Men, his eyes fairly popped.†

Finally it was time for Apollonius to depart. Iarchas provided him with camels and a guide, and presented him with seven healing rings—one for each planet and day of the week.

Ten days later Apollonius and his companions reached the sea, and boarded a ship that was bound for Babylon.

In the decades that followed, Apollonius of Tyana rose to

---

* The food and drink, Philostratus informs us, were served by self-propelling urns. And when the banqueters became drowsy, couches rose out of the floor. These marvels would seem to indicate an advanced technology.

† Did the Wise Men actually levitate? In a chapter on Apollonius in *Mystic Rebels* (1949), Harry C. Schnur writes:

"Damis and the others were admitted to their religious rites and a subsequent banquet. [The Wise Men] worshiped the light, after having purified themselves in a cold bath, and then, before Damis' gaping eyes, practiced levitation. Without judging here whether it is possible to those endowed with certain occult powers to overcome the so-called law of gravity, let us remain content with the knowledge that observers of greater keenness and, if we like, reliability than Damis have asserted throughout the ages the occurrence of this phenomenon."

prominence. Combining the wisdom of the East with that of Pythagoras, he became the foremost philosopher of the Græco-Roman world. And he continued to travel. For he saw himself now as having a mission: the restoration of religious practices to their original purity. "I shall never forget my Masters," he said of the Wise Men, "and journey through the world teaching what I have learned from them."

His fame and influence grew. Cities summoned him, to instruct their priests in the proper conduct of ritual. (Among the reforms that he advocated: the cessation of animal sacrifice.) And he busied himself with the standard duties of a sage: healing, interpreting dreams, installing talismans—and, of course, teaching and preaching. With his disciples he discussed matters both mundane and metaphysical. Nothing escaped his scrutiny, from the challenges of daily life to the nature of the soul.*

And always at his side was Damis, recording his words and deeds.

The Peripatetics were philosophers who supposedly walked as they talked; and Apollonius carried the practice to new heights. He was probably the greatest traveler of antiquity, roaming the length and breadth of the Roman Empire. He would lodge at temples, inns, and the homes of dignitaries. G. R. S. Mead lists the many places he visited (including the Upper Nile retreat of the Gymnosophists, or Naked Philosophers), and observes:

> Such then is the geographical outline, so to say, of the life of Apollonius, and even the most careless reader of the bare skeleton of the journeys recorded by Philostratus must be struck by the indomitable energy of the man, and his power of endurance.

Yet Apollonius was not just a wandering sage. He also

---

* Of the soul he remarked: "When the body is exhausted, the soul soars in ethereal space, full of contempt for the harsh, unhappy slavery it has suffered. But what are these things to you? You will know them when you are no more."

served as an advisor to emperors—in particular Titus and Vespasian. He lectured them on the duties of a wise ruler; and the emperors paid attention to him. Said Titus: "I have indeed captured Jerusalem, but you, Apollonius, have captured me."*

And like any philosopher, he wrote books—among them a life of Pythagoras, a treatise on sacrifices, and a treatise on divination. (Nothing has survived of these works save fragments.) Yet despite his intellectual acuity, Apollonius remained at heart a simple, pious man—one who thrice daily prayed to the sun.

He lived to be nearly a hundred years old. At that time he was still teaching, at a temple in Ephesus—the conclusion to a long and illustrious career as a philosopher.

Here are some comments on that career:

> There stands, in undiminished greatness, the image of a prophet and reformer. A man who strove for knowledge and self-improvement, and for the betterment of mankind. (Harry C. Schnur)

---

* Some emperors, however, sought to silence him. Nero was notorious for his public performances as a singer. When Nero fell hoarse, prayers for his recovery were dutifully said. But Apollonius wondered aloud whether the gods took an interest in "the antics of clowns." His remark was reported; and Nero had him tried for lèse-majesty. Asked by the prosecutor his opinion of Nero, Apollonius replied: "It's much better than yours. For you think he should sing, while I think it more dignified of him to remain silent." Apollonius was acquitted.

(Musonius Rufus, a friend and fellow philosopher, wasn't so lucky. Overheard to say that he would rather labor on the Corinth canal than listen to Nero sing, Musonius wound up laboring on the canal in chains. Apollonius was eventually able to have him released.)

And Emperor Domitian had Apollonius, who had gotten involved in the politics of the day, tried for treason. Apollonius was speedily acquitted—to his dismay, before he could deliver the lengthy and eloquent speech he had prepared in his defense. (The speech was preserved; and its text is quoted by Philostratus.)

[His] one idea seems to have been to spread abroad among the religious brotherhoods and institutions of the Empire some portion of the wisdom which he had brought back from India. (G. R. S. Mead)

From Apollonius I have learned freedom of will and understanding, steadiness of purpose, and to look to nothing else, not even for a moment, except to reason. (Emperor Marcus Aurelius)

But let Apollonius speak for himself on the calling of a philosopher. He and Damis were once visiting the island of Rhodes. As they viewed the Colossus of Rhodes, a towering statue of the god Helios, Damis said: "Can anything be greater than this?"

"Yes," said Apollonius. "A true man who pursues wisdom honestly and sincerely."

Such a man was Apollonius of Tyana—the very model of a philosopher.

Yet a curious fact is this: Philostratus portrays him also as a magician. He attributes to Apollonius supernatural doings—prophesies, exorcisms, miraculous healings, a resurrection, sudden disappearances, an encounter with the ghost of Achilles, and the like. How much of this Philostratus took from the diary of Damis, and how much is apocryphal—legendary material that had accrued to the life of a sage—is impossible to determine. (Much of it, I suspect, is apocryphal.) In any case, the portrayal of Apollonius as a magician was responsible for the controversy that has surrounded him, and contributed to the eclipse of his fame. Here are some criticisms of the magical aspects of the *Life*:

[Apollonius's life] is related in so fabulous a manner by his disciple that we are at a loss to discover whether he was a sage, an impostor, or a fanatic. (Historian Edward Gibbon)

We should deem it impertinent to direct argument against a mere romance and to subject a work of imagination to a grave discussion. (Cardinal Newman)

It would not surprise if, in the feverish religious atmosphere of the Severan court, Philostratus had turned a remarkable but not exceptional Pythagorean teacher of the first century into a holy man for a new age. (Translator Christopher Jones)

But let G. R. S. Mead—Theosophist and secretary to Madame Blavatsky—have the final word:

Was Apollonius, then, a rogue, a trickster, a charlatan, a fanatic, a misguided enthusiast, or a philosopher, a reformer, a conscious worker, a true initiate, one of the earth's great ones? This each must decide for himself, according to his knowledge or his ignorance.

I for my part bless his memory, and would gladly learn from him.

5.

King Herla

ONE DAY KING HERLA WAS ALONE IN THE FOREST. HE was resting after a day of hunting with his knights. Seated against a tree, he dozed off.*

Herla was awakened by a rustling sound. A goat was emerging from the forest. Riding it was a dwarf—a short, stocky creature with a ruddy face and full beard. And a crown upon his head.

The dwarf halted in front of Herla and introduced himself. He was the Dwarf King, he said. He had heard good things about Herla, and wished to honor the Briton by attending his wedding.

---

* King Herla was a ruler of the ancient Britons. Nothing is known of him, beyond the present tale. The source of the tale is Walter Map's *De nugis curialium* (Trifles of courtiers). Of Welsh ancestry, Map was a medieval chronicler.

Herla laughed and said he had no plans to wed. But the Dwarf King insisted that word would soon reach him—of a marriage proposal involving a French princess. Ambassadors from France were just now approaching his castle.

And the Dwarf King offered a pact. He would attend Herla's wedding, if—one year later—Herla would attend his. And without waiting for an answer, the Dwarf King slapped his goat and rode off into the forest.

Dwarfs were known for their mischief. So Herla suspected a prank. But no sooner had he returned to his castle than ambassadors from France appeared, with a marriage proposal. It was accepted; and preparations began for the wedding.

The appointed day arrived, along with scores of guests. They filled the banquet hall, which was crammed with tables and benches. And the festivities were about to begin, when a commotion was heard in the courtyard.

The Dwarf King entered the hall. He greeted King Herla and sat himself at a table. Meanwhile, out in the courtyard, other dwarfs were setting up tents.

And soon thereafter, a feast issued from the tents. Dwarf servants bustled about, serving the guests. Course after course was brought to the hall, along with flagons of wine. Herla's own servants shrugged and stood idle. The food they had prepared was left unserved.

So bountiful was the banquet, and so excellent the service, that the guests acclaimed the Dwarf King. And as dawn broke, he said to Herla:

"O king of the Britons. In compliance with our pact, I am present at your wedding. And I have provided a generous gift. If you are in need of anything else, just name it. But if not, I have fulfilled my obligation. And you must reciprocate at the proper time."

Without waiting for a reply, he departed with his dwarfs.

A year later the Dwarf King returned. He reminded Herla of their pact, and extended an invitation to his own wedding. Herla accepted, assembled his knights, and told them to ready their horses for a journey.

And with cartloads of food and drink, Herla and his knights followed after the Dwarf King.

He led them to a cave in the forest. They entered it on their horses; rode along a tunnel that descended into the earth; and emerged in a vast cavern. Lit by hundreds of lamps, it was richly furnished. The Dwarf King welcomed them to his palace.

Other guests arrived: scores of boisterous dwarfs. The nuptial ceremony was held; and the festivities began. Herla had reciprocated by bringing food and drink. For his part, the Dwarf King provided music and other entertainment. And for three days, the cavern reverberated with sounds of merriment.

Finally the guests began to leave. The Dwarf King thanked Herla and the knights for coming. And as a parting gift, he presented them with a small dog.

"On the ride homeward," said the Dwarf King, "carry this dog with you. *And do not dismount until it leaps to the ground.*"

"A strange warning, O king of the dwarfs," said Herla. "But we shall heed it. And I myself shall carry the dog."

Mounting their horses, Herla and the knights left the subterranean cavern; ascended via the tunnel; and exited the cave. And emerging into daylight, they were dumbfounded by what they saw.

For the forest was gone. In its place were fields and houses. Smoke curled up from chimneys. And nearby, an elderly shepherd was tending his flock.

They rode over to him. The shepherd stared at them blankly.

"Do you not recognize your king?" said Herla. "Are you not one of my loyal subjects? Greetings, shepherd. I am King Herla!"

"My lord," said the shepherd, "I speak your language but haltingly. For I am a Saxon and you are a Briton. As for 'Herla,' we have no such king—though legend tells of a Briton king by that name. He is said to have accompanied a dwarf into that cave, and to have been seen no more upon the earth. But that was long ago. We Saxons, having driven out the Britons, have possessed this land for nearly three centuries."

Herla's eyes widened with astonishment. "Three centuries!" he exclaimed. "Yet for us, only three *days* have elapsed. How can that be? What sorcery is afoot? What spell was cast upon us, whilst carousing in that cavern?"

Just then one of the knights dismounted from his horse —*and crumbled into dust.*

Herla recalled the warning they had been given. "Do not dismount!" he cried to his knights. "Not until this dog leaps to the ground. Come, let us ride—until it alights!"

And they galloped off in a thunder of hoofbeats.

•

What caused the plight of King Herla and his knights? The Dwarf King may be suspected of mischief.

And what became of these ancient Britons? It is said that they are riding still. Like a band of ghosts, they roam the countryside—waiting for the dog to alight.

Listen at night, and you may hear a sound like thunder. It is the rumble of their horses.*

---

* A visit to the Underworld can entail a distortion of time. For example, a person descends into Fairyland, is welcomed by the fairies, and enjoys a year of dancing, feasting, and other activities. Then he returns home—to discover that only an hour has elapsed.

Or the reverse takes place. One returns from a brief visit to Fairyland, and discovers that years have elapsed. The most celebrated case of this type is that of Rip Van Winkle. Having spent a night carousing with dwarfs, Rip returned in the morning to his village—to find it altered. For twenty years had passed!

And in his *Ming-shan tung-t'ien fu-ti chi* (Report concerning the Cave Heavens and Lands of Happiness in famous mountains), Tu Kuang-t'ing (850–933) describes a similar case in China. It involved a peasant who followed a passageway into a mountain, and emerged in a strange land of "fragrant flowers, densely growing willows, towers the color of cinnabar, pavilions of red jade, and far-flung palaces."

There a group of seductive women befriended him. They took him to a pleasure house and plied him with music and wine. And the peasant was about to yield to their blandishments, when he recalled his beloved wife and children—and fled. A dancing light led him back through the passageway.

Upon reaching his village, however, he recognized no one. And arriving at his house, he found it to be inhabited by strangers. To his amazement, they were his descendants! Hundreds of years ago, they told him, their ancestor had disappeared into the mountains, and was never seen again.

6.
Cuchulain

CUCHULAIN [COO-KHOO-LIN] OPENED HIS EYES AND became aware of a woman standing before him. Clad in crimson, she was smiling in what he took to be a seductive manner. The famed warrior of Ulster purred with expectation.

He was resting against a sacred pillar, near his stronghold of Dun Delgan. Intoxicated, Cuchulain had wandered from the stronghold; plopped down against the pillar; and fallen asleep. Just before dozing off, he had glimpsed a bird with crimson plumage, alighting at his feet. Now the bird was gone; and in its place, to his delight, this attractive woman.

But his delight turned swiftly to dismay. For the woman laughed and began to lash him with a horsewhip.

Later that day, he was found by his fellow warriors, still seated against the pillar. Afflicted by a mysterious malady, Cuchulain had fallen into a stupor, unable to move or to speak. They carried him back to the stronghold and laid him on his bed.

For weeks he continued in this state. His wife, Emer, would sit at the bedside and sing to him. *"Arise, O hero of Ulster,"* she sang. *"Come back to us, my love."* She also consulted with the local Druid. But even he, with his spells and potions, was unable to cure Cuchulain.*

Then one day a messenger arrived. He stated that he had been sent by Fand, the queen of the fairies; that Fand was

---

* The Druids were the wise men of Ireland in pre-Christian times. As repositories of knowledge, they served a wide variety of functions. They were priests, wizards, soothsayers, physicians, judges, historians, teachers, and royal advisors.

With the coming of Christianity, the Druids were suppressed and their records destroyed. (St. Patrick is said to have burnt 180 of their books.) And a vast body of knowledge was lost forever.

responsible for the malady; and that she was offering to cure Cuchulain, if he would come to Tir-nan-Og and visit her realm.*

His fellow warriors conferred. And deciding that he must go to Tir-nan-Og, they loaded Cuchulain onto his horse. Emer watched from a window, weeping and praying. And the messenger led the horse, with its human cargo, out of the stronghold.

Night was falling when the messenger arrived at a fairy hill. He clapped his hands and a portal opened. Leading the horse through it, he descended along a passageway. Slumped on the horse, Cuchulain murmured to himself. The *clomp clomp* of hooves echoed in the passageway.

Finally they emerged in Tir-nan-Og. And awaiting them in a meadow was Queen Fand—the woman in crimson. She introduced herself to Cuchulain and welcomed him to her realm.

Then she touched him. Instantly, he was cured of his malady. His sickly pallor vanished; his vitality returned. With a triumphant cry he sat up on the horse. The hero of Ulster was himself again.

"Come live with me and be my consort," said Fand.

And Cuchulain—entranced by her beauty—agreed to the proposal.

Fand escorted him to her palace. There he listened to celestial music; drank the nectar of the fairies; dined on delicacies. "This is indeed for me!" said Cuchulain. And they became lovers. A month went by (though Cuchulain had lost all sense of time).

Then he asked if he might pay a brief visit to his stronghold. For Cuchulain had decided to remain in Tir-nan-Og; and he wanted to make known his decision to his wife and

---

* Tir-nan-Og ("Land of Eternal Youth") was the Celtic Otherworld —the dwelling place of the gods, the fairies, and the dead. It was located inside the earth (although some accounts place it on an island in the Western Sea). One could enter it via a "fairy hill"— one of the mysterious mounds found throughout the British Isles. For there the Otherworld interpenetrated with our own.

warriors. Fand acceded to the request, after securing his promise to return to her. And she had him escorted back to the surface world.

Arriving at his stronghold, Cuchulain was greeted with jubilation. The warriors crowded about him, cheering and slapping him on the back. Emer tearfully embraced him. And there followed a day of feasting and celebration.

But finally he announced his intention. He was going to return to Tir-nan-Og and take up residence with the fairy queen.

Emer was devastated. She pleaded with him to change his mind. But Cuchulain was deaf to her pleas. He described the attractions of Tir-nan-Og—the nectar of the fairies; the freedom from care; the promise of eternal youth. And he extolled Queen Fand. In her presence, said Cuchulain, he felt like a divine being.

At the mention of Fand, his wife grew livid. "I am as good a woman as she!" cried Emer. And she predicted that, as the queen's novelty wore off, Cuchulain would tire of her. "New things are glittering," she told him. "But they soon tarnish and get tossed aside. Moreover, you are dishonoring your wife. The women of Ulster are laughing at me!"

But Cuchulain would not listen. His decision was firm, he said. He planned to return to Tir-nan-Og in the morning.

Emer let out a cry of anguish and fled to her chamber. There she brooded—and arrived at a decision of her own.

Slipping out of the stronghold, she went to visit the Druid. She found him sitting in his hut, amid jars of medicine and piles of manuscripts. A concoction was bubbling on the stove.

The Druid listened to her tale of woe. Emer told him of the conversation with her husband. And she described the pain she was feeling, and the rage.

"And what would you have me do?" he asked.

"Provide me with poison. For I wish to send Cuchulain to his grave. At least there he will still be mine."

"An extreme solution. One that should not be undertaken lightly. But listen, I have a better idea."

He searched through his potions, located a vial of amber liquid, and handed it to her.

"Take this. It is the *dcog dermaid*—the Potion of Forgetfulness."

The Druid instructed her on its use. Emer thanked him and returned to the stronghold. There she mixed the potion into a cup of ale, and took the cup to Cuchulain.

"Drink this, O husband," she said. "As a farewell toast to the years we have spent together."

"Gladly," said Cuchulain.

He drank from the cup. A shiver ran through him. And all of his recent memories were erased. His stay in Tir-nan-Og, his liaison with Fand, his promise to return to her—all were forgotten. It was as if none of it had happened. He looked at his wife and smiled lovingly.

Now she too drank from the cup. And her memories were likewise erased. Cuchulain's sojourn in Tir-nan-Og, his decision to leave her, her intent to poison him—all were

forgotten. She had no remembrance of any of it. And she returned his smile.

The Potion of Forgetfulness had brought them back together.*

---

* The tales of Cuchulain originated with the Celtic bards. Around the eighth century these tales (of which there were conflicting versions) were compiled and collated; and the resulting texts have survived in dusty archives. Pouring over them, Lady Gregory—a leading figure of the Irish Literary Revival—wrote *Cuchulain of Muirthemne*. In an introduction to the book, William Butler Yeats tells us that, while "no story has come down to us in the form it had when the storyteller told it in the winter evenings," Lady Gregory's retellings are the definitive version of the saga.

The above tale is based on a similar tale by Lady Gregory. Her ending, however, is somewhat different. She has a distraught Cuchulain wandering about the countryside. For Fand has ended their relationship, causing him to lose his mind. Whereupon—

"[The king of Ulster] sent the poets and the skilled men and the Druids of Ulster to visit him, that they might lay hold of him.... the Druids did enchantment on him, until they had laid hold of him, and until his wits began to come back to him. Then he asked them for a drink, and the Druids gave him a drink of forgetfulness. From the moment he drank that drink, he did not remember Fand, and all the things he had done. And they gave a drink of forgetfulness to Emer as well, that she might forget her jealousy, for the state she was in was no better than his own.

"And after that, Manannan [the husband of Fand] shook his cloak between Cuchulain and Fand, [so that] they should never meet one another again."

Was Cuchulain a historical personage, or merely a creation of the bards? Most likely he was both—a first-century warrior of Ulster, about whom nothing definite is known; and a legendary figure, of whom the bards spun tales. Says Yeats of those bards: "Surely they believed or half-believed in the historical reality of their wildest imaginations."

7.

Elidore

ELIDORE WAS A PRIEST WHO CLAIMED TO HAVE VISITED
—as a twelve-year-old boy—a subterranean kingdom. His tale was recorded by Giraldus Cambrensis, the medieval chronicler. Giraldus heard the tale from the bishop of St. David's, who had heard it from Elidore himself.*

Young Elidore, we are told, had been a pupil in the monastery school of St. David's. But he had resented the harsh discipline. ("'The root of learning is bitter, although the fruit is sweet,'" observes Giraldus, quoting from the Book of Proverbs.) So he had neglected his studies, and received frequent blows from his teacher. Finally he abandoned his books altogether and ran away.

For two days Elidore hid in the hollow of a river bank. Weary and hungry, he began to regret having run away. Then he heard a voice and looked up. Two little men were standing before him. "Come with us," said one, "and we shall lead you to a land of delights and games." Elidore assented, and followed them through a dark passageway that led down into the earth.

They emerged in a subterranean realm—"a most fair country," says Giraldus, "replete with rivers and meadows, forests and plains." Thick clouds obscured the sky; and a

---

* Giraldus Cambrensis ("Gerald the Welshman") included the tale in *Itinerarium Cambriae*, a chronicle of his journey through Wales. What kind of chronicler was Giraldus? An introduction to the English translation of the book refers to his "credulity in matters of faith and his shrewd common sense in things of the world, his wit and lively fancy, his eloquence of tongue and pen, his acute rather than accurate observation, his scholarship elegant rather than profound."

Giraldus (1146–1223) was friends with Walter Map, our source for the Herla tale.

kind of twilight cast an eerie spell upon the country.

The little men led Elidore to a palace. There he was presented to the king, who questioned him. Judging him to be suitable, the king had Elidore installed in the palace, as a playmate for one of the princes.

The men of this kingdom were knee-high to the visitor, with blond, shoulder-length hair. (Giraldus refers to them as *pygmaei*.) They rode horses the size of greyhounds; spoke a language that Elidore would one day recognize as having been Greek; and were vegetarians. "They have no form of religious worship," reports Giraldus, "devoting themselves simply to truth." And they were utterly upright, detesting nothing so much as a lie. They viewed the inhabitants of the surface world as hopelessly reprobate—greedy, treacherous, and untruthful.

During his stay in their kingdom—a stay he enjoyed—Elidore returned home occasionally to visit his mother. He described to her the splendor of the subterranean world; the manners and customs of its inhabitants; and his carefree life among them. Elidore also told her of the vast quantities of gold that the king possessed. Hearing this, his mother urged him to bring back some gold; and he agreed to do so.

The prince had a golden ball, which he and Elidore used as a plaything. One morning Elidore stole the ball. He hid it in his shirt, slipped out of the palace, and returned to the surface via the passageway. Unbeknownst to Elidore, the two little men were following close behind him.

Arriving at his house, Elidore stumbled on the doorstep and dropped the ball. The little men grabbed it and sped off. As they did so, they spit at Elidore and denounced him for his greed and treachery.

Ashamed of his deed, Elidore rebuked his mother for having suggested it. He ran after the little men; but they had vanished. And when he walked along the river and looked for the passageway, it was nowhere to be found.

In the months that followed, he searched repeatedly for the passageway. Alas, it seemed to have disappeared. There would be no returning, he realized, to that carefree land.

So he returned instead to school. And having resolved to mend his ways, he applied himself to his studies. Eventually, he entered the priesthood.

Many years later, Elidore—now an elderly priest—told the bishop of St. David's about his visit to the subterranean kingdom. And recalling his happy days there, he burst into tears.

Giraldus recorded the tale in his chronicle. But what was his appraisal of it? Was it credible? His conclusion was this:

> If a scrupulous inquirer should ask my opinion of this story, I answer with Augustine: "Divine miracles are to be wondered at, not debated or discussed." I would neither, by denial, place a limit on God's power; nor, by assent, insolently overstep the bounds of credibility. But on such occasions I always call to mind the saying of St. Jerome: "You will find many things incredible and improbable, which nevertheless are true."... This story, therefore, and others like it, I would

place—as Augustine implied—among those things which are neither to be strongly affirmed nor denied.

That is to say, Elidore may well have visited such a place. But Giraldus was withholding judgment.

8.

Sir Owen

A CAVE IN IRELAND ONCE SERVED AS AN ENTRANCE TO Purgatory. Located on an island in Lough Derg, the cave was known as St. Patrick's Purgatory. For St. Patrick himself had discovered it.

The discovery took place in the year 445. St. Patrick had retreated to the island to pray. While asleep in the cave, he experienced a vision of Purgatory. And a voice revealed that the cave was an entrance to Purgatory—and that by spending a night in it, one might be purged of one's sins. Years later, his disciple Dabheoc founded a monastery on the island; and the monks served as keepers of the cave.*

Its fame spread; and by the twelfth century, St. Patrick's Purgatory had become a major destination for pilgrims. They came from throughout Ireland and from abroad. The site (which now comprised two islands: a monastery on one, the Purgatory on the other) was administered by Augustinian monks. They would greet the pilgrim; try to dissuade him from entering the Purgatory; and (if he persisted) supervise him in a regimen of fasting and prayer. He was then shut up inside the cave. The next day the gate was unlocked;

---

* St. Patrick also discovered a menhir, or sacred stone, on the island. In *The Life and Writings of St. Patrick* (1905), Archbishop Healy describes the stone:

"There is an upright circular stone shaft, about four feet high, and eight inches in diameter, with spiral flutings and a plain iron cross fixed on the top. This stone shaft is said to be the genuine 'clogh-oir,' or golden-stone, from which the diocese of Clogher has derived its name. It was originally a pagan idol, and, like Apollo Pythius, seems to have delivered oracular responses, until it was exorcised and blessed by our Apostle."

This ancient relic has survived on the island to the present day, as has the stone pillow upon which St. Patrick experienced his vision.

and the pilgrim (if he had survived the ordeal) was released. He had undergone the torments of Purgatory. And he was a new man—reassured of the reality of Heaven, and cleansed in advance of his sins.

One such pilgrim was Sir Owen, an Irish knight who had fought in the Crusades.

Upon his return to Ireland, Sir Owen found himself racked with guilt. He felt remorse for the life of violence and plundering that he had led as a Crusader. And he wished to do penance, that he might be absolved of his sins. The Church had a penitential system: contrition; confession; punishments and austerities; and then, amendment of one's ways. Yet so overwhelming was his sense of guilt that Owen wished to perform an extreme act of penance: the descent into St. Patrick's Purgatory. So in the summer of 1147, he mounted his horse and set off for Lough Derg.

Days later he arrived at his destination. Nestled in the hills of Ulster, Lough Derg was a small, placid lake. A monk rowed Owen out to the island.*

The monks welcomed him as a pilgrim. They sought to dissuade him, however, from descending into the Purgatory. But Owen was steadfast; and his fifteen days of preparation began. He fasted and prayed; joined the monks at Mass; made out a will. And finally he was ready for his descent.

Marching and chanting in a solemn procession, the monks led him to the cave. An iron gate blocked the entrance. They opened it, sprinkled holy water on him, and pronounced a benediction. And Owen—determined to wash away his sins—entered the cave.

The gate clanged shut behind him, leaving him in darkness. He heard the key turn in the lock.

Owen proceeded further into the cave, as instructed, groping his way along a steep descent. The air was cold and

---

* Archbishop Healy on the ambience of the surrounding hills: "There was no flora except moss and heather. In fact, nature here clothes herself in sackcloth and ashes; the very aspect of the place induces solemn thought, and makes it [a fit] shrine for penance."

damp, with a sulphurous smell. Breathing it, he began to feel drowsy. A weariness overcame him; and Owen lay down to rest. Lulled by the sound of dripping water, and by a low murmuring (the lament, according to the monks, of souls in Purgatory), he dozed off.

Then, rising from the stone floor, he pressed onward. A dim light became visible ahead; and Owen groped his way towards it. And he arrived in the courtyard of a cloister.

Monks in white robes emerged from the cloister. They warned him that he was about to be attacked by demons. To defend himself, he must invoke the name of Jesus. And the monks disappeared back into the cloister.

Owen stood there in the courtyard. Suddenly the ground shook. And he was engulfed by a dark cloud of demons. Only their red eyes were visible.

"Turn back!" they chanted.

"Jesus give me strength to go on," said Owen.

Taking hold of him, the demons carried him down into the earth. And Owen was given a tour of Purgatory. He was shown souls that were immersed in freezing water; that were attached to a fiery wheel; that were dragged by a dragon. The purpose of these torments was to purify them of their sins.

Then it was Owen's turn to be punished. The demons flew him to a fiery abyss and dropped him into it. He plummeted through flames. The heat was unbearable. Sulphurous vapors seared his lungs. In agony he cried out: "Jesus Christ, Son of the living God, have mercy on me, a sinner." And he was lifted out of the abyss, as if by an invisible hand.

The demons took him next to a river of fire. Spanning it was a narrow bridge—barely a foot wide. "This is the River of Hell," they told him. "Cross it if you can!" Owen started across. But so narrow was the bridge, and slippery, that he could not gain a foothold. Flames were shooting up from below. And the demons were taunting him and throwing stones.

"O Jesus help me," said Owen. And the bridge widened, as if stretched by an invisible hand. He scampered across.

On the opposite bank was a wall. A gate in it swung open; and he entered a garden. There he was met by an angel, who welcomed him to the earthly paradise. This was a temporary residence, explained the angel—a way station for souls that had been purified in Purgatory and were bound for Heaven. The angel pointed to a gate that shimmered in the distance: the Gate of Heaven.

Owen asked if he could remain here. No, said the angel; he must return to the world and complete his allotted span. One could reside in the earthly paradise only after relinquishing one's flesh and bones.

Then the angel gave him a taste of heavenly food. Owen grew faint with rapture. And then it was time to return to the cave.

When morning came, the monks unlocked the gate and found him asleep on the floor of the cave. They roused him and led him back to the monastery, for further fasting and prayer.

And finally, they said farewell to the knight. A monk rowed him from the island. He mounted his horse and headed home.

Sir Owen was a new man. He had been purged of his

sins—relieved of a heavy burden—and restored to God's grace.*

---

* Many in Europe were soon learning about Owen and his descent. Here is how that happened:

In 1156 Gilbert of Louth, an English monk, was sent to Ireland to establish a monastery. In need of an interpreter, he was introduced to the bilingual Owen. (After his return from Lough Derg, the knight had joined a monastic order.) During their time together, Owen described his descent into Purgatory.

Upon his return to England, Gilbert passed the story on. Among those who heard it was Henry of Saltrey, who committed it to writing. Henry titled his manuscript *Tractatus de Purgatorio Sancti Patricii* (A treatise on Saint Patrick's Purgatory). It began with a discourse on the nature of Purgatory, then recounted the visit there of Sir Owen. Copies of the *Tractatus* were widely circulated—a medieval bestseller. (Some 150 manuscripts have survived.) Moreover, the Latin text was translated and adapted into vernaculars.

But what was one to make of it? Was Owen's tale to be taken literally? Did he actually descend into Purgatory? According to Henry, Owen denied that his experience had been a dream or a vision. No, insisted Owen, *he had descended bodily into a real place.* And a local bishop, reported Henry, had affirmed the authenticity of his account.

The *Tractatus* inspired many pilgrimages to Lough Derg. Such pilgrimages would continue into the present—with one dark interlude. In 1632 the English Parliament condemned St. Patrick's Purgatory, deeming it a flagrant instance of "Papist" superstition. The pilgrimage was banned; the monks were expelled; and the monastery was demolished. In *Lough Derg and Its Pilgrimages* (1879), Father Daniel O'Connor laments:

"The apostate English determined to destroy that shrine of religion, where their forefathers in the Ages of Faith had done penance; where King Aldfred of Northumbria had prayed to St. Patrick...and where Harold, afterwards King of England (not to speak of many other princes and nobles of that country, who had done likewise), made pilgrimage about the year 1050 to the 'miraculous cave of St. Patrick.'"

Yet it was not long before pilgrims were showing up again, despite the threat of punishment. Finally the monks returned;

and rebuilding began.

"'Mid weal and woe," says Father O'Connor, "the Irish heart had entwined round the holy island of Lough Derg.... the ruined church and crosses and oratories were again put in some sort of repair by loving hands; and the pilgrimage rose again, phoenix-like, from its ashes."

Today the shrine of Lough Derg is the most revered in Ireland. Tens of thousands of penitents arrive each summer. The cave is long gone, destroyed by the English. But penitential exercises are conducted. The pilgrims fast (dry toast and black tea are allowed); pray in a modern basilica; conduct all-night vigils; confess their sins; and perform barefoot circuits of the island. Though a far cry from the fiery abyss, the experience can be profoundly affecting.

9.

Thomas the Rhymer

THE QUEEN OF THE FAIRIES LIKED TO PUT A SPELL ON young men; take them to her castle in Fairyland; and enslave them. She preferred those who were handsome and skilled at reciting poetry. Such a one was Thomas of Ercildoune—or Thomas the Rhymer, as he was known.

Thomas was a Scottish laird of the thirteenth century. He dwelt in a tower at Ercildoune, in the Eildon Hills. Little is known of his life or family. But Thomas was known in his day as both a poet and a prophet. He wrote a rhymed narrative titled *Sir Tristrem*—the earliest such work in English. As for his prophecies, they invariably came true. And a tale began to circulate—of how Thomas the Rhymer acquired the power of prophecy.*

•

Thomas was lounging, the tale began, on a river bank. Young and handsome, he was admiring his reflection in the water. Suddenly, he heard hoofbeats. And a woman on a white horse emerged from the woods, rode up to him, and halted.

---

* The tale was preserved in a popular ballad, and in *Thomas of Ercildoune*, a fourteenth-century romance. Included in the romance were his prophecies. Then, beginning in the sixteenth century, these prophecies were published as chapbooks. Every Scottish farmhouse had a copy—a collection of the sayings of True Thomas (as he was dubbed). A sample of his sayings:

> When Finhaven Castle runs to sand,
> The world's end is near at hand.

Nostradamus, move over!

She wore a velvet cape and a green silk gown. There was an unearthly quality to her beauty; and Thomas wondered if he was having a vision. "Are you Mary, the Queen of Heaven?" he asked. The woman laughed. "I am a queen," she replied, "but not of Heaven." And she asked Thomas to kiss her.

Taken with her beauty, he did so—and his fate was sealed. For the kiss cast a spell upon Thomas. He was now in the thrall of the queen of the fairies. She told him to get up behind her on the horse. Thomas complied. And together they rode off into the forest.

At dusk they arrived at a fairy hill. The queen clapped her hands; and a portal opened. They entered the hill and followed a passageway down into the earth. The horse trotted along, its bells jingling. Its hoofbeats echoed from the walls, which were luminous.

The sound of rushing water became audible. The sound grew louder; and they came to a subterranean river. Dark waters flowed into the depths of the earth. The horse waded through them and trotted on.

Finally a light became visible; and they emerged from the passageway. Before them lay a vast plain, strewn with boulders. A gray sky hung oppressively low, like the roof of a cavern. Bats were gliding about.

"We are in the Underworld," said the queen.

She spread her cape on the ground; brought out food and wine; and sat down with Thomas to dine. Then she drew his attention to a roadway, which branched into four separate roads. And she said:

> "Yonder right-hand path conveys the spirits of the blessed to Paradise; yon downward and well-worn way leads sinful souls to the place of everlasting punishment; the third road, by yonder dark breake, conducts to the milder place of pain [Purgatory] from which prayer and mass may release offenders. But see you yet a fourth road, sweeping along the plain to yonder splendid castle? Yonder is the road to Elfland to which we are now bound. The lord of the castle

is the king of the country, and I am his queen."*

The castle shimmered in the distance like a mirage. That road to Elfland led directly to its gate. They got back on the horse and set out for the castle.

What was Thomas's state of mind during all this? He was spellbound—bewitched by a kiss. And like someone in a trance, he was oblivious to the singular nature of what was happening. A single thought gripped him: he must accompany the queen and serve her.

They arrived at the castle and rode inside. In the hall a banquet was in progress. Seated at long tables were scores of fairies. They were feasting, singing, laughing. Servants circulated with platters of food. A clown cavorted from table to table. The scene was one of boisterous merriment.

The queen took her seat at the head table, and directed Thomas into the seat beside her. They were served goblets of nectar. Whispering in his ear, she told him to relax and enjoy himself. And she pointed to a corpulent fairy who was holding forth at the far end of the table. That was her husband, the king of the fairies. Ignore him, she said.

And ignore him they did. For that night Thomas and the queen became lovers. And for seven days he recited his poems for her, and enjoyed her company. But on the eighth day, she informed Thomas that it was over. It was time for him to leave Fairyland and return home. He protested, but to no avail. His captivity had ended.

The queen took him back to the river bank. She thanked him for his poetry and handed him an apple. "Take this for your wages. It will bestow on you the gift of prophecy."

Finally, she made him pledge that—if summoned—he would return to her. And with that, she rode off into the forest.

Pocketing the apple, Thomas walked into town. And the

---

* This speech is from Sir Walter Scott's version of the tale, which he based on interviews with local peasants. Sir Walter was quite taken with the tale. So much so that he purchased the spot where Thomas was said to have kissed the queen; incorporated it into his estate; and would lead visitors to "the Rhymer's Glen."

townsfolk crowded about their missing laird. They were amazed at his return. For seven *years* had elapsed.*

Thomas explained his absence: the queen of the fairies had been holding him captive. But the explanation drew a mixed reaction. Some of the townsfolk believed him. But others were skeptical. Surely, they insisted, he had simply been roaming the countryside as a vagabond.

"Here's proof," he said, and showed them the apple. "A gift from the queen of the fairies. And it will grant me the power of prophecy."

Thomas returned to his tower. There he resumed his life

---

* See note in chapter 5 regarding the passage of time in Fairyland.

as a laird and a poet. In addition, he began to prophesy.

The years passed. And Thomas the Rhymer became famous for his prophecies. He foretold deaths, political events, crop failures—all with uncanny accuracy, thanks to the apple. Thomas could foresee the future. Yet in private, he looked back to the past. For he had spent a week with the queen of the fairies. And the memory haunted him.

Then one night Thomas was dining with guests, when a neighbor burst into the tower. He had a marvelous sight to report. Two *white deer* had emerged from the forest. They were approaching the tower at a stately pace, their coats gleaming in the moonlight.

"She has summoned me," said Thomas, rising slowly from his chair.

He excused himself and went outside. When the deer saw him, they turned and headed back to the forest. Thomas followed after them.

He was never seen again.*

---

* Or perhaps he was—by an eighteenth-century horse-dealer known as Canobie Dick.

While traveling one night in the Eildon Hills, Canobie Dick encountered "a man of venerable appearance, and singularly antique dress." (The description is Sir Walter Scott's.) It was Thomas the Rhymer. The horse-dealer bargained with Thomas, sold him a horse, and accompanied him to a cave.

Deep in the cave was a stable, lit by torches. And in each stall was a horse and a knight, both of them asleep. For since his disappearance, Thomas had become a caretaker—of King Arthur and his knights!

Thomas paid Canobie Dick for the horse, and gave him a tour of the stable. On a table, gleaming in the torchlight, was a horn. Thomas explained that it was for awakening the knights. For they were to be roused in an hour of national crisis. Canobie Dick picked up the horn and examined it.

And unable to resist the impulse, he blew on it.

Immediately, there was a stirring throughout the stable. Horses snorted and shook themselves. Knights stirred, murmured, and began to awaken. King Arthur himself—on a velvet couch—bolted upright.

"False alarm, false alarm!" shouted Thomas. "Go back to sleep!" And he ushered the horse-dealer out of the cave.

10.
Paiute Chief

There appeared in the September 1949 issue of *Fate* magazine an article titled "Tribal Memories of the Flying Saucers." Its author was identified as Oge-Make, a Navaho Indian.

Oge-Make tells of going to the foothills of the Panamint Mountains; seeking out an old man of the Paiute tribe; and asking him about the "mystery ships" that were being seen in the skies. Were flying saucers something new? asked Oge-Make. Or had Indians known about them in earlier times, and preserved that knowledge in legend?

At dusk the two sat beside a fire and smoked together. And the old man told Oge-Make a tale.

•

Long ago, said the elderly Paiute, a tribe called the Hav-musuv migrated to the Panamint Mountains. And in a subterranean cavern, they built a city. For they wished to dwell in seclusion, hidden from the warring tribes of the region.

The nearby Paiutes, however, were aware of their presence. For the Hav-musuvs were both technologically and culturally advanced; and when they traveled, they did so in silver airships—flying disks that would emerge from the cavern and disappear into the clouds.*

The Paiutes feared their subterranean neighbors and

---

* That issue of *Fate* had two articles on flying saucers. For editor Ray Palmer was zealously promoting the phenomenon. Initially, he proposed an extraterrestrial origin for UFOs. But he would later change his mind, and argue that they came from inside the earth.

The career of Ray Palmer (who has been called "the man who invented flying saucers") will be examined in chapter 20.

avoided contact with them. But on one legendary occasion, the Paiute chief visited the Hav-musuvs.

The chief's young wife had died suddenly. Overwhelmed with grief, he had wandered off into the mountains. His intent was to perish there at the hands of the Hav-musuvs, and join his wife in the Spirit-land. For the Hav-musuvs were reputed to slay—with a kind of ray-gun—anyone who approached their cavern.

The Paiutes mourned their chief. But after many weeks, he returned to them. And as they gathered round, the chief described his experience in the mountains.

The Hav-musuvs had welcomed him, he said, and escorted him into their underground city. There they had taught him their language, their legends, and their wisdom. Taken with the beauty of the city, and impressed by the advanced ways of its inhabitants, he had wished to remain with the Hav-musuvs. But they had insisted that he return to his people, and pass on the wisdom he had acquired.

So that is what he did.

•

When the old man had concluded his tale, Oge-Make

asked if he believed it to be true. The Paiute took a few puffs of tobacco and was silent for a moment. Then he acknowledged that the chief may have imagined the encounter. His grief, coupled with the isolation of the mountains, could have affected his mind.

But then the old man gestured at the mountains.

"Look behind you at that wall of the Panamints. How many giant caverns could open there, being hidden by the lights and shadows of the rocks? How many could open outward or inward and never be seen? How many ships could swoop down like an eagle, on summer nights? How many Hav-musuvs could live in their eternal peace away from the noise of white-man's guns in their unscaleable stronghold?"

And staring into the fire, he said: "This has always been a land of mystery. Nothing can change that."

He passed the pipe to Oge-Make, who gazed out at the mountains and wondered what lay hidden therein.*

---

* Oge-Make was actually L. Taylor Hansen (1897–1976), a magazine writer and ethnologist. And "L. Taylor Hansen," her usual by-line, was itself a kind of pseudonym. Her full name was Lucile Taylor Hansen; and she wrote a monthly column for *Amazing Stories* that explored Indian legend and lore. In the 1940s ethnology was still largely a male enterprise; and Hansen apparently concealed her gender that it might not diminish her credibility.

But why present herself in this case as a Navaho? Conceivably, Hansen was an honorary member of the tribe, which she had visited and written about. (She had been inducted into at least one other tribe, the Ojibway.) More likely, Ray Palmer, the editor of *Fate*, sought to enhance the authenticity of the article by having it appear to have been written by an Indian.

Oge-Make was not Hansen's first incarnation as an Indian. In the December 1946 issue of *Amazing Stories* (also edited by Palmer) was an article titled "America's Mysterious Race of Indian Giants." The writing style, learned and literate, was recognizable as that of columnist L. Taylor Hansen. Yet the article was attributed to "Chief Sequoyah," supposedly a hunter and fisherman. Chief Sequoyah (that is to say, Hansen) is worth quoting at length, for his evocative prose, and for the lore about giants:

"The very first stories I heard as a boy were those of a mysterious race of Indian Giants which the Indians of the Pacific Coast called the Se-at-kos. Whether sitting before a friendly campfire or snugly wrapped in furs on a long canoe voyage up and down the Puget Sound, the story teller would always eventually turn to the colorful Giants who roamed up and down the Olympic peninsula as well as the Rocky Mountain range; who were such swift runners they ran their game down and killed it with their hands; whose strange sex-life moved them to kidnap Indian women into wifely bondage; who understood and could talk fluently the different parent tongues of the Pacific Coast Indians; who knew the art of mass hypnotism beyond the knowledge of any modern hypnotist; whose peculiar Nietzschean philosophy often made them ruthless; who were past masters in the art of ventriloquism; who were psychic and had strange mystical powers and yet had such an original sense of humor that they appeared at times like boisterous irresponsible children, playing practical jokes upon people and laughing their way through life....

"Occasionally, the Puget Sound Indians heard strange, soul stirring songs just before winter set in, as the Giants mobilized in the Olympic Range and started their long march to the south. I have gathered from Indian mystics who heard their songs, that it sounded like the rhythmic rumblings of muffled thunder symbolically attuned to sidereal harmonics, to the cosmic chant of the stars, to the music of spheres, to the crashing of systems in the four great cycles of Man, to the querulous chirp of the hungry people in the dead ashes of time, to the cool tumult of elemental conflicts as cyclonic winds went questing in the darkened void for atoms and Man, to the flaming up of America in the primeval darkness of the fire age, to the onset of tidal waves crashing over the hum of gnats, the trumpeting of mastodons, the barking of dogs, the coughing of lions, the melody of the thrush, the bull-roar of Giants and the wailing voice of man....

"The Puget Sound Indians are not the only tribe that have seen and talked with the mysterious race of Indian Giants. The Okanagans, the Iroquois, the Coeur D'Alenes, the Kalispels, the Pend Oreilles, the Nez Perce, and the Cherokees tell of them in song and legend."

As a chronicler of Indian lore, Hansen was both erudite

and eloquent. Yet her monthly columns—never collected into a book—are slowly disappearing. For the pages of old issues of *Amazing* (which was printed on pulp paper) are turning brittle and crumbling. Like the culture she sought to commemorate, these writings by L. Taylor Hansen are vanishing.

For more on Hansen, see *Partners in Wonder: Women and the Birth of Science Fiction* by Eric Leif Davin.

11.

Robert Kirk

ON THE EVENING OF MAY 14, 1692, A SCOTTISH CLERGY-man was abducted by fairies. They took him to their underground realm and held him captive. His attempts to escape failed; and the clergyman became a resident of Fairyland.

He is apparently still there.

His name was Robert Kirk. He grew up in Aberfoyle (known today as "the gateway to the Highlands"), where his father was the local minister. After studying at Edinburgh University, Kirk was himself ordained and assigned to the town of Balquidden. For twenty years he served as minister there. He then succeeded his late father at Aberfoyle—where he remained until that fateful evening.

In both places Kirk attended diligently to the needs of his parishioners. Yet he also had time for scholarship. He translated the Psalms into Gaelic. And he supervised the publication of a Gaelic Bible—that the Holy Scriptures might be read in the Highlands. But an endeavor of a different sort would come to preoccupy him.

For the Reverend Kirk had begun a study of local folklore—specifically, of fairy lore. Notebook in hand, he would visit his parishioners and record what they had to say (in Gaelic) about "the little people." His notebooks filled, with traditions about the fairies—and with eyewitness accounts. For some of his informants, endowed with second sight, spoke of personal encounters.*

---

* Second sight was not uncommon in the Scottish Highlands. The term referred to psychic gifts, such as the ability to see into the future, to heal, to find lost objects, or to see the fairies. Kirk himself may have possessed second sight. He was the seventh son in his family; and it was believed that seventh sons possessed such abilities.

Over the years, Kirk gathered a sizable collection of lore. Some fairies were human-sized, his parishioners told him; but most were smaller. They were fond of mischief, and would pilfer from kitchens at night. They dressed in tartan, just like Highlanders, and were similarly divided into tribes. They had rulers and laws. The fairies loved to dance and make music. They dwelt underground, in large houses, and held banquets in subterranean halls. They married and died, though living to a ripe old age. They were quarrelsome. And they were godless—utterly irreligious.

Kirk was told how to see the fairies. You sought out a seer—a person with second sight—and placed a foot on his foot. The seer then placed his hand on your head. And looking over his right shoulder, you would see the fairies!

And he was told about the fairy hills—the earthen mounds scattered throughout the Highlands. Beneath them dwelt the fairies. (Though some said it was the souls of the dead who dwelt there.) It was dangerous, he was warned, to remove wood from a fairy hill, or to otherwise disturb it.

But Robert Kirk already knew about fairy hills. For he had grown up in the shadow of one.

The Kirk family had resided in the Manse—the parsonage at Aberfoyle. A short walk from the Manse was a mound, on which young Robert and his siblings had played. They knew, of course, who dwelt beneath the mound. For it was called Dun Shi, or "mound of the fairies." Dun Shi was overgrown with trees and bushes. At its summit was a clearing, in which grew a solitary pine. The river Forth flowed nearby. And the mound seemed to be brooding beneath the gray skies of Aberfoyle.*

In 1685 Kirk succeeded his father as Aberfoyle's minister. He returned to the town and moved back into the Manse, his boyhood home. And in addition to preaching the gospel, he began to write a treatise. It was based on the lore he had collected over the years—lore he had come to believe was factual. *Fairies were real.* By 1691 the manuscript was complete. He made a copy for an interested party in London; tucked away the original in a drawer; and went about his pastoral duties.

Now it had become his habit to take a stroll in the evening, on Dun Shi. Roaming the mound in his nightshirt, Kirk was a ghostlike figure, and a peculiar one, too. For he was sometimes seen with his ear to the ground—listening for fairies. On the evening of May 14, the Reverend Kirk took such a stroll.

Later that night he was found collapsed on the mound—the apparent victim of a heart attack. Carried back the Manse, Kirk was pronounced dead. He was 48 years old.

---

* Sir Walter Scott describes Aberfoyle and its environs: "These beautiful and wild regions, comprehending so many lakes, rocks, sequestered valleys, and dim copsewoods, are not even yet quite abandoned by the fairies, who have resolutely maintained secure footing in a region so well suited for their residence."

As for that solitary pine atop the mound, it would become a tourist attraction: the "Minister's Pine." Visitors to Aberfoyle tie ribbons to its branches, inscribed with wishes. And children run around it seven times, in hope of seeing a fairy.

A funeral was held. And Robert Kirk—*or what was believed to be him*—was buried in the churchyard. And there, presumedly, his tale had ended.

But there was more to come. For a few days later Kirk—still clad in his nightshirt—appeared to a relative in a dream. And he said:

> "Go to my cousin Duchray, and tell him that I am not dead; I fell down in a swoon, and was carried into Fairyland, where I now am. Tell him, that when he and my friends are assembled at the baptism of my child [Kirk had left his wife pregnant], I will appear in the room, and that if he throws the knife which he holds in his hand over my head, I will be released, and restored to human society."*

The relative neglected to deliver the message. So Kirk appeared to him a second time, threatening to haunt him until he complied. The message was delivered. And on the day of the christening, cousin Duchray came prepared with a knife.†

Family and friends gathered in the Manse. The child was baptized. And suddenly, *Robert Kirk entered by the front door.* The apparition was seen by everyone. Alas, so astonished was Duchray that he failed to throw the knife. And Kirk (no doubt sorely disappointed) passed through and exited by the rear door.

Now what exactly had happened to him? Kirk had apparently been taken captive by the fairies—something known to occur in the Highlands. But why? According to Sir Walter Scott, his abduction was a punishment—for gathering information about the fairies, and for trespassing on their hill. Sir Walter describes his final moment

---

* This speech is found in Patrick Graham's *Sketches of Perthshire* (1812). The Reverend Graham, who succeeded Kirk as minister in Aberfoyle, was quoting a local tradition.

† It was believed in the Highlands that fairies had an antipathy to iron, and that an iron object—such as a knife—would counteract their spells.

on Dun Shi:

> He sunk down in what seemed to be a fit of apoplexy, which the unenlightened took for death, while the more understanding knew it to be a swoon produced by the supernatural influence of the people whose precincts he had violated.

His more grievous offense, though, had been to delve into their secrets:

> It was by no means to be supposed that [the fairies], so jealous and irritable a race as to be incensed against those who spoke of them under their proper names, should be less than mortally offended at the temerity of the reverend author, who had pryed so deeply into their mysteries, for the purpose of giving them to the public.

For these transgressions, Kirk was spirited away—"a terrible visitation of fairy vengeance."

But what about the body that was found on Dun Shi and brought back to the Manse? For that the local Highlanders —wise to the wily practices of the fairies—had a ready explanation. The body was a "stock"—a facsimile—a kind of changeling. The fairies had taken Kirk and left behind a substitute.

Buried in the churchyard was that substitute. And Kirk, it was widely believed, was a captive in Fairyland.

•

In the years that followed, he appeared in dreams to residents of Aberfoyle, with a plea for help. And occasionally, someone crossing the bridge near Dun Shi would feel a sudden burden on his back—the soul of Robert Kirk, seeking to escape. But the clergyman's fate had been sealed. And he remained among the fairies.

Three centuries have passed since his abduction; and Kirk has probably become resigned to his captivity. And he may even be making the best of it. Perhaps he is joining the fairies at their banquets (along with Thomas the Rhymer)... visiting them in their homes...taking notes for a sequel to his treatise (the fairies themselves now his informants).

And—futile as it may seem—preaching the gospel to the fairies.*

---

* That manuscript that Kirk left behind in a drawer? It fell into the possession of his eldest son, and was eventually deposited in a library in Edinburgh. And in 1815 *The Secret Commonwealth* was published in a limited edition.

The book begins with a preamble:

"AN ESSAY on the Nature and Actions of the Subterranean (and, for the most Part) Invisible People, heretofore going under the names of ELVES, FAUNS and FAIRIES, or the like... as they are described by those who have the SECOND SIGHT; and now, to occasion further Inquiry, collected and compared, by a Circumspect Inquirer residing among the Scottish-Irish in Scotland."

The Secret Commonwealth of Elves, Fauns and Fairies (as later editions were titled) is a study of the inhabitants of Fairyland—by a man who believed in their existence. It describes their origin, appearance, customs, crafts, food, social organization, and lifestyle—information that Kirk had collected from his parishioners. And it includes a discourse on second sight, in which he seeks to show that the talent is "not unsuitable to Reason nor the Holy Scriptures." For Kirk viewed such subjects as second sight, ghosts, and fairies through a dual lens: the scientific spirit that arose in the seventeenth century, and the traditional world view of a Christian.

He discusses in his treatise the nature of fairies. Materially, they evince "a middle Nature betwixt Man and Angel, as were Dæmons thought to be of old... somewhat of the Nature of a condensed Cloud and best seen in Twilight." As for their character, fairies can be as troublesome as humans. "These Subterraneans have Controversies, Doubts, Disputes, Feuds, and Siding of Parties; there being some Ignorance in all Creatures.... they transgress and commit Acts of Injustice, and Sin."

And sadly, the fairies are godless. They have "no discernible Religion, Love, or Devotion towards God, the blessed Maker of all: they disappear whenever they hear his Name invoked, or the Name of JESUS."

Clearly, such creatures bear little resemblance to the dainty fairies—the sprites with gossamer wings—of the Victorian era.

Robert Kirk was a folklorist, who specialized in traditions about the supernatural. And he holds a unique position among folklorists. For not only did Kirk believe in the factual nature of the lore he collected; he became, with his alleged abduction, the stuff of lore himself.

12.

Hans Dietrich

The ISLE OF RÜGEN IS LOCATED IN THE BALTIC SEA, and has become a popular tourist destination. Its principal inhabitants are of German descent. But they share the island with another people—a mysterious race who dwell underground; are short of stature (barely knee-high to the Germans); and are known as *zwergen*, or dwarfs.

The dwarfs reside beneath the Nine Hills, near the village of Rambin. There they labor as silversmiths and goldsmiths. During the winter the dwarfs keep to their workshops, deep within the earth. But in the spring they emerge from the hills, to enjoy the sunshine and flowers. And at night they cavort upon the grass, making music and dancing. The villagers hear the music, but cannot see the dwarfs, who make themselves invisible.

Now a family named Dietrich once resided in Rambin. The youngest child was Hans—an intelligent, well-behaved, and studious boy, whose passion was to listen to stories.

One summer Hans was sent to work on an uncle's farm. He was eight years old at the time. His job was to help old Klas, the cowherd, graze the cows on the Nine Hills. As they worked together, Klas entertained him with tales. Thus did Hans learn about the dwarfs who dwelt beneath the hills.

And he yearned to visit their subterranean home. Klas had even revealed the means of doing so: the cap of a dwarf. Donning such a cap, one could see the dwarfs, descend safely into their realm, and even master them.

Finally, Hans could restrain himself no longer. During the night he slipped away from the farm; made his way to the hill where, according to Klas, the dwarfs held their nocturnal revels; and lay there, pretending to be asleep.

A distant church bell tolled midnight. And soon thereafter, a medley of sounds arose: humming and drumming, whispering and singing, jingling and whirling. *The dwarfs were dancing on the hill.* But peeking out, Hans could see nothing of them. For they were as invisible as the wind.

So he did not see the prank: one dwarf snatching the cap of another and tossing it. But as it landed near Hans, the cap—peaked and topped with a bell—became visible.

"A dwarf cap!" cried Hans. And leaping to his feet, he picked it up and donned it.

The dwarfs became visible. Dozens of them were cavorting on the hilltop. They were all dressed alike. Glinting in the moonlight were the bells on their caps—the buttons on their vests—the buckles on their shoes.

The cap's owner approached Hans and tried to snatch it back. When Hans dodged him, the dwarf begged for its return. But Hans refused to give it up. "I shall keep your cap," said Hans, "for it makes me your master. Dwarf, you are my servant now! You shall cater to my needs. And you shall take me underground to the dwelling place of your people."

The dwarf wept, but to no avail. Hans ordered him to fetch food. And as the dancing continued, Hans feasted.

At dawn a trumpet sounded. A portal opened in the hill;

and the dwarfs swarmed into it. Led by his servant, Hans too entered the hill.

Inside, the dwarfs were crowding into tubs. The tubs—attached to chains drawn from below—were rising and descending in a shaft. Hans and his servant climbed into a tub. Ethereal music rose from below; and as they descended in the shaft, Hans was lulled into sleep.

When he awoke, Hans found himself lying in a bed. He was in a richly furnished room. His servant entered with breakfast. And thus began his visit with the dwarfs—and his ten-year stay among them.

Later that day, Hans joined the dwarfs at a banquet. His servant had provided him with suitable clothes; and Hans still wore the cap that was his passport to the subterranean realm. The banquet hall was lit by luminescent gems that were embedded in the ceiling. Entering the hall, Hans had been welcomed by all; introduced to the dwarf leaders; and seated between two females, who fawned upon him. Amid general merriment an elaborate meal was served.

The servers, Hans noted with surprise, were human children like himself. Wearing white jackets, they bustled from table to table. These children, he learned, had been taken from their homes and made to serve the dwarfs. After fifty years they would be allowed to return to their villages. Hans pondered their fate for a moment. Then he said to himself: "The children seem happy enough. And they're not so badly off, serving the dwarfs. It's better than tending cows!"

Mechanical birds had been launched into the air; and their singing filled the hall. When the meal ended, the bird song became livelier; and it served as music for dancing. Hans joined in the dancing. Finally, the merriment ended; and the dwarfs filed out of the hall—some to their workshops, others to their quarters.

Hans was an honored guest of the dwarfs—a status conferred upon him by the cap. So he was given no work to do. But as the weeks went by, he developed a routine of activities. After the daily banquet, he would wander about the Abode (as their rambling residence was called). He looked at the pictures on the walls, and explored nooks and crannies. Hans played on a flute. He went outside and took walks in the subterranean fields. And most agreeably, he played games with the human children. For when not serving the dwarfs, they were free to do as they liked.

This pleasurable idleness continued for a while. Then Hans learned that the dwarfs had a school. Its classes were taught by the Wise—elderly dwarfs with long white beards. Some of the Wise were thousands of years old, and had acquired vast stores of knowledge over the millennia.

Hans was permitted to enroll in the school. He began with classes in Latin and math. An apt pupil, he went on to study chemistry and other scientific subjects. And he mastered the art of riddle-making, which was highly esteemed among the dwarfs.

Hans was pleased with the new life he had found. The world of the dwarfs offered all that he might want. And as he pursued his studies, played with the servant children, and danced at the banquets, his former life was forgotten. He gave no thought to the cows on the Nine Hills, the village of Rambin, or the family he had left behind. And so the years passed.

Now among his playmates was a girl named Elizabeth. Two years younger than he, Elizabeth was also from Rambin; her father was its minister. Unlike the other servants, she had not been stolen from her home. Rather, she had joined the children of the village in a ramble through the hills. Lying down to rest, she had fallen asleep in the grass—and been left behind. When she awoke, Elizabeth found herself in the Abode. The dwarfs had discovered her asleep in the grass, and taken her as a servant.

As they played together, Hans and Elizabeth grew fond of one another. The fondness blossomed into love. And by the time he was eighteen and she, sixteen, the two had become inseparable.

They delighted in taking walks together. Hand in hand, they would stroll through the subterranean fields. And they would marvel at the stone sky and mysterious light of the home of the dwarfs. Elizabeth enjoyed these walks, yet found herself saddened by them, too. For gazing up at the sky, she was reminded of the world beyond it. Of the sun, the moon, and the stars. And of the parents who had loved her.

One evening, while strolling, they passed the entrance to the shaft. From the world above, they heard the crowing of a cock. It was a sound neither of them had heard since leaving that world. Elizabeth broke into tears. And she said:

"The dwarfs have always been kind to me. Yet I have never felt truly at home here. And I have you—yet that isn't enough. How I miss my father and mother, and the church where we worshipped God. Every night I dream of that church! Hans, it is no Christian life that we lead among the dwarfs. Nor can we ever marry, without a minister to bind us. Let us find a way to leave this place and return to Rambin. That we may dwell among Christian folk and worship God."

Hans too had been affected by the crowing of the cock. And listening to Elizabeth, he realized that his own feelings were no different than hers. His family, his village, his church—how could he have gone for so long without giving them a thought? How could he have succumbed so totally to the blandishments of the Abode? Surely he had been bewitched!

"You are right," said Hans. "It is wrong for us to dwell among the dwarfs. That crowing was a wake-up call. Let us return to Rambin. It was a sin for me to have come to this place—may I be forgiven on account of my youth. But I shall remain here no longer! For am I not free to leave when I wish?"

At these final words of his, Elizabeth turned pale—for she recalled the terms of her servitude. As their captive, she was bound to serve the dwarfs for fifty years.

"Alas, I may not accompany you," she said. "For I must remain in the home of the dwarfs for fifty years. Such is the law. We'll both be gray-haired when I join you in Rambin. And my parents will be gone!"

But Hans swore he would not leave without her. And the

next day he approached the dwarf leaders. They were seated together in the banquet hall, drinking and singing. Hans greeted them respectfully, and announced that he was leaving. The dwarfs expressed regret at his decision, and wished him well. Then Hans asked if he might take with him one of the servant girls. For he wished to marry her.

The dwarf leaders denied his request. It was a fixed law, they said—servants must complete their fifty years of service before departing. The girl would have to wait until then. Hans begged them to make an exception. But the dwarfs were adamant. And turning away from him, they resumed their merrymaking.

That evening Hans and Elizabeth stood outside the entrance to the shaft, and gazed at it wistfully. Hans assured her that a solution would be found. But Elizabeth shook her head. "There is the gateway to the surface world," she said. "Yet for me it is sealed shut. For the dwarfs are not going to let me go."

Just then a toad came hopping out of the shaft. And Hans recalled something old Klas had told him—that dwarfs could not endure the smell of a toad. Indeed, just seeing one was a torment to them. One could threaten a dwarf with a toad, and compel him to do anything. Hans picked up the toad and took it back with him to the Abode.

The next day he again petitioned the leaders. And again they turned him down. The law was inflexible, they insisted. The girl would have to complete her fifty years of service.

"In that case," said Hans, "I have a present for you." And pulling the toad from his pocket, he dangled it in front of them.

At the sight of it, the dwarfs were overcome with revulsion. They began to whimper, howl, and roll about on the floor. "Take that odious creature away!" cried one of them.

"Gladly. If you'll agree to my request. Allow the servant girl to depart."

"Take her! We'll suspend the law."

"One more thing—we'd like a wedding gift. How about a sackful of gold coins?"

"You shall have it!"

That afternoon the pair were escorted to the shaft. They were given a sackful of coins, loaded into a tub, and drawn to the top of the shaft. The portal opened; and they emerged into sunlight.

They were on top of the hill. Hans tossed away the cap. And they headed for Rambin.

The villagers greeted them with amazement; for both had long ago been given up as lost. Rejoining their families, Hans and Elizabeth rejoiced to be back. And that summer they were wed.

With the sackful of coins, Hans was now a wealthy man. He purchased a farm of his own. And he performed many charitable acts. Among them was the building of a new church for Rambin—which stands to this day.*

---

* My source for this account has been *The Fairy Mythology* (1850) by Thomas Keightley, an Irish scholar. Keightley (who deemed himself to be a "Fairy historian") describes fairies as "beings distinct from men, and from the higher orders of divinities. These beings are usually believed to inhabit, in the caverns of the earth, or in the depths of the waters, a region of their own. They generally excel mankind in power and in knowledge." And the subject of his book, he says, is "those beings who are our fellow-inhabitants of earth, whose manners we aim to describe, and whose deeds we propose to record."

He recounts several tales of the Isle of Rügen, including that of Hans Dietrich. And he gives as his source a book titled *Märchen und Jugenderinnerungen* (Fables and memories of youth) by Ernst Moritz Arndt. And Arndt's source? A native of Rügen, he had heard the stories from a local magistrate.

"We therefore see no reason to doubt of their genuineness," says Keightley, "though they may be a little embellished."

13.

Reuben

In the town of Koretz, on the Korchyk River, dwelt Rabbi Pinchas (1728–1790). The rabbi was a Hasid—a disciple of the Baal Shem Tov.*

Rabbi Pinchas was both saintly and scholarly. His days were devoted to prayer, meditation, and study. He was particularly devoted to the Zohar, the central text of Jewish mysticism. He studied it daily and urged his own disciples to do likewise. Those disciples revered Rabbi Pinchas, and believed him to possess special powers.†

Oblivious to mundane matters, Rabbi Pinchas lived a life of poverty. He dwelt in a dilapidated house with his wife and daughter. There he was always available to those who sought his guidance, knowledge, or working of wonders. And one day a young man named Reuben appeared on his doorstep.

A yeshiva student, Reuben had come to Koretz from a distant town—prompted by a series of dreams. In these dreams his late father had appeared to him. The father had told him to travel to Koretz and seek out Rabbi Pinchas.

Summoned to the door, Rabbi Pinchas welcomed Reuben

---

* The Baal Shem Tov ("Good Master of the [Divine] Name") was the founder of Hasidism, a form of Judaism emphasizing mysticism and religious fervor. He had numerous disciples, but none like Pinchas. "A soul such as that of Rabbi Pinchas," said the Baal Shem Tov, "comes down to this world only once in 500 years."

† It was said, for example, that Rabbi Pinchas could read minds. A man in Koretz once had doubts as to whether God could know his thoughts. So he decided to get Rabbi Pinchas's opinion on the matter. Going to the rabbi's house, he knocked on the door. Rabbi Pinchas opened the door and said: "Look, *I* know what you are thinking at this moment. So if I can know, surely God knows!"

to Koretz. He told his wife to prepare a meal for their "special guest." For a moment he gazed intently at the young man. Then he suggested that Reuben visit the *mikvah*. For the Feast of the New Moon was to begin that evening.*

Reuben made his way to the mikvah hut, which was located behind the house. He stepped through the doorway. Before him a stairway descended into darkness. Reuben peered into the darkness, but could not discern the pool. A warbling sound, like that of a bird, rose from below.

He began to descend the stairway. Oddly, no pool presented itself. Instead, the stairs continued downward.

As he descended further, the darkness enveloped him. Reuben kept on going, as if drawn by the warbling, or impelled by some hypnotic force. His footsteps echoed as he descended into the earth.

Finally he reached the bottom of the stairway and emerged into light. To his astonishment, he found himself in an underground forest. A bird warbled in a canopy of foliage. A bluish light illumined the trees. There was no mikvah pool in sight.

Puzzled, Reuben took a stroll through the forest. And he was about to return to the stairway, when he heard voices approaching. Frightened now, he climbed a tree and hid in the foliage.

Two men emerged from the woods. They were drinking from a jug and laughing. Near the tree in which Reuben was hiding they came to a halt, dug a hole, and buried something.

"What a prize we have stolen!" said one of the men. "Come, let us go celebrate."

When they were gone, Reuben climbed down from the tree. "Thieves have buried their loot here," he said. "What

---

* The mikvah is a pool in which ritual baths are taken, for purposes of purification. Hasidic men immerse themselves on the eve of the Sabbath and of certain holidays.

The practice is said to have originated with Adam. As an act of penitence, Adam immersed himself in a river that flowed out of Eden.

am I bound to do?"

Digging in the ground, he uncovered a bag. Inside was a large emerald. Like a living thing, it glowed and pulsated.

"What a marvelous gem," said Reuben. "And surely of great value. But I must return it to its rightful owner, or at least make a sincere attempt to do so. For so we are taught by our sages."

And pocketing the emerald, he set off in the direction from which the men had come.

He soon emerged from the forest and beheld a vista of rolling hills. A road wound through them; and rising in the distance were the ramparts of a castle. A gray mist obscured the sky. No habitation was visible, except for the castle. So he set out on the road and headed towards it.

When he reached the castle, its residents were in an uproar. A guard informed him that a theft had occurred. The royal emerald—a jewel that brought good fortune to the kingdom—had been stolen. And the king was offering a reward for its return.

"What sort of reward?" asked Reuben.

"His daughter's hand in marriage."

"Indeed? Well, I have news of the emerald."

Admitted to the throne room, Reuben gave the emerald to the king and explained how it had come into his possession. The king was overjoyed to have it back. And true to his word, he summoned his daughter; introduced her to Reuben—her name was Rachel; and announced their betrothal. Soon thereafter, the two were wed.

The marriage was a happy one. For as it happened, Reuben and Rachel were suited to one another. They settled into a wing of the castle. And in the years that followed, three children were born to them.

Then one day the sky darkened. Thunder shook the castle. And torrents of rain came pouring down.

The flood waters rose; and the castle was inundated. The waters surged about its walls and poured in through its windows. And suddenly a colossal wave swept through the castle.

Caught up in the wave, Reuben was borne away. Like a

piece of debris, he was swept out a window and carried away from the castle. Away from his wife and children!

Gasping for breath, he struggled to stay afloat. But a whirlpool drew him downward. Reuben fought to rise to the surface—

And the next thing he knew, he was in a mikvah hut. He was standing before its pool, at the foot of a brief stairway. Reuben looked at the stairway, and recalled a longer one that years ago he had descended. In a daze, he climbed the stairs and exited the hut.

"Come, your meal is ready."

It was Rabbi Pinchas, calling to him from the house. Reuben went inside.

"We've been awaiting your return," said Rabbi Pinchas. "You've been gone an entire hour."

"An *hour*?"

Reuben rubbed his eyes, as if awakening from a dream. Bewildered, he told Rabbi Pinchas of having spent *years* in a subterranean kingdom. The rabbi nodded knowingly. And he summoned his daughter from the next room.

The daughter entered, carrying a tray of food. Reuben

stared at her in disbelief. For it was the daughter of the king.

"Rachel!" he cried. "My wife from the kingdom!"

"Allow me to explain," said Rabbi Pinchas. "Recently I had a dream. In it I saw the young man who was destined to wed my daughter. Then this afternoon you came knocking at our door. And I recognized you—the young man in my dream!

"So I cast upon you a hypnotic spell; and as you entered the mikvah hut, an illusion took hold of you. You imagined a stairway that went down into the earth. And you imagined a subterranean kingdom, in which you won the hand of Rachel, raised a family, and lived in happiness—until it all came to an abrupt end.

"Why did I subject you to this illusion? First of all, to make you aware of your destiny—to reveal that you were fated to marry my daughter.

"Secondly, to remind you that a man's destiny is influenced by his actions. Had you kept that emerald for yourself, you would not have married Rachel. For one's destiny is subject to revision!

"But my primary aim in creating that illusion? To impress upon you that *nothing lasts in this world*—that happiness can vanish in an instant—that our blessings can be swept away, like debris in a flood! Therefore, enjoy them while they endure."

"That is sound advice, Rabbi. I shall endeavor to do so."

"So Reuben—will you accept Rachel here as your wife?"

"Indeed I shall. For I have loved her for years—however illusory those years may have been."

"And you, Rachel? Will you accept Reuben as your husband?"

"I shall indeed," said Rachel. "Dare I oppose a destined bond? Moreover, we would seem to be already well acquainted."

Rabbi Pinchas clapped his hands. "Then the marriage has my blessing. But Reuben, you must be hungry. Come, let us eat."

Reuben and Rachel were duly wed. They resided in Koretz and raised three children. According to Reuben, the children resembled exactly those in the illusion.

Reuben was grateful to God for the restoration of his wife and children of the subterranean kingdom. And he held them even dearer than before. For he knew now how abruptly they could be taken from him.*

---

* Like most Hasidic tales, this story was transmitted orally for many years. In 1881 a version was included in *Maaysiot ve'shichot Tsaddikim*, a collection of tales published in Warsaw. And most recently, Howard Schwartz has retold it in *Gabriel's Palace*. The tale describes one of the many wonders that Rabbi Pinchas is said to have performed.

As for the teachings of Rabbi Pinchas, they were preserved in a near miraculous fashion. His teachings had been recorded by his disciples. Finally they were gathered together in a manuscript, which remained unpublished. During World War II the manuscript vanished.

But a few years later, a parcel was brought to the Jewish community house in Breslau. It contained that manuscript. Attached was a letter, written in Yiddish by Rabbi Chodorov of Tarnov. The letter read as follows:

"To him into whose hands this manuscript may fall: These papers contain one volume of commentaries by the illustrious Rebbe Pinchas of Koretz, one of the disciples of the Baal Shem Tov. They are the only originals extant. They contain a vast treasure of priceless holy thoughts and insights.... Since I left my home three years ago, a deportee, driven from place to place, I have carried these papers in my valise, never abandoning them—until now. Now that the 'rage of the oppressor' has overtaken us (my dear wife and son and daughter have been stolen from me, may it be the will of our Father in Heaven that I will see them again), and we, the ones who remained, the life we face is precarious and we do not know what the day will bring. Therefore I decided to give these manuscripts which are so dear to me to one of my non-Jewish acquaintances who will hide them until G-d will return the captives from among His people.

"I fervently pray that the One Above has decreed that I may live, and that I myself will have the merit of publishing these manuscripts. But if, G-d forbid, my tracks will not be known, I ask him into whose hand this letter will fall, to be aware that Heaven bestowed on you this holy treasure in order that you bring to light the teachings of the saintly Rebbe Pinchas of Koretz. My request is that you include also my own commentaries, so that they be an everlasting memorial for me.

"My hands are extended to G-d in prayer that I may live to see the consolation of His oppressed nation and the return of G-d to Zion."

14.
Captain Seaborn

IN THE SPRING OF 1818, HUNDREDS OF UNIVERSITIES AND learned societies in America and Europe, along with individual scientists, heads of state, and members of Congress, received a circular in the mail. It contained a startling announcement:

> TO ALL THE WORLD!
> I declare the earth is hollow and habitable within; containing a number of solid concentric spheres, one within the other, and that it is open at the poles 12 or 16 degrees. I pledge my life in support of this truth, and am ready to explore the hollow, if the world will support and aid me in the undertaking....
> I have ready for the press a Treatise on the Principles of Matter, wherein I show proofs of the above positions....
> I ask one hundred brave companions, well equipped, to start from Siberia, in the fall season, with Reindeer and sleighs, on the ice of the frozen sea; I engage we find a warm and rich land, stocked with thrifty vegetables and animals, if not men, on reaching one degree northward of latitude 82; we will return in the succeeding spring.

The circular had been mailed from St. Louis, and was signed by one John Cleves Symmes. Appended to it was a letter—signed by prominent citizens—attesting to Symmes's good character and sanity.

Who was this fellow, who had authored so provocative a notice? Who had spent a considerable sum to print and disseminate it? (500 copies had been mailed out.) And who feared (not unreasonably) that his sanity might be questioned?

Born in New Jersey, John Cleves Symmes (1779–1829) had enlisted as a young man in the Army. He had served with distinction in the War of 1812, rising to the rank of captain. After the war he had been posted to a fort in Missouri, where he had married the widow (with six children) of a soldier. Finally, he had resigned his commission and moved with his family to the frontier town of St. Louis. There he had run a trading post, furnishing supplies to the Army and the local Indians.

The proprietor of a trading post enjoyed an abundance of free time; and Symmes had occupied himself with the study of science and mathematics—and with the formulation of a theory. His formal education had ended early; but he had the self-discipline, enthusiasm for knowledge, and unfettered imagination of an autodidact. The result was that circular, which was soon followed by Circular No. 2 and Circular No. 3.*

But business at the trading post was declining. So Symmes packed up his books, loaded his family (four more children had been added) onto a steamboat, and moved to a town near Cincinnati. And now began in earnest the crusade that would occupy him for the rest of his life. Obsessively, he sought to promulgate his theory of a hollow earth, and to seek financial support for an expedition.

Symmes wrote newspaper articles. (Deemed a crackpot, he also inspired them.) He issued circulars, published pam-

---

* The contents of the circulars were engaging; but the writing lacked polish. As Captain Symmes himself admitted: "I am, perhaps, better fitted for thinking than writing—reared at the plough, I seldom used a pen (except in a commonplace book) until I changed my ploughshare for a sword, at the age of 22."

Of Symmes's educational attainments, disciple James McBride would write: "During the early part of his life he received what was then considered a common English education, which in after-life he improved by having access to tolerable well-selected libraries; and, being endued by nature with an insatiable desire for knowledge of all kinds, he thus had, during the greater part of his life, ample opportunities to indulge it."

He was self-educated—and self-directed in his thinking. According to an acquaintance, Symmes had "attractive blue eyes that gave indication of a mind absorbed in speculation."

phlets, sent off letters. And he traveled about, giving lectures and soliciting donations. Despite his deficiencies as a speaker ("the arrangement of his subject was illogical, confused, and dry, and his delivery was poor," laments one account), Symmes's lectures attracted large audiences. The topic was enticing; and the props he used—a globe with openings at the poles; spinning bowls of sand; magnets and iron filings—provided a theatrical touch. And indeed, his audiences came more for entertainment than for edification. To many, Symmes's theory of a hollow earth was risible; and he was regularly heckled. (Heckling him could be dangerous. On at least one occasion, Captain Symmes physically ejected a heckler from the lecture hall.)*

Symmes also petitioned both Congress and the General Assembly of Ohio, urging them to finance an expedition. For he believed that the interior of the earth could be settled and made part of the Union. (In fulfilling its Manifest Destiny, the U.S. could expand downward as well as westward!) And Congress did in fact consider such a project. In 1823 Representative Johnson of Kentucky proposed that the fed-

---

* His theory became a national joke, with the polar openings referred to derisively as "Symmes's Hole." According to a historical cyclopædia of Butler County, Ohio:

"[The theory's] reception by the public can easily be imagined; it was overwhelmed with ridicule as the production of a distempered imagination, or the result of partial insanity. It was for many years a fruitful source of jest with the newspapers.

"The Academy of Science, of Paris, before which the circular was laid by Count Volney, decided that it was not worthy of consideration. The scientific papers of Europe generally treated it as a hoax, rather than believe that any sane man could issue such a circular or uphold such a theory.

"Circulars and newspaper articles soon followed circular No. 1, and were kept up for years, despite of the ridicule which was poured on the unfortunate author from all sides."

As consolation, Symmes no doubt told himself that he was not the first original thinker whose ideas had met with contempt.

(The expression "It's gone down Symmes's Hole" is still to be heard in the Cincinnati area, referring to misplaced objects.)

eral government launch an expedition "to claim the lands inside the earth"—an expedition to be led by "Captain John Cleves Symmes, late of the United States Army." Though receiving a measure of support, the proposal was voted down.

But material aid was forthcoming from a private source. Attending one of the lectures was James McBride, a wealthy resident of Hamilton, Ohio. McBride was taken with Symmes's theory; befriended him; and bankrolled his travels. Symmes had been lecturing and raising funds in the general vicinity of Cincinnati; now he could range further afield. McBride also published a monograph: *Symmes's Theory of Concentric Spheres; demonstrating that the earth is hollow, habitable within, and widely open about the poles.* It elucidated, and enthusiastically embraced, the hollow-earth theory.*

What exactly was that theory? Symmes believed that the earth consisted of five or more concentric spheres—hollow globes, one within the other. (He later changed his mind, deciding that the earth was a single hollow globe.) Each sphere was surrounded by an atmosphere. And each had an opening at its north and south poles.

The openings in the outer sphere were thousands of miles wide. Upon reaching them, the sea flowed into the earth. The waters clung to the descending rim of the opening; then—inverted now—to the inner surface of the sphere. (Symmes had original ideas about gravity too.) But the curvature of the rim was gradual. Thus, a ship's crew would be unaware (initially at least) that they had sailed into an opening.

As evidence for his theory, Symmes cited the annual migrations that had been observed in the Arctic. In March or April herds of reindeer moved southward along the ice; in October they returned northward. Vast shoals of fish, and flocks of birds, migrated in a similar fashion. Where were they coming from and returning to? *The interior of the earth,* insisted Symmes. And the odd behavior of compasses

---

* An example of McBride's enthusiasm: "Go to the mineralogist and...he cannot perceive anything more derogatory from the power, wisdom, or divine economy of the Almighty, in the formation of a hollow world, than in that of solid ones; and he is rather of opinion, that a construction of all the orbs in creation, on a plan corresponding to Symmes's theory, would display the highest possible degree of perfection, wisdom, and...a great saving of stuff."

in northern latitudes? Further evidence of a polar opening. But Captain Symmes was a man of action as well as a thinker. To confirm his theory—and to serve his country—he was prepared to lead an expedition. The idea was to visit the Arctic in October, follow the reindeer across the ice, and see where they went.

To this goal of polar exploration Symmes devoted himself—publicizing his theory, soliciting funds, and petitioning the government. Yet his efforts might have been in vain, were it not for those of an equally determined disciple.

•

Jeremiah Reynolds was a young newspaper editor in Wilmington, Ohio. He heard Symmes lecture and became a believer. Reynolds wound up joining Symmes on the lecture circuit, serving as his manager and co-lecturer. Together, they embarked on a nationwide tour.

But the two men eventually had a falling out. The point of contention was the hollow earth. While Reynolds continued to credit the idea (or at least to deem it a possibility), it became increasingly less important to him. What should be emphasized, he felt, was the goal of polar exploration—for the sake of scientific advancement, commercial gain, and national prestige. But Symmes refused to downplay his theory of polar openings. The partners split and became rivals, each offering his own version of the lecture. On one occasion, they gave competing lectures in Manhattan on the same day.

Symmes had been a vigorous crusader in behalf of his theory. The rigors of travel, however, led to a deterioration of his health. In 1827 he suffered a collapse, and was forced to retire from lecturing and writing. His years of crusading had ended.

Reynolds now assumed the mantle. As chief advocate for a polar expedition, he spoke in numerous places and to sizable audiences. He was a better lecturer than Symmes: articulate, and endowed with a sense of humor. And his talks scarcely mentioned the hollow earth. His subject was the need for polar exploration.

He also wrote a report on the South Polar regions. It was based on interviews with those who had been there: the captains of whaling and sealing ships. Finally, he succeeded in eliciting government support for an expedition. President John Quincy Adams endorsed the idea; a Navy sloop was fitted out; and plans began to be laid. Unfortunately, Adams was not reelected; and the project was canceled.

Reynolds, however, was determined. He turned now to the private sector, and was able to interest a group of investors in financing an expedition. And in October 1829, three ships—the *Annawan,* the *Seraph,* and the *Penguin*—set sail for the Antarctic. Their purpose was threefold: to hunt seals (and thus earn a profit for the investors); to gather scientific data; and to make a landing in Antarctica. The captains of the ships were all veterans of the seal trade. And included among the scientific corps was Reynolds himself.

But the enterprise was ill-starred. Few seals were found; and the crew (whose pay was to be shares of the catch) began to grumble. Barriers of ice prevented the ships from reaching Antarctica. And when a landing party in a longboat attempted to circumvent the ice, it got separated from the ships and nearly perished.

Finally, as the ships made stops along the coast of Chile, crew members began to desert. Faced with a deficiency of manpower, the captains decided to head home. Reynolds (for reasons that remain unclear) was put ashore in Chile.

For some time he wandered about the country. Then the USS *Potomac*—on its way back from a mission in Sumatra—docked in Valparaiso. Reynolds was taken aboard. And for the next eighteen months, he served as private secretary to the commodore. Upon returning to the U.S., he published an account of the voyage of the *Potomac.**

---

* Its full title was *Voyage of the United States Frigate Potomac, Under the Command of Commodore John Downes, During the Circumnavigation of the Globe, in the years 1831, 1832, 1833, and 1834; Including a Particular Account of the Engagement at Quallah-*

But Reynolds had not given up on Antarctica. He continued to lecture and to call for exploration of the South Polar regions. And in 1836 he was invited to address the House of Representatives. He delivered a speech that was both impassioned and persuasive.

The result was the United States Exploring Expedition of 1838–1842, or Wilkes Expedition, after its commander. Six American ships surveyed islands of the South Pacific; charted the coastline of Antarctica; and collected specimens of flora and fauna. (The specimens would become the nucleus of the Smithsonian collection.) No entrance to the hollow earth was discovered—though admittedly, the Antarctic remained largely unexplored. But much scientific data was gathered.

Reynolds's only disappointment was personal. Due to a clash with the Secretary of the Navy, he had not been permitted to accompany the expedition. Still, he could be proud of his achievement. His efforts had brought about a major advance in knowledge, and had established the gov-

---

Battoo, on the Coast of Sumatra; with All the Official Documents Relating to the Same. In its opening pages, Reynolds describes his acquisition of a post aboard the ship:

"The signal announced a man-of-war, southwest from Playa Ancha, with all sail set, standing directly for the port. The wind was fresh, and she approached rapidly. The stripes and stars were seen waving from the mizzen peak of a stately frigate, which was now pronounced by all to be the Potomac. She entered the harbour late in the afternoon, making several seamanlike tacks against a strong southerly breeze.... On the following day I went on board, with the view of visiting several of the officers with whom I had been previously acquainted. Here I received an invitation from the commodore to join the Potomac as his private secretary, the gentleman who had previously filled that station having died at sea. This is a pleasant birth on board a flag-ship, and I accepted it, as the stay of the commodore on the station promised me a fine opportunity to improve my knowledge of the institutions, natural capacities, commercial resources, and political condition and prospects of so large a portion of South America, which hitherto I had not been able to visit."

ernment as a patron of scientific research.*

---

* Reynolds also left his mark on American literature. He wrote an article about a white whale, known as Mocha Dick, that had sunk a ship off the coast of Chile, and among his readers was Herman Melville. And the alleged polar openings that he and Symmes had publicized? They found their way into the writings of Edgar Allan Poe. Both "MS. Found in a Bottle" and *The Narrative of Arthur Gordon Pym* conclude with their protagonist sailing into the South Polar abyss. In *Pym,* Poe quotes from the address Reynolds delivered to the House of Representatives. And Poe later reviewed a pamphlet by Reynolds, commending its author in no uncertain terms:

"To the prime mover in this important undertaking [the Wilkes Expedition]—to the active, the intelligent, the indomitable advocate of the enterprise—to him who gave it birth, and who brought it through maturity, to its triumphant result, this result can afford nothing but an unmitigated pleasure. He has seen his measures adopted in the teeth of opposition, and his comprehensive views thoroughly confirmed in spite of cant, prejudice, ignorance and unbelief.... With mental powers of the highest order, his indomitable energy is precisely of that character which will not admit of defeat."

The relationship between the two men has been the subject of speculation. Poe may have heard Reynolds lecture, and could have known him when both were living in Manhattan. But what prompted the speculation were the deathbed cries of Poe. According to Dr. Moran, the attending physician: "This state [of delirium] continued until Saturday evening...when he commenced calling for one 'Reynolds,' which he did through the night until three on Sunday morning."

Why would Poe, in his final hours, have called for Reynolds?

It has been suggested that he was calling for *Henry* Reynolds, a carpenter who lived nearby. But the standard view among Poe's biographers is that he was calling for Jeremiah Reynolds, the polar advocate. Why would he have done so? Arthur Hobson Quinn offers an explanation:

"On Saturday night he began to call loudly for 'Reynolds!' Perhaps to his dim and tortured brain, he seemed to be on the brink of a great descending circle sweeping down like the phantom ship in the 'Manuscript Found in a Bottle' into 'darkness and

•

The Wilkes Expedition conducted the first organized exploration of the Antarctic. But informal exploration had been going on for years (as Reynolds had learned from his

---

the distance.'"

And Robert Almy offers a similar explanation:

"Is it not likely, therefore, that in his last illness, when Poe called to Reynolds, he was calling from the verge of that polar chasm whose shadow was as the shadow of death and whose concentric circles led downward to the incommunicable?"

Perhaps. Yet such speculation makes an assumption: that Dr. Moran correctly transcribed what he heard. But what if the doctor was mistaken? What if Poe had called out, not "Reynolds!" but some other word?

What might that word have been?

Poe had a problem with alcohol. But a month prior to his death, he had joined the Sons of Temperance and taken the oath of abstinence. (He had gotten engaged to a woman in Richmond; and a precondition to the marriage may have been that he swear off alcohol.) A common form of the oath of abstinence was this: "I am now fully determined to *renounce* this destructive beverage, from this day, to the day of my death. Yes, I do *renounce* it, fully, totally." [emphasis added]

He seems to have adhered to the pledge—until a fateful day in October. As described by J. P. Kennedy, a friend in Baltimore:

"On Tuesday last Edgar A. Poe died in town here at the hospital from the effects of a debauch.... He fell in with some companion here who seduced him to the bottle, which it was said he had *renounced* [emphasis added] some time ago. The consequence was fever, delirium, and madness, and in a few days a termination of his sad career in the hospital. Poor Poe!...A bright but unsteady light has been awfully quenched."

Poe—susceptible to the worst effects of alcohol—was dying and delirious. Yet surely he was aware of the lapse that had caused his condition. And as if possessed by the voice of Temperance, he had cried out: *"Renounce! Renounce!"*

Alas, it was too late. That same morning he uttered his last words—"Lord help my poor soul!"—and expired.

interviews with sea captains). Whaling and sealing ships had penetrated, and charted, the southernmost latitudes. But these were highly competitive enterprises; and the captains kept their findings secret.

One of them, however, made an astounding discovery (or so he claimed). And in 1820 he published an account of it. The book was titled *Symzonia: A Voyage of Discovery*. It was printed in New York by the firm of J. Seymour. Its author was identified as Captain Adam Seaborn—clearly, a pseudonym. Few copies were sold; and the book attracted little notice. Yet its contents (if factual) were momentous.

Captain Seaborn prefaced his account with these remarks:

> The Author of this work, and of the discoveries which it relates, leaves it to his readers to decide whether he excels most as a navigator or a writer, and whether he amuses as much as he instructs. If he has any professional vanity, arising from his enterprises upon the sea, it does not tempt him to conceal that, in the achievements here recorded, he availed himself of all the lights and facilities afforded by the sublime theory of an internal world, published by Captain JOHN CLEVE SYMMES.

Inspired by Symmes's theory, Seaborn—a veteran sealer—had custom-built a ship; dubbed it the *Explorer*; and sailed for the Antarctic with a crew of fifty. He intended to hunt seals and turn a profit. But his ultimate aim was to enter the South Polar opening and explore the internal world. The benefits of exploring that world? "I flattered myself that I should open the way to new fields for the enterprise of my fellow-citizens, supply new sources of wealth, fresh food for curiosity, and additional means of enjoyment." But he kept this goal secret from the crew, who believed they were simply looking for seals.

The *Explorer* was equipped with a steam-powered paddle wheel, for breaking through ice. (According to Symmes, an "icy hoop" surrounded the polar opening.) The ship's frame was reinforced against the anticipated rigors. And no iron nails had been used in its construction—only wooden pegs and copper bolts. For a colossal lodestone was believed to rise out of the polar waters. "I remembered the misfortune of the discoverer SINDBAD," writes Seaborn, "whose ship, when he approached the magnetic mountain, fell to pieces, in consequence of the iron being all drawn out of it."

Thus prepared, the *Explorer* cruised the Antarctic. Few seals were found; and as the ship passed deeper into uncharted waters, the crew grew mutinous. But Seaborn was hopeful:

> I concurred in the opinion published by Capt. Symmes, that seals, whales, and mackerel, come from the internal world through the openings at the poles; and was aware of the fact, that the nearer we approach those openings, the more abundant do we find seals and whales.

Finally, a welcome discovery was made: a continent, its coast teeming with seals! Seaborn planted a flag, claiming the land for the United States. With the unanimous consent of his crew, he dubbed the continent Seaborn's Land. (It would come to be known as Antarctica.) A portion of the crew was selected to remain behind, establish a station, and hunt seals.

And the *Explorer* sailed on, toward its secret goal.

The hours of daylight grew fewer. The sun's path through the sky was increasingly eccentric. And the compass had become useless, spinning this way and that. These developments excited Seaborn, but frightened his men. It was as if, said one of them, the ship were descending into a hole in the earth.

And in fact, such was the case. For they had entered the South Polar opening and were sailing downward—*into the earth's interior.*

As they sailed on, an island was spotted.

> We discovered land, just at sunset, and immediately hove to, to keep a good offing until day-light. I walked the deck all night, and was very impatient for the morning of that

day which was to disclose to me the wonders of the internal world, and probably to decide the question whether it was or was not inhabited by rational beings.

In the morning a landing party went ashore; and the island was found to be uninhabited, save for turtles and seabirds. But the wreck of a ship was discovered—an "outlandish vessel," unlike any they had ever seen. To Seaborn the wreck strongly suggested that the interior world was inhabited.

Once again the *Explorer* put to sea. The sun was visible now for only a quarter of the day. When it set, a subdued, reflected light illuminated the sea. But a fear had gripped the crew—that total darkness might soon be enveloping the ship; and again there were murmurings of mutiny.*

Then came a cry from the masthead: "Sail ho!" The lookout had spotted a ship in the distance; and the *Explorer* gave chase. But despite its speed, it could not overtake the vessel, which disappeared over the horizon.

Then, as the sun was setting, another cry rang out: "Land ho!"

They drew in slowly, wary of unseen hazards. Scanning the shore with his telescope, Seaborn was able to discern buildings and moving objects. He could barely contain his excitement.

> I was about to reach the goal of all my wishes; to open an intercourse with a new world and with an unknown people; to unfold to the vain mortals of the external world new

---

* The internal world is lit, explains Seaborn, by sunlight that enters via the polar openings. He describes the quality of the light: "The soft reflected light of the sun, which was now no longer directly visible, gave a pleasing mellowness to the scene, that was inexpressibly agreeable, being about midway between a bright moonlight and clear sunshine. I had great cause to admire the wonderful provision of nature, by which the internal world enjoyed almost perpetual light, without being subject at any time to the scorching heats which oppress the bodies and irritate the passions of the inhabitants of the external surface."

causes for admiration at the infinite diversity and excellence of the works of an inscrutable Deity.... My imagination became fired with enthusiasm, and my heart elated with pride. I was about to secure to my name a conspicuous and imperishable place on the tablets of History, and a niche of the first order in the temple of Fame.

When morning came, a striking landscape revealed itself. Rolling hills and groves of trees lay at the foot of a lofty mountain. The *Explorer* sailed into a cove and anchored.

Seaborn surveyed the land he had discovered in the interior of the earth. And he gave it a name.

At noon, on the 24th of December, we anchored in 14 fathoms water, on a fine sandy bottom. This land, out of gratitude to Capt. Symmes for his sublime theory, I immediately named SYMZONIA.

To prepare for his encounter with its inhabitants, Seaborn retired to his cabin. He shaved and donned formal clothes. And he hung a saber at his side, "to make my appearance as imposing as possible." Then, arming seven of his best men, he climbed with them into the longboat.

The landing party headed for the shore. Seaborn stood at the prow of the boat, preening himself in the breeze. The American flag fluttered at the stern.

They landed at a pier. As a signal of peaceful intent, Seaborn removed his saber. (He instructed his men, however, to remain at the ready with their muskets.) And ordering the men to remain in the boat, he disembarked alone.

He walked along the pier, approaching what seemed to be a public building. A number of Symzonians had been gathered on its portico, but had fled inside as he came near. Seaborn removed his hat and bowed toward the building.

When no one appeared, he bowed again. Then he recalled the experience of Captain Ross, the Arctic explorer. Ross had encountered men—from inside the earth?—who had greeted him by pulling their noses. The gesture was an insult in the external world; but within the earth, it was perhaps a mode of salutation. So Seaborn redonned his hat, stood erect, and pulled his nose. The action had the desired effect. A few individuals, then a crowd, emerged from the building. They stared at the American, talking among themselves. Finally one of them stepped forward, put his thumb to his nose, and waved. Seaborn waved back in a similar fashion. Then the two tried to converse, but were mutually unintelligible.

> Seeing him still in doubt whether it was a mortal or a goblin that stood before him, I bethought me to show him that I had some sense of a Supreme Being. I therefore fell on my knees, with my hands and eyes upraised to heaven, in the attitude of prayer. This was distinctly understood. It produced a shout of joy, which was followed by the immediate prostration of the whole party, who seemed absorbed in devotion for a few minutes.

The crowd rose. And the Symzonian with whom he had tried to converse, now came up to Seaborn and shook his hand. The man then walked around him, surveying the explorer with curiosity.

Captain Seaborn, meanwhile, was examining *him*. The Symzonian was about four-feet tall (as were all the adults in the crowd). His complexion was pale—no doubt from the dearth of sunlight inside the earth. He wore a white tunic (as did everyone else); and woven into his hair was a tuft of feathers.

> Having both satisfied our eyes, I again endeavoured to make myself intelligible to him; and, by the aid of signs, succeeded so far as to convince him that I came in peace, and meant no harm to any one. He pointed to the building, which I took as an invitation to go in, and walked towards the portico, with the Internal by my side.

It was the beginning for Seaborn of a six-month stay among the Symzonians. During that time he would be introduced to what was no less than a utopian society.

His stay was supervised by an elder named Surui. The Symzonian arranged living quarters for him; acted as an interpreter (Surui was able to learn English with astonishing ease); and conducted him about. And Surui was pleased to instruct him in the civic polity, customs, manners, and habits of the Symzonians.

Their mode of government, Surui explained, was democratic. Public affairs were directed by a Grand Council (hundreds of thousands of members); an Ordinary Council (one hundred members); and a chief executive known as the Best Man. The Best Man was elected by the Grand Council, and held the position for life. He was advised in day-to-day matters by the Ordinary Council.

The Councils were comprised of men known as Worthies. Selected from the general populace, the Worthies consisted of three orders: the Good, the Wise, and the Useful. The Good were men of benevolence and exemplary conduct, who had worked to promote the happiness of their fellow citizens. The Wise were the philosophers of the land, who had benefitted society by adding to its store of knowledge. And the Useful were individuals with practical skills, whose resourcefulness and inventiveness had advanced the various arts.

Contrary to what might be expected, the Wise men constituted only a small percentage of the Worthies. For their pursuit of knowledge was deemed largely irrelevant to the daily needs of people. And who was eligible for selection as a Worthy, or as the Best Man? One trait that disqualified a candidate was ambition. Anyone who sought an office was —*ipso facto*—considered unfit for it. Thus, Symzonia was governed by the most valuable and upright of its citizens, chosen with the sole aim of advancing the best interests of the nation.

Seaborn was impressed by the Symzonian form of government—a fact that he made known to his host:

> I could not refrain from expressing my admiration of a system so wisely calculated to give the state the benefit of all the talents, information, and tried integrity of the nation. Surui asked me with apparent surprise, if we the Externals did not select men to fill the places of honour, power, and trust, with the same scrupulous attention to their character, purity of life, usefulness in society, and goodness of heart. I was ashamed to acknowledge the truth, and gave him a specimen of the veracity of an External by replying, "yes,

much the same, at least in the State of New-York, where I am best acquainted."

As for the diet of the Symzonians, it was strictly vegetarian. Such a regimen was deemed to be physically beneficial as well as righteous. Symzonians were strong, could leap thirty feet, and lived to be over 200 years old. Their diet was one of moderation, too. When first brought food, Seaborn had eaten—in the eyes of his astonished hosts—enough for ten. He would come to understand the dangers of indulgence:

> Men feeding upon animal food and costly drinks, and given to the indulgence of inordinate passions, must of necessity become very unequal in their condition, depraved in their appetites, and miserable in proportion to their aberrations from the strictest temperance, virtue, and piety.

The Grand Council was in session, with the Best Man presiding. And Seaborn was invited to visit the place of assembly—located on a river, many miles inland—and meet with the Best Man. He and Surui boarded a boat and began the journey.

> We ascended the river, the banks of which, and all the country near them, appeared like one beautiful and highly cultivated garden, with neat low buildings scattered throughout the scene. No crowded cities, the haunts of vice and misery, hung like wens [disfiguring growths] upon the lovely face of nature. An appearance of equality in the condition and enjoyments of the people pervaded the country. The buildings were all of them large enough for comfort and convenience, but none of them so large, or so charged with ornament, as to appear to have been erected as monuments of the pride and folly of the proprietor....The active inhabitants all seemed engaged in something useful.

For several days they traveled up the river. At each stopover they were surrounded by a crowd of the curious, who wished to view the visitor from the outer world. Seaborn describes his "extreme mortification" as Symzonians gazed upon him "with evident pity, if not disgust." He was treated kindly, though, with gifts of food and flowers.

Finally they arrived at the place of assembly, known as the Auditory. It was a colossal structure, covering eight acres and roofed with a dome. Gazing at it, Seaborn was struck with awe and admiration. The Council had adjourned for the day; and the two men were allowed to enter the empty building.

They stood amid its vastness and silence. Rising in tiers were hundreds of thousands of seats—for the Worthies who comprised the Council. The seats surrounded a platform, which held a seat for the Best Man. And another platform held the chairs and music stands for a 500-man orchestra. Each assembly, said Surui, began with sacred music and silent prayer. For the Auditory was both the seat of government and a temple. The idea was for the Council to deliberate in the presence of the Supreme Being.

The next day Seaborn was granted an audience with the Best Man. They met in the garden of his modest residence. Graciously received by the head of state, Seaborn was put at ease by his frank, unaffected manner. And with Surui translating, they conversed.

The Best Man inquired as to whence he had come. Seaborn replied that his country was on the surface of the earth. And the Best Man expressed amazement—that humans could survive in the direct rays of the sun.

And why, the Best Man inquired, had he ventured inside the earth?

> My motive I stated to be, a desire to gain a more extended knowledge of the works of nature; adding, that I had undertaken this perilous voyage only to ascertain whether the body of this huge globe were an useless waste of sand and stones, contrary to the economy usually displayed in the works of Providence, or, according to the sublime conceptions of one of our Wise men [i.e., Symmes], a series of concentric spheres, like a nest of boxes, inhabitable within and without.

Seaborn refrained from mentioning an additional motive: his desire to profit financially from the venture. For he was sufficiently acquainted by now with Symzonian high-mindedness, to know that such a disclosure would arouse aversion and contempt.

Other matters were equally problematical:

> [The Best Man] expressed a desire to be made acquainted with the form of government, the religion, habits, sentiments and practices of the people of the external world... on all which subjects I was extremely disinclined to converse, being aware that if I spoke the truth I should fill him with disgust.

Seaborn described briefly the American form of government, taking care to say nothing of the means that men employed to advance themselves in office. He did mention —expecting approval—that a "Wise man" had once occupied the presidency. But the Best Man reacted with horror, and told him that Symzonia minimized the influence of its Wise men; for they were notorious for their impracticality.

Regarding the habits of the externals, Seaborn was careful to describe only those of the most virtuous and refined individuals. But when he revealed that even they indulged in animal flesh and fermented liquors, the Best Man expressed surprise—that such harmful and deplorable practices were permitted at all, and that the race of externals had not become extinct.

An embarrassed Seaborn sought to change the subject:

> Finding that the longer we conversed on the habits, manners, and sentiments of the externals, the lower they would sink in the estimation of this truly enlightened man, I endeavoured to turn the discourse to our acquisitions in useful knowledge, in full confidence that on this subject I should have a decided advantage, and be able to raise the people of the external world to a high place in his consideration.

Seaborn boasted of the costly apparel and ornaments manufactured by his countrymen. He mentioned cashmere shawls, so exquisitely made as to be valued at two years' labor of a farmer; and works of gold and silver, so beautifully wrought as to become objects of adoration.

> The Best Man could hear me no further on this subject; he pronounced these things to be useless baubles, the creation of vanity, pernicious in their influence upon the foolish, who might be so weak as to place their affections on them, and the production of them a most preposterous perversion of the faculties bestowed upon us by a beneficent Creator for useful purposes.

Again Seaborn sought to change the subject. Confident of impressing the Best Man, he spoke of the skill in arms that the externals had acquired. He described their invention of gunpowder, and their creation of mighty fleets of ships, for the transport of armies and the vanquishing of foes.

> This was the most unhappy subject I had yet touched upon. Instead of exciting his admiration, I found it difficult to convince him that my account was true, for he could not conceive it possible that beings in outward form so much like himself, could be so entirely under the influence of base and diabolical passions, as to make a science of worrying and destroying each other, like the most detestable reptiles.

As his meeting with the Best Man came to a close, Seaborn made a request. Might he moor his ship in a more secure location, and await a more favorable season before sailing home? The Symzonian leader gave permission; but he stipulated that Seaborn's crew remain aboard the ship.

> Enough had been already discovered of our sentiments and habits to convince the Best Man that a free communication with my people would endanger the morals and happiness of his.

And with assurances that, during the remainder of his

stay, information on any subject that interested him—*with the exception of the Engine of Defense*—would be made available, Captain Seaborn took his leave.

In the months that followed, he was able to speak with Worthies; meet again with the Best Man; and observe Symzonians in their daily activities. And he learned about the way of life of this enlightened people. They had simple tastes in both food and dress (everyone wore that white tunic). Greed and selfishness, he discovered, were virtually unknown among them. Instead, doing good was deemed the highest of earthly satisfactions. Symzonians strove to benefit one another. And while an economic system was necessarily in place, it was rational and just. Taxes were light —the equivalent of one or two days' labor per year. At the same time, the accumulation of wealth was disreputable; and most Symzonians devoted any surplus to the wellbeing of their fellows.

Seaborn was able to learn much about Symzonia. He discovered, for example, that pearls—abundant in the local waters—were ground up for use as paint. (He resolved to acquire a rich supply of these pearls.) But in one regard, his curiosity remained unsatisfied. What was that Engine of Defense, he wondered? Against whom did it defend? And why were Symzonians reluctant to speak of it?

He made discreet inquiries; and eventually the facts came out. The Engine of Defense was a highly destructive machine, which had been instrumental in winning the war with Belzubia.

Seaborn already knew about the Belzubians, from conversations with Surui. They were a people on the northern continent of the interior world, descended in part from expelled Symzonians. These Symzonians had yielded to base instincts, formed pernicious habits, and turned to crime. Considered dangerous to society and incorrigible, they had been exiled to the northern continent, and left to pursue their vicious ways.*

---

* When Seaborn had first learned of Belzubia, and of its proximity to the North Polar opening, a sobering thought had

Over the course of centuries, the two countries had maintained an uneasy relationship. Then one day, Belzubian warships showed up and began to conquer Symzonia. Unarmed and adverse to bloodshed, the Symzonians stood by helplessly. The total subjection of their country, and the termination of their way of life, seemed to be at hand.

At this juncture, a citizen named Fultria came forward with an invention. The Engine of Defense, as he called it, was a huge machine on wheels. It shot flames, and could destroy anything in its path. Fultria demonstrated his invention, and urged that it be used to exterminate the invaders.

But the Worthies denounced his proposal. It was barbarous and inhumane, they declared. Not even the most righteous end could justify such a means.

In response, Fultria appeared before the Council, and delivered an eloquent and impassioned speech. His argument was compelling. War could be abolished, he insisted, by making inevitable the destruction of those who would wage it. "Let all who take the sword perish by the sword, and war will be known no more."

The Worthies deliberated. And while remaining steadfast in their principles, they arrived at a plan.

> It was thought that the exhibition of this terrible machine, with all its engines in operation, in sight of the Belzubians and their adherents, would impress them with such dread and horror, as to drive them immediately from the country, and effectually deter them from ever returning. This expedient was therefore tried, and it was completely suc-

---

occurred to him. "I felt not a little humbled by this account of the origin of the northern internal people, and cautiously avoided any observation that might discover, to my intelligent conductor, the suspicion which darted through my mind, that we the externals were indeed descendants of this exiled race; some of whom, penetrating the 'icy hoop' near the continent of Asia or America, might have peopled the external world. The gross sensuality, intemperate passions, and beastly habits of the externals, all testified against us."

cessful. The enemy fled.... and since that time war had not been known.

Seaborn wished to know more about the Belzubians. But given their warlike nature, he thought it best not to inquire about them. For his own people were equally warlike—a fact that might come out if Belzubia were discussed.

Yet the character of his people did become known. For Surui had been borrowing books from the *Explorer*; translating them; and reporting on their contents. The Best Man studied these reports, with growing concern. And finally he summoned Seaborn to his residence.

The two men met in the garden. And in a grave voice, the Best Man announced that he had come to a resolution. *The Americans were to leave Symzonia and never return.* For given the character of their race, they presented a danger to the welfare of his people.

> That, from the evidence before him, it appeared that we were of a race who had either wholly fallen from virtue, or were at least very much under the influence of the worst passions of our nature; that a great proportion of the race were governed by an inveterate selfishness, that canker of the soul, which is wholly incompatible with ingenuous and affectionate good-will towards our fellow-beings; that we were given to the practice of injustice, violence, and oppression, even to such a degree as to maintain bodies of armed men, trained to destroy their fellow-creatures; that we were guilty of enslaving our fellow-men for the purpose of procuring the means of gratifying our sensual appetites; that we were inordinately addicted to traffic, and sent out our people to the extreme parts of the external world to procure, by exchange, or fraud, or force, things pernicious to the health and morals of those who receive them, and that this practice was carried so far as to be supported with armed ships.

His decision was based on the contents of the books. He had concluded that the externals were motivated by a thirst for gain; that such a thirst had prompted Seaborn's voyage;

and that commerce with this people would be harmful to Symzonia. Therefore, Seaborn was to return to his vessel and, when conditions were favorable for sailing, depart for home. Nor was he to take with him any goods that might arouse the cupidity of his countrymen. For Symzonia wanted no further contact with externals.

Captain Seaborn was devastated by this lecture, and by his expulsion from Symzonia.

> I was petrified with confusion and shame, on hearing my race thus described as pestiferous beings, spreading moral disease and contamination by their intercourse, and by thus seeing all my hopes of unbounded wealth at once laid prostrate; and I did not recover from the despondency which overwhelmed me, till I recollected that Mr. Boneto [his first mate] would no doubt have a full cargo of seal skins ready against my return to Seaborn's Land, which would ensure me a handsome fortune.

He attempted to dissuade the Best Man, representing the books as the work of benighted Englishmen—not of Americans, who were "the most enlightened people on the face of the earth." And he argued that limited commerce might prove mutually beneficial:

> The Symzonians would, in that case, enjoy the sweet reflection, that they had contributed to the reformation of many of the externals, by the beauty and loveliness of their example, and at the same time have the benefit of more expanded views of the works of a beneficent Creator, through the information which they might derive from the externals.

But the Best Man would not relent. And within a few weeks, the *Explorer* was weighing anchor and sailing away. The ship was headed towards the polar opening.

By the time they had sailed through it and reemerged in the Antarctic, Seaborn was feeling elated. He was thinking of the celebrity he would acquire, as the discoverer of a new world, and of the "unbounded encomiums" that would be lavished upon him. He was also thinking of the fortune that would be his, if the seal hunt had been successful.

It had been. Arriving at Seaborn's Land, he learned that tens of thousands of seals had been slain. Seaborn had the skins further preserved and loaded onto the ship. And the *Explorer* headed for China, to trade its cargo.

During the passage, Seaborn had time to reflect. And he arrived at a decision. Though avid for celebrity, he would not disclose his discoveries. Such disclosure, he feared, would be met with disbelief and ridicule. Or if believed, others would take advantage of it, fitting out their own expeditions.

Thus resolved, he assembled the crew and made them an offer. If the men would take an oath of secrecy, they could join him on future voyages—to Seaborn's Land, and even to Belzubia. The profits would be shared by all. Enthusiastically, the men accepted.

After weeks at sea, they reached the bustling port of Canton. There the sealskins were exchanged for tea, silks, and porcelain. And laden now with finished goods, the *Explorer* set out on the last leg of its journey.

The passage was uneventful, save for a hurricane off the coast of Africa. And finally the spires of New York appeared on the horizon. The men cheered as the ship sailed into the harbor.

Seaborn engaged an agent to dispose of the cargo. And his tale concludes with a rise to riches—and an abrupt fall.

> Mr. Slippery [as Seaborn refers to this agent] was undoubtedly a great merchant. He lived in a spacious house in Broadway, rode in a splendid coach, walked like a man of consequence in Wall-street, was a bank director, and had the handsomest carpeted compting room in the city, and I know not how many clerks writing in the next room.... I was charmed with him, poor fool that I was, little dreaming that it was the prospect of handling the half million of dollars, which my cargo would produce, that excited his cupidity.

Seaborn signed over his goods. And for several months, he was able to draw sums of money from Slippery's account. He purchased a spacious house of his own; assisted friends and relatives; and "felt myself perfectly secure of all the good things of this world for the remainder of my days."

But the good things came suddenly to an end. One morning he opened the newspaper and learned that Slippery had cheated him of his fortune. Not only was he now destitute, but heavily in debt.

Seaborn entered into a period of mortification and misery. He lost his house. His friends deserted him. And he was forced to declare bankruptcy.

On account of his debts, he was confined to the garret of a debtors' prison. There he wrote *Symzonia: A Voyage of Discovery*. For he hoped to raise money from sales of the book, and free himself from "my present uncomfortable situation."

And there too he found solace—in his memories of Symzonia and the lesson they offered. As we learn in the final chapter:

> With neither the means of subsistence for my family, nor liberty to go in pursuit of them, my misfortunes and privations often weighed down my spirits, and became almost insupportable. When I thought of my situation, I felt no longer like a man. But the remembrance of the pious resignation, the humility, the contentment, the peacefulness and happiness of the Symzonians, recalled me to a conviction of the truth, *that with a temper of calm and cordial submission to the will of Providence* [emphasis added], a man may be happy under any circumstances, but without it must be wretched.

Having completed his voyage of discovery, Captain Seaborn was imprisoned in a garret. And there he discovered a liberating truth.

•

What are we to make of *Symzonia: A Voyage of Discovery*? Is it fact or fiction? And who was its author?

The work presents itself as a factual account. Its title page lists "Captain Adam Seaborn" as the author. In his preface, the author claims to have "discovered and explored a world before unknown." And he asks the reader to decide "whether he excels most as a navigator or as a writer."

But was he in actuality a navigator? Or simply a writer, whose imagination ventured into uncharted waters? Certainly, "Captain Seaborn" is versed in nautical matters. His descriptions—of maritime commerce, routines aboard a ship, the effects of a hurricane—are detailed and accurate, and suggest an intimate acquaintanceship. The man has clearly been to sea, and is able to evoke the seafaring world with his pen.

Whether he has been to Symzonia is another matter. He fears that his claims will be met with disbelief—and they have been. His book has been deemed by most commentators (with one notable exception) to be fiction. It has been described as a utopian fantasy; a satire on voyages of discovery; the first American science-fiction novel. The work is presumed to be an imaginative exercise—a tall tale in the tradition of *Gulliver's Travels*. Bibliographers have classified it under "Voyages, Imaginary."

Nor have the bibliographers been fooled by the pseudonym. The probable author, they tell us, was none other than John Cleves Symmes. That is to say, *Symzonia* was the secret creation of Symmes himself. Who else would have composed so eccentric a tale, with its defense of the hollow-earth theory? And who else would have referred to Symmes as "that profound philosopher"? And named a utopia after him!

But the attribution is surely erroneous. It is unlikely that Symmes (whose middle name the book misspells) was the author. His writings are not distinguished by their prose style; whereas *Symzonia* is the work of a polished writer—an elegant stylist. Nor was Symmes familiar with the sea: aside from his service during the Battle of Lake Erie, he was a landlubber. And his theory—which obsessed him—is barely mentioned in the book. The interior of the earth is simply a convenient place to locate a utopia. As for that reference to a "profound philosopher," it comes with a wink. We are meant to hear "crackpot."

And finally, Symmes was an avid supporter of American expansionism. The earth's interior, in his view, was waiting to be colonized. The author of *Symzonia* condemns such rapacity.

Who then wrote the book, if not Symmes? Who was "Captain Adam Seaborn"? Whose was the plume behind the nom de plume?

One guess is that it belonged to Nathaniel Ames. The son of a Massachusetts congressman, Ames (1796–1835) dropped out of Harvard, ran away to sea, and later wrote newspaper sketches recounting his experiences. Did he also write *Symzonia*? He had the requisite knowledge of seafaring; had visited some of the places mentioned in the book; and displays a satiric bent in his writings. But there is nothing to connect him directly with *Symzonia*—the evidence for authorship is wholly circumstantial. And most critically, Ames fails the style test: his prose, while engaging, is scarcely elegant.*

So who wrote *Symzonia*? No one knows. The book is a minor classic—a gem of American literature. Yet the identity of its author remains a mystery.†

---

* For the theory that Ames was "Seaborn," see "The Authorship of *Symzonia*: The Case for Nathaniel Ames" by Hans-Joachim Lang and Benjamin Lease (*New England Quarterly*, Vol. 48, No. 2).

† During the first half of the nineteenth century, America's most esteemed writer was Washington Irving. Could *he* have been the author of *Symzonia*? A case can be made. Consider the following:

1. Irving published all his early works under pseudonyms: "Jonathan Oldstyle," "Launcelot Langstaff," "Anthony Evergreen, Gent.," "Diedrich Knickerbocker," "Geoffrey Crayon." Might not "Captain Adam Seaborn" be added to the list?
2. Like Captain Seaborn, Irving was a New Yorker.
3. Irving is credited with having dubbed the city "Gotham"—a name that appears in his earliest writings. It also appears

in *Symzonia*.

4. Washington Irving was no stranger to literary hoaxes. His *History of New York* claimed to be the work of Diedrich Knickerbocker, an elderly Dutchman who had vanished and left the manuscript behind in a hotel room.

5. While not a sailor like Ames, Irving had been a passenger on transatlantic vessels—and was observant. Moreover, as a youth he had been an avid reader of tales of exploration. "Books of voyages and travels became my passion," he recalls in *The Sketch Book,* "and in devouring their contents I neglected the regular exercises of the school. How wistfully would I wander about the pier-heads in fine weather, and watch the parting ships bound to distant climes—with what longing eyes would I gaze after their lessening sails, and waft myself in imagination to the ends of the earth!"

6. The Irving family business went bankrupt in 1818; whereupon, Washington turned to writing to make money. Captain Seaborn does likewise after his own bankruptcy.

7. *Symzonia* must have been written between 1818 (when Symmes announced his theory) and 1820 (when the book was published)—the very period in which Irving began to write

•

There were some, however, for whom the authorship of *Symzonia* was no mystery at all. For whom the work was just what it claimed to be: a seafarer's account of his voyage to the earth's interior. Among the believers was Americus Vespucius Symmes, for whom *Symzonia* was confirmation that the earth was hollow.

Americus was the son and disciple of John Cleves Symmes. In 1878 he published *The Symmes Theory of Concentric Spheres*, which reprinted his father's circulars and articles. And the book included a theory of his own: that the inhabitants of the earth's interior were the Ten Lost

---

professionally.

8. Compare these passages (published within eighteen months of one another) that describe sailing up a river:

"As we sailed up the Mersey, I reconnoitered the shores with a telescope. My eye dwelt with delight on neat cottages, with their trim shrubberies and green grass-plots." (*The Sketch Book*)

"Much occurred to gratify my senses...and delight my heart. We ascended the river, the banks of which, and all the country near them, appeared like one beautiful and highly cultivated garden, with neat low buildings scattered throughout the scene." (*Symzonia*)

9. Irving was a skilled satirist, as was the author of *Symzonia*. At the same time, he was known for his geniality. The author of *Symzonia* was described by the *Literary Gazette* of Philadelphia as "good-natured."

10. Irving was an elegant stylist—again, like the author of *Symzonia*. (By his own admission, Nathaniel Ames may be excluded in this regard. When a critic recommended that his next book "should savor more of the style of Goldsmith or Washington Irving," Ames responded: "I should have no objection whatever to writing like either of these distinguished authors, *if I could*; but as the case is, I must be content to write as well as I can.")

Thus, it is conceivable that *Symzonia* was written by Washington Irving. But until a publisher's account book turns up ("$50 pd. to W. I. for Sym."), or some other evidence, the attribution remains purely speculative.

Tribes of Israel.

The book was not his only tribute to his late father. Years before, Americus had arranged for a monument to be placed on his father's grave. It was a stone obelisk, topped with a hollow globe that was open at the poles.

The monument still stands, fenced off in a park in Hamilton, Ohio. A local curiosity, it is weathered and forlorn, with inscriptions that are barely legible. One inscription reads as follows:

> CAPT. JOHN CLEVES SYMMES WAS A PHILOSOPHER, AND THE ORIGINATOR OF "SYMMES' THEORY OF CONCENTRIC SPHERES AND POLAR VOIDS." HE CONTENDED THAT THE EARTH IS HOLLOW AND HABITABLE WITHIN.

15.
Saint-Yves d'Alveydre

IN 1886 THE MARQUIS JOSEPH ALEXANDRE SAINT-YVES d'Alveydre had been about to publish, at his own expense, a work titled *Mission de l'Inde en Europe* (Mission of India in Europe). But no sooner had the books arrived from the printers than he destroyed them all—except for one copy. Threats had been received from India, Saint-Yves would confide to friends; he had been warned not to reveal secrets. Not until after his death, in 1909, would the book be reprinted and released to the public.*

Who was Saint-Yves d'Alveydre? And what were the secrets revealed in his book—a book with this dedication:

> To the Sovereign Pontiff who wears the Tiara of Seven Crowns, the current Brahatma of the ancient Metropolitan Paradesa of the Cycle of the Lamb and the Ram

Born in Paris in 1842, he was the son of a psychiatrist (or alienist, as such physicians were then known). Brilliant but rebellious, young Saint-Yves was removed from school by his father and privately tutored by eminent scholars. He went on to study briefly at a medical college; spent time in London (reading in a desultory fashion at the British Museum); served as a soldier in the Franco-Prussian war; and found employment as a clerk in the Ministry of the Interior.

The clerkship provided a decent livelihood. But in his spare time Saint-Yves was reading widely. And he was writing: poems, essays, a treatise on the agricultural potential of

---

* That sole surviving copy passed into the possession of his stepson, who allowed it to be reproduced. Confusingly, the copy (which resides today in the library of the Sorbonne) is labeled "Third Edition." Such misrepresentation was a common practice of the day, as publishers sought to make new books appear to be bestsellers.

marine algae. Eventually, in his mid thirties, he married a countess. The marriage was a love-match; but it also provided Saint-Yves with financial independence. He was able to quit his job, devote himself to scholarship and writing, and underwrite the publication of his books. To top off his good fortune, the countess procured for him the title of marquis.

Though largely forgotten today, Saint-Yves was a well-known—and controversial—figure of his day. A prolific writer, he was both a political philosopher and an occultist. As a philosopher, he advocated a system called Synarchy. Synarchy was government by an elite group of wise, benevolent men. These sages were without formal power; but they ruled from behind the scenes. Their rule was based on authority: those in positions of power looked to them for guidance. Thus, Synarchy—a system that put the ordering of society in the hands of an unelected elite—was profoundly antidemocratic. In a series of books that combined political theory with occult speculation, Saint-Yves elaborated upon and promoted this idea.

Then, in 1885, he decided to learn Sanskrit, in order to delve deeper into the occult. For this purpose he engaged a teacher: a mysterious Easterner named Haji Sharif. (The fellow was rumored to be an Afghan prince, or else a Brahmin priest who had fled India after the Sepoy Rebellion.) Sharif, who possessed a wealth of arcane knowledge, styled himself "Guru Pandit of the Great Aghartan School." Agharta, he explained to Saint-Yves—into whose house he had moved—was a subterranean kingdom. Located deep beneath the Himalayas, it was governed by sages.

And it dawned on Saint-Yves that this teacher had been sent to him by "the universal occult government of humanity." Sharif's mission was to reveal the existence of Agharta, and to elucidate its spiritual and political organization. Saint-Yves listened avidly.

The Sanskrit lessons, and the esoteric instruction, continued for a year and a half. But then the two men had a falling out. During a dispute about spiritualism, the Guru

Pandit threatened his student with a knife. Saint-Yves evicted him from the house; and Sharif disappeared from Paris. (Years later, he was spotted in Le Havre, supporting himself as a dealer in exotic birds.)

But the mysterious Easterner had fulfilled his mission. Obsessed now with Agharta, Saint-Yves began to receive telepathic messages from its sages. And he began to travel to Agharta via astral projection! These communications and dream journeys would confirm the principles of Synarchy. And they would inspire the writing of a book.

In *Mission de l'Inde* Saint-Yves describes the kingdom of Agharta and its system of government. Agharta is a utopia, hidden away inside the earth. It is a place of advanced technology and exotic architecture. (The main building is a

colossal temple—a "subterranean dome where the Sages celebrated their mysteries.") Its inhabitants speak Vattanian, the original language of mankind. They are vegetarians. And they are healthy and happy.

Agharta is governed, we are told, by a hierarchy of wise men. There is a Sovereign Pontiff; his two assistants, Mahatma and Mahanga; twelve *archis,* who sit on a council; 360 *bagwandas*; and 5000 *pundits.* A kind of "sacred university," these sages govern Agharta. But they also take an interest in the upper world, using their powers to combat its negative energies. And from time to time they even send an emissary to the surface, to instruct its wayward inhabitants.

The Sovereign Pontiff (to whom the book is dedicated) dwells in a palace. And in the palace library, accessible to the sages, is the accumulated knowledge of mankind. With its miles of shelves, the Aghartan library is a storehouse of ancient wisdom—much of it derived from Atlantis. For the original settlers of Agharta were refugees from Atlantis.

Saint-Yves made repeated visits to Agharta. He did so via astral travel—an out-of-body technique he refers to as "attunement." In *Mission de l'Inde* he describes the kingdom that he visited in these dreams. And he insists that a similar society could be established in the West. But first, Christianity must promote its own teachings (Saint-Yves was a devout Catholic); and government must base itself on the principles of Synarchy. For Synarchy is the cure for the ills of society.

A Synarchical society would be governed by three councils, representing the executive, economic, and spiritual powers. Comprised of wise men, these councils would rule indirectly. By dint of their moral authority, they would guide and inspire the governmental powers; and as a result of this tutelage, class strife and other social pathologies would disappear. And Saint-Yves offers a warning to those powers: "O emperors and kings of Europe, and presidents of republics—without an authority above you, you are doomed to the mutual destruction of your peoples, your powers, and your might."

Would such a system work? It already has, he declares. During the Middle Ages, the Knights Templar controlled the political, financial, and religious life of Europe—in effect, a Synarchical state. And those centuries represented the highest achievement of the West.

After his death, a collection of his later writings was

published, titled *L'Archéomètre*. Archeometry was described as "the key to all the religions and all the sacred sciences of Antiquity." A complex system of symbols and interpretations, it sought to "measure" the principles of the universe. These measurements were made with a cardboard disk called the planisphere. The device (which Saint-Yves had patented) contained signs of the Zodiac, letters of the Atlantean alphabet, musical notes, and colors. One put questions—relating to philosophical or spiritual matters—to the planisphere, and received answers. It was a kind of Ouija board for advanced thinkers.

So what are we to make of the Marquis Saint-Yves d'Alveydre—in particular, his claims regarding Agharta? Did he in fact travel to such a place? Did he receive messages from its sages? And did the planisphere really work?

Some considered him to be mad. (His psychiatrist father is said to have remarked: "Of all the lunatics I have known, my son is the most dangerous.") Others denounced him as a fraud, or dismissed him as a crank. Yet to judge from his writings, Saint-Yves was sane, sincere, and clear-thinking. He was a serious intellectual (awarded the Legion of Honor medal), who moved in the highest circles of French society. So he must be taken seriously, whatever one's view of those visits to Agharta.

And what exactly *were* those visits? Were they merely dreams, expressive of his deepest concerns? Or were they visionary experiences, with a reality of their own? Or even actual travels?*

---

* In his introduction to the English translation of *Mission de l'Inde,* Joscelyn Godwin concludes that the visits were visionary. And he explains them:

"What is the source, and the ontological status, of such visions? There are, one gathers, definite places or complexes in the Astral World...which present to the clairvoyant visitor certain invariable features. I have heard reliable reports, for instance, that libraries are to be found there, in which the initiate is able to further his philosophical study while his body rests. But the incidental circumstances of such a place vary, according to the visitor's

In other words, did Saint-Yves visit the Inner Earth? Or simply plumb the depths of his inner self? Where, that is to say, is Agharta?

•

Our awareness of this mysterious place began in the nineteenth century, with another Frenchman. Louis Jacolliot was an official in colonial India, who befriended the local Brahmins. They showed him ancient texts—palm-leaf manuscripts moldering in a temple. And they told him about Agharta: a subterranean kingdom, ruled by a semi-divine priest called Brahatma. In his book *Le Fils de Dieu* (The Son of God, 1873), Jacolliot relates what he learned about Agharta.

A decade later, Saint-Yves d'Alveydre began to travel to Agharta in his dreams. In *Mission de l'Inde* he describes these visits, and reveals the general location of Agharta: somewhere beneath the Himalayas.

The book (when it was finally published) found an audience among occultists. And a year later, Agharta was mentioned in a magazine article by Swami Narad Mani:

> The true Hindu Center, spiritual in essence, which none of the leaders of Blavatskyism have ever been in touch with, is "AGARTTHA." And let him who has ears, hear; it is located, so said Saint-Yves d'Alveydre, in "certain regions of the Himalayas, among twenty-two temples representing...the twenty-two letters of certain sacred alphabets," where it forms "the Mystic Zero, the Unfindable."

We next hear of Agharta in *Beasts, Men and Gods* (1922),

---

own cultural conditioning and expectations. Some find themselves, for example, in what they believe to be the Alexandrian Library, or in Atlantis, i.e. a place of the past. To others, it seems current and contemporary, though preferably in an inaccessible location like the Himalayas....I can accept that in some state of altered consciousness he saw what he claims to have seen."

a travel diary and adventure tale by Ferdinand Ossendowski. Fleeing the Bolsheviks, Ossendowski (a Polish chemist who had been working in Siberia) traveled through Buddhist Mongolia. As he did so, he spoke with monks and lamas. They told him about the "King of the World," who ruled from the underground realm of Agharta. Agharta, he was told, was a land of wonders and wisdom. It was illuminated by a strange light that brought growth to crops and longevity to people; and it was connected by tunnels with other such realms.

Ossendowski sought to learn more about Agharta. And he tells of being shown a cave:

> A Soyot from near the Lake of Nogan Kul showed me the smoking gate that serves as the entrance to the "Kingdom of Agharti." Through this gate a hunter formerly entered into the Kingdom and, after his return, began to relate what he had seen there. The Lamas cut out his tongue in order to prevent him from telling about the Mystery of Mysteries. When he arrived at old age, he came back to the entrance of this cave and disappeared into the subterranean kingdom, the memory of which had ornamented and lightened his nomad heart.

Beasts, Men and Gods was a bestseller; and it drew another French occultist, René Guénon, into the fray. In 1927 Guénon published *Le Roi du Monde* (The King of the World). The book describes Agharta as the spiritual center of humanity, and gives its precise location: the interior of Mount Meru (mythic home of the Hindu gods). Guénon also defended Ossendowski—whose description of Agharta closely paralleled that of Saint-Yves—against charges of plagiarism. The similarities between the two accounts, argued Guénon, served as confirmation—Agharta was a real place!

Meanwhile, a Russian artist named Nicholas Roerich was trekking through Mongolia. And in 1930 he published a breezy yet poetic travelogue titled *Shambhala*. In it he tells how his guides would point to caves and declare them to be entrances to a subterranean kingdom:

> Every entrance to a cave suggests that some one has already entered there. Every creek—especially the subterranean creeks—draw one's fantasy to the underground passages. In many places of Central Asia, they speak of the Agharti, the subterranean people. In numerous beautiful legends they outline the same story of how the best people abandoned the treacherous earth and sought salvation in hidden countries where they acquired new forces and conquered powerful energies.

And in the Altai Mountains, Roerich was regaled with additional lore:

> When we saw entrances of caves, our caravaneers told us, "Long ago people lived there; now they have gone inside; they have found a subterranean passage to the subterranean kingdom. Only rarely do some of them appear again on earth. At our bazaar such people come with strange, very ancient money, but nobody could even remember a time when such money was in usage here." I asked them, if we could also see such people. And they answered, "Yes, if our thoughts are similarly high and in contact with these holy people, because only sinners are upon earth and the pure and courageous people pass on to something more beautiful."

Apparently, our thoughts were not sufficiently high; and for some time Westerners were accorded no further information about Agharta. Then, in the mid 1940s, a series of nonfiction articles appeared in *Amazing Stories*. In one of them, "Tales from Tibet," author Vincent Gaddis revealed the following:

> The existence of Agharti is widely known among the natives of Central Asia, but very few know the exact location of its carefully guarded entrance. This secret city of the caverns is ruled by an individual known as the "King of the World," and he actually has a political influence on events in Mongolia and Tibet today.... Agharti is supposed to be

a vast, underground region containing several thousand inhabitants. Science has been greatly developed; plants are grown by the aid of a special light; and cars travel through the caverns at great speeds.... The story of Agharti is by no means a myth.

And an editorial titled "The King of the World?" appeared in the May 1946 issue of *Amazing Stories*:

> Is there an underground cave city called Agharti ruled by a Venusian who holds our future hopes?
> All through the world today are thousands of people who claim to have knowledge of an underground city, not specifically located though generally assumed to be in Tibet, called Agharti, or Shambala. In this city, they say, is a highly developed civilization ruled by an "Elder" or a "Great One" whose title is among others "The King of the World." Some claim to have seen him, and it is also claimed that he made at least one visit to the surface....
> To quote the words of a "witness": "He came here ages ago from the planet Venus to be the instructor and guide of our then just dawning humanity. Though he is thousands of years old, his appearance is that of an exceptionally well-developed and handsome youth of about sixteen. But there is nothing juvenile about the light of infinite love, wisdom and power that shines from his eyes...."

A drawing of this ruler accompanied the text. With his ornate helmet, flowing cape, and Roman-style armor, he seemed to have stepped out of a Flash Gordon serial.

These issues of *Amazing Stories* must have been seen by Robert Ernst Dickhoff. For in 1951 Dickhoff—a New Yorker who fancied himself "the Sungma Red Lama and Messenger of Buddha," and who dressed in a glimmering robe—published a book called *Agharta*. It provided further (and no less fantastical) information about the kingdom. Located beneath the Sangpo Valley of China, Agharta had been co-founded (millions of years ago) by humans and Martians; but it was subsequently overrun by Venusians. Eventually it became a spiritual center, inhabited by holy men. From his lamasery on East 107th Street, Dickhoff urged seekers to "attach thyself to the Wise"; promoted Buddhism ("the Aghartan philosophy"); and marketed his books. (Other titles included *Homecoming of the Martians* and *The Martian Alphabet and Language*.)

Among Dickhoff's admirers was Walter Siegmeister, or Raymond Bernard, as he called himself. (The name-change was due to difficulties with the postal authorities, who had banned Siegmeister's pamphlets, with their medical claims, from the mails.) Dr. Bernard was a philosopher, health-food advocate, and Inner Earth researcher. (The doctorate was in education.) In 1960 he published *Agharta: The Subterranean World*. The book reveals that the Aghartans are fruitarians (and thus long-lived); that their weather is perfect, due to cool air from the North Polar opening; and that their capital city is Shambhala. Also, they were the originators of Buddhism. The religion was brought to the upper world by Aghartan sages, who traveled there via UFOs.

As for UFOs, Dr. Bernard has this to say about them:

> On the other hand, if flying saucers came from the Subterranean World, then we can understand why they are so much alike, since they were made by the same subterranean race and are really atlantean aircraft, or "vimanas," which have been visiting us since time immortal, but were never studied nor reports about them credoted 1/2ropr tp tjeor ,ass vosotatopm fp;;pwomg tje Jorpsjo,a arp,oc ex1/2;psion [*sic*!] of 1945, when they first came to the world's attention. [The original edition of the book was typewritten and mimeographed; and that slip of the fingers has gone uncorrected in subsequent editions.]

For potential visitors to Agharta, Bernard provided a map. It shows a number of entrances to the Inner Earth (including Mammoth Cave, the Great Pyramid, and King Solomon's Mines). And on the rear cover of the book is a declaration: "For the first time in history, a philosopher has dared to unveil the mystery of mysteries which has hitherto been concealed from the masses under the most severe of penalties."

Since then, two additional books have sought to unveil that mystery. One is *The Lost World of Agharti* (1982). In this comprehensive study, Alec Maclellan examines what is known about Agharta, and concludes:

> Such a mountain of evidence... plus the legends and histories I have recounted, convince me that Agharti *is* a reality. That somewhere below the plateau of Tibet lies the heart of this nation, a super-race of remarkable people who still exist and live out their lives: as much a mystery as any of the other mysteries which still flourish in our world and which likewise only our lack of knowledge prevents us from understanding.

And in 2003 *My Visit to Agharta* was published. Its author, Lobsang Rampa, was a genuine Tibetan lama.*

●

Where then is Agharta? Deep within the earth, according to our sources.

And how does one get there? Those entrances shown on Dr. Bernard's map await the intrepid traveler.†

---

* Or was he? The strange career of Lobsang Rampa will be examined in chapter 22.

† See Appendix 1 for practical tips on visiting the Inner Earth.

16.
Olaf Jansen

WILLIS GEORGE EMERSON (1856–1918) WAS A LOS Angeles banker and novelist. His fiction (such titles as *The Treasure of Hidden Valley* and *My Pardner and I*) is largely forgotten today. But he also published, in 1908, a work that presented itself as a factual account, and that has continued to provoke controversy. Titled *The Smoky God, or A Voyage to the Inner World*, it tells the story of Olaf Jansen.

Emerson describes the work as "a truthful record of the unparalleled experiences related by one Olaf Jansen." And he claims that Jansen, an elderly neighbor, summoned him one night. On his deathbed, Jansen spoke to the novelist of an ocean voyage he had made as a young man. And Jansen entrusted him with a manuscript—an account of the voyage—and elicited a promise to have it published.

Dutifully, Emerson tells us, he fulfilled his promise to the dying man. He edited the manuscript; wrote a foreword and an afterword; and placed the book with Forbes & Company, his own publisher. And the story of Olaf Jansen's voyage became known at last.

•

The story begins in the spring of 1829, with two Norwegian fishermen setting out in a small sloop. But what started as a fishing trip for Olaf and his father became a voyage of discovery. For they decided impulsively to seek out the Land beyond the North Wind—a land legendary among fishermen.

They steered their vessel northward. "Our little fishing-sloop," recalls Olaf, "sprang forward as if eager as ourselves for adventure." And they soon found themselves navigating a wilderness of icebergs.

> These monster bergs presented an endless succession of crystal palaces, of massive cathedrals and fantastic mountain ranges, grim and sentinel-like, immovable as some towering cliff of solid rock, standing silent as a sphinx, resisting the restless waves of a fretful sea.

A storm arose; and for hours their fragile craft was battered and tossed by tremendous waves. When the waters calmed, the two men found themselves in a green sea. The sky had turned purple; the icebergs flashed like prisms.

Sailing onward, they noted that their compass was behaving oddly. The needle was pressing up against the glass. They noted too that the air was growing warmer. And they were struck by an apparition that had appeared on the horizon: a small reddish sun surrounded by haze. The rumored "mock sun" of the far north! This mirage would soon fade away, they assumed.

But as they sailed on, the sun gradually climbed in the sky. And they realized that it was no mirage, but a reality—"a planet of some sort."

The Jansens took naps in the cabin of the sloop. And Olaf was slumbering, when he was roused by his father. "Olaf, awaken; there is land in sight!" Visible in the distance was a shoreline green with vegetation.

For several days they sailed along the shore. Finally they anchored in a river, waded ashore, and gathered nuts from gigantic trees. A tropical forest, in the northernmost clime of the globe! How was it possible?

Then came an even greater surprise. For they heard *voices singing*. And a huge ship sailed into view—filled with singing giants.

The ship approached them. A boat was lowered; and a party of giants—twelve-feet-tall, bearded, garbed in tunics and knee breeches—rowed over to inspect the voyagers. The giants were friendly and curious; and communicating with gestures, they invited the two men to board their ship.

Olaf and his father were taken to the country of the giants. There they dwelt for nearly two years, learning the language (similar to Sanskrit) and observing the customs and lifestyle of this gargantuan race. Housed with a family,

they were taken on tours and shown natural and technological wonders. But the most startling revelation was geographical. For they learned that the country of the giants—the Land beyond the North Wind—was located *inside the earth.*

The earth was hollow, it was explained to them. The globe had a thick crust enclosing its vacancy, with an opening at each pole. Into these openings, and down the sides of an abyss, passed the waters of the ocean. The waters then continued along the underside of the crust—held in place by "the immutable law of gravitation."

A single continent rose from the interior ocean. And its inhabitants suffered no lack of warmth or illumination. For at the center of the earth was a small sun. This central sun had come into view as the Jansens, unaware that they were doing so, had entered the abyss and sailed down along its side. And finally—as they sailed "upside down" on the interior ocean—the sun had hovered overhead.*

During their stay in the Land beyond the North Wind, the Jansens became acquainted with its inhabitants. The giants were wise and knowledgeable, and had life spans of up to 800 years. They were good-natured—possibly due to the ionized atmosphere inside the earth. The air "was a constant vitalizer," reports Olaf. "I never felt better in my life." And the giants were musical. "Their cities were equipped with vast palaces of music, where not infrequently as many as twenty-five thousand lusty voices of this giant race swell forth in mighty choruses of the most sublime symphonies."

Their capital was a garden city called Eden—the same Eden, Olaf learned, that was the cradle of the human race. The giants worshipped a deity who dwelt in the haze of their sun, and whom they called the Smoky God. And ruling over them, from his residence in Eden, was the High Priest.

One day an emissary of the High Priest visited the Jansens, and questioned them about their homeland. They

---

* Around the time that Symmes and Reynolds were calling for a government-sponsored expedition, these fishermen had discovered the North Polar opening on their own.

were then taken to Eden (via a monorail) for an audience with the ruler himself.

Garbed in rich robes and taller even than his subjects, the High Priest questioned them further. Then he invited them to tour the cities of his realm. And he informed them that their sloop had been preserved. They were free, he said, to return home if they wished; but the journey would be difficult and dangerous.

Accepting his invitation, Olaf and his father toured the cities. But finally, "we decided to cast our fortunes once more upon the sea, and endeavor to regain the 'outside' surface of the earth."

Loading the sloop with provisions, they sailed toward the South Polar opening (to take advantage of the prevailing winds). And they succeeded in returning to the outer world. But the dangers had not been exaggerated. His father perished in the Antarctic; and Olaf got stranded on an iceberg. Rescued by a whaling ship, he eventually returned home.

But more woe was in store for him there. Olaf's story was not believed. And deemed to be mad, he was committed to a mental asylum and confined for many years.

Finally released, Olaf resumed his life as a fisherman. He prospered and was able to retire to a cottage in California. And there the old man set down "the record of my strange travels and adventures."

Which he bequeathed to a neighbor, the novelist Willis George Emerson.

•

And that is the tale of Olaf Jansen. But how is it to be taken? Is it fact or fiction?

In an afterword, Emerson discusses his editing of the manuscript, affirming that "the original text has neither been added to nor taken from." And he gives a list of literary and historical works that "are strangely in harmony with the seemingly incredible text found in the yellow manuscript of the old Norseman, Olaf Jansen, and now for the first time given to the world."

So what is *The Smoky God*? A novel by Emerson—one that employs the literary device of a found manuscript? The delusional memoir of a lunatic? Or indeed a factual account, entrusted to Emerson and corroborated by the works of others?

It is a question that the reader—wary of found manuscripts—must decide for himself.*

---

* Manuscripts that are allegedly left on one's doorstep, found in a cave, thrust upon one by a stranger, or otherwise unexpectedly or fortuitously acquired—by an author who then dutifully serves as editor, annotator, or translator—are a tradition in literature. For examples of found manuscripts, see Appendix 3.

As for *The Smoky God*, Emerson said he was donating the original manuscript to the Smithsonian. Perhaps it will someday turn up there.

17.

Morgan

A CURIOUS BOOK WAS PRIVATELY PRINTED—AN "AUthor's Edition"—in Cincinnati in 1895, and sent to newspapers, journals, and select individuals to be reviewed. (For some of their reactions, see Appendix 2.) Its title page suggests the eccentric character of the book:

ETIDORHPA

OR

THE END OF EARTH.

THE STRANGE HISTORY OF A MYSTERIOUS BEING

AND

The Account of a Remarkable Journey

AS COMMUNICATED IN MANUSCRIPT TO

LLEWELLYN DRURY

WHO PROMISED TO PRINT THE SAME, BUT FINALLY
EVADED THE RESPONSIBILITY

WHICH WAS ASSUMED BY

JOHN URI LLOYD

The man who assumed that responsibility—securing the copyright and engaging a printer—was well-known to the citizens of Cincinnati. John Uri Lloyd (1849–1936) was a pharmacist, chemist, and businessman—one of the proprietors of Lloyd Brothers Pharmacists, the leading manufacturer in the U.S. of botanical medicines. He was the author of a *materia medica*—a pioneering guide to the medicinal plants of North America. And as Professor Lloyd, he taught chemistry at the Eclectic Medical Institute.*

Lloyd was a prolific writer, having published several books and hundreds of scientific articles. So his fellow Cincinnatians would not have been surprised to learn of a forthcoming publication. When *Etidorhpa* appeared, however, they were perhaps puzzled by the fact that only its preface was credited to Lloyd. And surely they were taken aback by its subject matter: a journey to the Earth's interior.

In his preface Lloyd discusses the manuscript of *Etidorhpa*. It has been in his possession for seven years, he says; but he is not permitted to reveal the circumstances of its acquisition. Due to the controversial nature of the material, he has been reluctant to publish it. But at last he is honoring his commitment to do so.

As the reader learns, *Etidorhpa* is actually a composite of two manuscripts. One (the bulk of the book) had been in the custody of one Llewellyn Drury, who had received it from a mysterious stranger. The other was penned by Drury himself, and describes his encounters with this stranger. All of this material was passed on to Lloyd.

Drury's contribution—a prologue, a series of interludes, and an epilogue—serves to frame the story that is narrated by the stranger. In the prologue Drury introduces himself; assures the reader of his "sincerity and responsibility"; and warns that what he is about to describe will be "strange, not to say marvelous." But he urges the reader to maintain an open mind.

He lived alone, Drury tells us, amid a "unique library largely on mystical subjects, in which I took the keenest

---

* The distinguishing feature of Eclectic Medicine was its exclusive use of herbal remedies. Eclectic physicians vied unsuccessfully with their chief rivals, the allopathic physicians (today's M.D.s), and eventually faded from the scene. However, their discipline has survived in the healing science known as naturopathy.

The name "Eclectic Medicine" was coined by Constantine Rafinesque, a backwoods doctor who lived among the Indians and studied their medical use of plants.

delight." One wintry night in November—the bells of the nearby cathedral had just chimed eleven o'clock—he was sitting in his library, restless and morose.

As he stared into the fire and pondered a Latin quotation, Drury was startled by a voice. And he discovered that he was not alone in his library. Seated on the opposite side of the room, gazing at him intently, was a white-haired man.

> He was nearly six feet tall, and perfectly straight; well proportioned, with no tendency either to leanness or obesity. But his head was an object from which I could not take my eyes,—such a head surely I had never before seen on mortal shoulders.... surmounted by a forehead so vast, so high, that it was almost a deformity, and yet it did not impress me unpleasantly; it was the forehead of a scholar, a profound thinker, a deep student. The nose was inclined to aquiline, and quite large. The contour of the head and face impressed me as indicating a man of learning, one who had given a lifetime to experimental as well as speculative thought. His voice was mellow, clear, and distinct, always pleasantly modulated and soft, never loud nor unpleasant in the least degree. One remarkable feature I must not fail to mention—his hair; this, while thin and scant upon the top of his head, was long, and reached to his shoulders; his beard was of unusual length, descending almost to his waist; his hair, eyebrows, and beard were all of singular whiteness and purity, almost transparent, a silvery whiteness that seemed an aureolar sheen in the glare of the gaslight. What struck me as particularly remarkable was that his skin looked as soft and smooth as that of a child; there was not a blemish in it. His age was a puzzle none could guess; stripped of his hair, or the color of it changed, he might be twenty-five—given a few wrinkles, he might be ninety. Taken altogether, I had never seen his like, nor anything approaching his like, and for an instant there was a faint suggestion to my mind that he was not of this earth, but belonged to some other planet.

This unbidden guest (whom Drury initially feared to be a maniac, but quickly came to accept) disclosed the purpose of his visit. He had come to acquaint Drury with "a narrative of unusual interest." It was contained in a manuscript that the stranger had drafted, and which he intended to read aloud. The reading would take place over the course of several visits. As it proceeded, Drury would be able to ask questions and engage in discussion. Subsequently, he was to take possession of the manuscript; safeguard it for thirty years; then publish it.

Intrigued, Drury agreed to this plan. Whereupon, the mysterious stranger (who never reveals his name) said, "I will see you again—good night," and departed.

No sooner was he alone than Drury wondered if he had imagined the encounter. "Had not my peculiar habits of isolation, irregular and intense study, erratic living, all conspired to unseat reason?"

But the stranger (whom we shall refer to as "Morgan"—see note in Appendix 2) did eventually return to the library. He had with him the manuscript. Seating himself, he began to read it aloud. And Drury listened spellbound to his tale.

●

In upstate New York, the tale began, flourished a "fraternity of adepts"—a secret society devoted to esoteric knowledge. But within the society, a tiny faction had arisen. This dissenting group wished to share the knowledge with all of mankind.

To that end they communicated with Morgan, a student of alchemy, and induced him to join the society, learn its secrets, and write a book revealing those secrets. But when his project became known, the society "endeavored to prevail upon me to relent of my design." Morgan refused, and was condemned by the membership, for violating his oath of secrecy.

For a time he was harassed and persecuted. Then one night he was abducted. Men in top hats and overcoats forced him into a carriage. And they informed him of his punishment. He was to be initiated into *highly secret* knowledge. For the society was benevolent; and its rule was that a punishment must both instruct the offender and elevate the human race.

> "You wished to become a distributor of knowledge; you shall now by bodily trial and mental suffering obtain unsought knowledge to distribute, and in time you will be commanded to make your discoveries known."

Morgan was imprisoned in a cabin in the woods. There his appearance was altered, by alchemical means, to that of an elderly man. Thus transformed, he was taken on a ride in a carriage. Soon to be revealed to him, said his captors, were hidden truths of existence—truths hidden from both ordinary men and most of the adepts. He was about to embark upon "a journey of investigation, for the good of our order and also of humanity." And after several days they reached their destination: a cave in rural Kentucky.*

A strange creature emerged from the cave. Short, blue-skinned, and blind, it was a kind of moleman. Morgan was asked by his captors if he was ready for the journey. He replied that he was.

> "Then farewell. This mystic brother is to be your guide during the first stages of your subterrene progress. You are to go into and beyond the Beyond, until finally you will come to the gateway that leads into the Unknown Country."

Morgan followed the guide into the cave. After wading through water, they made their way along a descending passageway and emerged in a cavern. And they descended now through a series of caverns. Their way was lit by a faint light —a luminous haze in the air. Strangely, the light seemed

---

* *Etidorhpa* gives no further information as to the location of the cave (referring to it only as "Zoroaster's Cave"). But researcher Bruce Walton (author of *A Guide to the Inner Earth*) believes it to be Puckett Spring, a spring cave near Salem, Kentucky.

always to be strongest in their immediate vicinity.

Like an accompanying and encircling halo the ever present earth-light enveloped us, opening in front as we advanced, and vanishing in the rear.

For hours they walked, descending into the earth. Morgan was struck by the acoustics of the caverns.

The sound of our footsteps gave back a peculiar, indescribable hollow echo, and our voices sounded ghost-like and unearthly, as if their origin was outside of our bodies, and at a distance. The peculiar resonance reminded me of noises reverberating in an empty cask or cistern. I was oppressed by an indescribable feeling of mystery and awe that grew deep and intense.

Morgan was struck too by the didactic nature of the guide. For during their descent the creature gave frequent lectures. He was learned in science, and spoke on a variety of topics—light, motion, volcanos, the ether.

As they passed through cavern after cavern, Morgan lost track of time. Yet oddly, he grew neither hungry nor thirsty. This was due, the guide explained, to the atmosphere inside the earth, which had "an intrinsic vitalizing power." That power sustained one's life force, making food and drink—and even air!—unnecessary.

They trekked through an eerie, subterranean world. Stalactites, stalagmites, and other formations gleamed like baroque sculptures. One cavern sparkled with immense crystals. Another was overgrown with giant fungi, of diverse shapes and colors. And another contained a vast lake, which they traversed in a boat that had been left by the shore.

At one point Morgan tried hopping into the air—and bounded upward a full six feet! This feat was attributable, said the guide, to two factors: the diminishing gravity, and the vitalizing effect of the atmosphere.

As they penetrated deeper into the earth, Morgan found himself becoming lighter and lighter. And his impulse to breathe was waning. Finally, these physical effects, along with the eerie surroundings, were too much for him.

> I impulsively turned my face toward the passage we had trod; a feeling of alarm possessed me, an uncontrollable, inexpressible desire to flee from the mysterious earth-being beside me, to return to men, and be an earth-surface man again, and I started backward through the chamber we had passed.
> The guide seized me by the hand. "Hold, hold," he cried; "where would you go, fickle mortal?"
> "To the surface," I shouted; "to daylight again. Unhand me, unearthly creature, abnormal being, man or devil; have you not inveigled me far enough into occult realms that should be forever sealed from mankind? Have you not taken from me all that men love or cherish, and undone every tie of kith or kin? Have you not led me into paths that the imagination of the novelist dare not conjure, and into experiences that pen in human hand would not venture to describe as possible, until I now stand with... utter loss of weight; with a body nearly lost as a material substance, verging into nothing, and lastly with breath practically extinguished, I say, and repeat, is it not time that I should hesitate and pause in my reckless career?"
> "It is not time," he answered.

Pressing onward, they entered a cavern filled with giant mushrooms. Among them was a specimen from which berries had sprouted. The guide broke open a berry, revealing a green liquid; and he bid Morgan drink.

Morgan drank. Then the guide—lecturing on the history of intoxicants—led him into another cavern. And there, as the green liquid took effect, he experienced a terrifying vision.

"Listen!" said the guide. "Do you not hear them? Listen!"

Morgan listened to a cacophony of shrieks and groans. And he saw a creature emerge from a mushroom. It had the form of a man, yet writhed like a serpent. It grasped Morgan; moaned "Back, back, go thou back"; and returned into the mushroom.

Morgan was set upon now by monstrous figures. Among these hallucinations were huge hands that whispered and pointed: "Back, back, go thou back."

Meanwhile, the guide was lecturing on the pernicious effects of alcohol. A temperance lecture in the depths of the earth! This particular cavern, he said, was called the Drunkard's Den. Its inhabitants had been transformed by alcohol into monsters. He urged Morgan to keep going and leave the place behind.

But the monstrous forms were still swarming about Morgan. And a figure with an angelic face appeared and handed him a cup. It was filled, the figure told him, with "the elixir of life," and would provide an hour of bliss—after which he would be returned to the surface.

And he was about to drink, when the true face of the figure became visible. Grinning at him from behind a mask was a demon.

"No, I will not drink!" shouted Morgan, dashing the cup to the ground. And the monstrous forms vanished.

His vision took on now a different character. First, a faint music became audible. It grew louder. And the musicians appeared.

> From the corridors of the cavern, troops of bright female forms floated into view. They were clad in robes ranging from pure white to every richest hue....Thus it was that I became again the center of a throng, not of repulsive monsters, but of marvelously lovely beings. They were as different from those preceding as darkness is from daylight.

The throng of females sang and danced before him. Then it parted, to make way for a single advancing figure. Slender, lithe, and radiant, she floated to his side and spoke.

"My name is Etidorhpa. In me you behold the spirit that elevates man....Behold in me the antithesis of envy, the opposite of malice, the enemy of sorrow, the mistress of life, the queen of immortal bliss....The noblest gift of Heaven to humanity is the highest sense of love, and I, Etidorhpa, am the soul of love."

Then Etidorhpa too delivered a lecture—on the nature of love. At its conclusion she and her entourage faded away. The vision had ended. The effects of the green liquid had worn off; and Morgan was himself again.*

---

* In a footnote John Uri Lloyd asks: "If in the course of experimentation, a chemist should strike upon a compound that in traces only would subject his mind and drive his pen to record such seemingly extravagant ideas as are found in the hallucinations herein pictured, would it not be his duty to bury the discovery from others, to cover from mankind the existence of such a noxious fruit of the chemist's or pharmaceutist's art?"

They resumed their trek, through a fantastical landscape.

> For a long time thereafter we journeyed on in silence, now amid stately stone pillars, then through great cliff openings or among gigantic formations that often stretched away like cities or towns dotted over a plain, to vanish in the distance. Then the scene changed, and we traversed magnificent avenues, bounded by solid walls which expanded into lofty caverns of illimitable extent, from whence we found ourselves creeping through narrow crevices and threading winding passages barely sufficient to admit our bodies.

Finally they arrived at the edge of an abyss. The guide walked out on a ledge. Trembling with fear, Morgan crawled out after him. And he looked down into the abyss.

Light was streaming up from a luminous void. This

chasm was seven thousand miles deep, said the guide. They had reached the terminus of the earth's crust—and a choice had to be made. Morgan could return now to the surface; most seekers did just that, lacking the courage to go on. Or he could descend into the abyss. If he chose to turn back, the guide would accompany him. But if he was willing to descend, an awesome revelation was promised.

After a brief hesitation, Morgan chose to keep going. Whereupon, the guide drew him to his feet, grasped him about the waist, and *leapt into the abyss.*

> I recall a whirling sensation, and an involuntary attempt at self-preservation, in which I threw my arms wildly about with a vain endeavor to clutch some form of solid body, which movement naturally ended by a tight clasping of my guide in my arms, and locked together we continued to

speed down into the seven thousand miles of vacancy. Instinctively I murmured a prayer of supplication.

They were plunging into a sea of light and accelerating. Yet the lack of atmospheric friction left Morgan feeling motionless. He was oddly calm and elated, "oblivious to everything save the delicious sensation of absolute rest that enveloped and pervaded my being." He asked to where they were descending.

"Into the earth's central space," said the guide. And even as they plummeted, he lectured—on the nature of gravity.

A silver crescent came into view. As they neared it, a robed figure could be discerned, standing on a cliff. Morgan asked if it was a mortal. The guide replied:

> "It is a being of mortal build, a messenger who awaits our coming, and who is to take charge of your person and conduct you farther. It has been my duty to crush, to overcome by successive lessons your obedience to your dogmatic, materialistic earth philosophy, and bring your mind to comprehend that life on earth's surface is only a stop towards a brighter existence."

Morgan became apprehensive. "Do not desert me now," he pleaded, "after leading me beyond even alchemistic imaginings into this subterranean existence."

They landed on the cliff. The guide bid him adieu, flew back upwards, and disappeared from view. The robed figure was approaching him. Morgan fell to his knees.

> In all my past eventful history there was nothing similar to or approaching in keenness the agony that I suffered at this moment, and I question if shipwrecked sailor or entombed miner ever experienced the sense of utter desolation that now possessed and overcame me. Light everywhere about me, ever-present light, but darkness within, darkness indescribable, and mental distress unutterable.

"Come, my friend," said the robed figure, "let us enter the expanses of the Unknown Country. You will soon behold the original of your vision, the hope of humanity, and will rest in the land of Etidorhpa."

> Arm in arm we passed into that domain of peace and tranquillity, and as I stepped onward and upward perfect rest come over my troubled spirit. All thoughts of former times vanished. The cares of life faded; misery, distress, hatred, envy, jealousy, and unholy passions, were blotted from existence. Excepting my love for dear ones still earth-enthralled, and that strand of sorrow that, stretching from soul to soul, linked us together, the past became a blank. I had reached the land of Etidorhpa—
>
> THE END OF EARTH.

•

The reading of the manuscript had concluded. Drury's visitor put down the final sheet and gazed into the fire. Then he reminded his listener of their agreement—Drury was to become custodian of the manuscript.

But Drury protested that the tale had ended abruptly. Did not more remain to be told? What lay beyond the end of the earth? What was the nature of the Unknown Country?

The mysterious stranger shook his head. Nothing further could be revealed, he said. Men were not yet ready for the full story—nor were they ready for the contents of the manuscript. Therefore, thirty years were to elapse before its publication. Drury was to place it in his safe. And he was to draw up a will, providing for a new custodian in the event of his death. Finally, the visitor held up a sealed envelope. It was to be opened thirty years hence, and would provide more detailed instructions.

He tied the manuscript into a bundle and gave it to Drury. And the stranger began now to weep. For he was forbidden, he said, to meet with his loved ones, or to visit the scenes of his former life. Rather, he had to return to the Unknown Country—to the realm of Etidorhpa.

And he bid Drury farewell.

He held out his hand, I grasped it, and as I did so, his form became indistinct, and gradually disappeared from my gaze, the fingers of my hand met the palm in vacancy, and with extended arms I stood alone in my room, holding the mysterious manuscript.

In the days that followed, Drury pondered the manuscript that this spectral visitor had placed in his custody. And he did not know what to make of it. "Misgiving still possessed me concerning the truthfulness of the story. If these remarkable episodes were true, could there be such a thing as fiction? If not all true, where did fact end and fancy begin?"

Nonetheless, he preserved the manuscript as directed.
Thirty years later he opened the envelope. Inside was a letter, with instructions concerning publication. Drury was to make any necessary revisions to the text; engage an illustrator; and find a publisher. Also, he was to add a prologue describing his connection with the author of the book. "Write the whole truth, for although mankind will not now accept as fact all that you and I have experienced, strange phases of life phenomena are revealing themselves, and humanity will yet surely be led to a higher plane." And enclosed was a photograph of the author, to be used as a frontispiece.

Though aware that the publication would subject him to accusations, Drury set out to follow the instructions. He composed a prologue. And in an epilogue he challenged the reader:

> Whether I have been mesmerized, or have written in a trance, whether I have been the subject of mental aberration, or have faithfully given a life history to the world, whether this book is altogether romance, or carries a vein of prophecy, whether it sets in motion a train of wild speculations, or combines playful arguments, science problems, and metaphysical reasonings, useful as well as entertaining, remains for the reader to determine.

But in the end, Drury failed to publish *Etidorhpa*. Instead, the responsibility was assumed by John Uri Lloyd. And Lloyd had this to say about his own role in the affair:

> [The reader] can now formulate his conclusions as well perhaps as I, regarding the origin of the manuscript....Whether Mr. Drury brought the strange paper in person, or sent it by express or mail—whether my hand held the pen that made the record—whether I stood face to face with Mr. Drury in the shadows of this room...is immaterial. Sufficient be it to say that the manuscript of this book has been in my possession for a period of seven years, and my lips must now be sealed concerning all that transpired in connection therewith.

18.

Doreal

IN THE MOUNTAINS OF COLORADO, THE BROTHERHOOD of the White Temple survives to this day. Founded in 1930, the Brotherhood is dedicated to the study and dissemination of ancient wisdom. That wisdom was uncovered by the founder of the group: a shadowy figure known as Doreal.

Doreal was born on an Indian reservation in Oklahoma. His original name was Claude Doggins. After serving in the Signal Corps during World War I, he began his pursuit of esoteric knowledge. Doreal claimed to have spent a number of years in Tibet, studying with the Dalai Lama and others.*

During his lifetime Doreal published dozens of pamphlets, about such things as Kabbala, reincarnation, and UFOs. He is best-known, however, for a book: *The Emerald Tablets of Thoth the Atlantean*. This work purports to be a translation of the original Emerald Tablets. The Tablets were engraved, says Doreal, 38,000 years ago—by Thoth, the High Priest of Atlantis. Thoth took the Tablets to Egypt, where he built the Great Pyramid as a repository for them. The Tablets were later taken to the Yucatan; and there, in the ruins of a Mayan temple, Doreal discovered them. According to an ad for the book, "The powerful and rhythmic verse of Thoth is wonderfully retained in Doreal's translation."†

---

* While there, he may have run into George Adamski, who likewise claimed to have studied in Tibet during the 1920s. Professor Adamski (as he styled himself) went on to found the Royal Order of Tibet, a New Age study group. And he achieved fame as a flying saucer contactee. (See my *How to Make the Most of a Flying Saucer Experience* [Top Hat Press, 1998].)

† Doreal describes the Emerald Tablets as "the most stupendous

With his store of esoteric knowledge (much of it derived from Theosophy), Doreal gave lectures, issued pamphlets, and guided the Brotherhood. His leadership style was flamboyant. A reporter from *Time* magazine visited the group's headquarters in Denver. He describes Doreal as wearing a gold-trimmed robe of purple silk and sitting on a throne.*

In 1946 Doreal—anticipating a nuclear war—moved the Brotherhood to a secluded valley in the Rocky Mountains. There he continued to serve as its "Supreme Voice," until his death in 1963.

Doreal is said to have accumulated a sizable library: 30,000 volumes of occult, metaphysical, and science-fictional works. Yet he was not simply a scholar. For besides his international travels, Doreal made several visits to the Inner Earth.

The first occurred during his sojourn in Tibet. He traveled in his astral body, says Doreal, to a library located deep beneath Lhasa. There he studied the ancient wisdom of Tibet, which was recorded on spools of wire.

Back in the U.S., he visited the underground home of the Deros. (These malevolent creatures will be discussed in chapter 20.)

And in 1931 Doreal visited a subterranean city, located beneath Mount Shasta in California. In a pamphlet titled "Mysteries of Mount Shasta," he describes the visit. It began when two strangers took him to the top of the moun-

---

collection of the Ancient Wisdom available to mankind." A sampling of that wisdom:

"Order and balance are the Law of the Cosmos. Follow and ye shall be One with the ALL."

"Light is thine, O man, for the taking. Cast off the fetters and thou shalt be free."

Eventually, Doreal restored the Tablets to the Great Pyramid. Their current location is unknown.

* The article in *Time* (September 16, 1946) is clearly biased against Doreal. It describes him as "a chubby, bald little man" who "turned up" in Denver, and his students as "goggle-eyed followers."

tain. Doreal stood with the pair on a large flat rock. A section of the rock then descended like an elevator into the mountain. They traveled miles into the earth, arriving finally in a vast cavern.

There Doreal was escorted into "a small city of beautiful white houses...so beautiful that they almost blinded the eye." Inhabited by several hundred people, the city beneath Shasta was a former colony of Atlantis. His guides led him about the city; showed him its temple; and demonstrated the transmutation of sand into gold. (The gold, they explained, was used to purchase supplies from the outer world.) They also gave him instruction in secret matters.

> After they had finished they showed me certain things in the Great Plan and outlined work for me to do in the outer world, which I am doing now, so that gradually the consciousness of man could be made more and more aware of the great mysteries behind matter and substance and behind life.

And what better symbol of those mysteries than Mount Shasta—thrusting itself to the heavens, and whispering of hidden depths.*

---

* If the U.S. may be said to have a sacred mountain, it is Shasta. In nearby towns, various New Age organizations have hung out their shingles. These groups—with such names as the Radiant School of Seekers and Servers, Sree Sree Provo, and Astara—have been drawn to this dormant volcano by its cosmic energies. Also drawn have been a steady stream of pilgrims—spiritual seekers who wish to commune with the mountain, and who sometimes wind up making it their home.

No less attuned to the mystic vibes of Shasta were its original inhabitants. To the local Indians, Wai-i-ka was the home of the gods. It also served as a bridge between the heavens and the underworld; for the mountain—believed to be hollow—was deemed a passageway into the depths of the earth. Legends about Wai-i-ka abounded. According to one, it was the wigwam of the Great Spirit, with sulfurous bursts issuing from its smoke-hole. According to another, it was inhabited by a diminutive race, who were rarely seen, but whose laughter could be heard.

The white settlers who replaced the Indians preserved these legends. But they were soon coming up with lore of their own. Much of it originated with a book titled *A Dweller on Two Planets*. *A Dweller on Two Planets* was published in 1905 (though it had been written twenty years earlier). Its author was Frederick Spencer Oliver, a resident of Yreka—a town just north of the mountain. But Oliver was no ordinary author; for he claimed to be channeling "Phylos the Thibetan." He describes the process of taking dictation from Phylos, via automatic writing: "At such times I am as fully conscious of my surroundings as at any other time, though I feel lifted as into a Master's presence, and gladly do for him the work of an amanuensis." Phylos revealed that a secret brotherhood dwelt within Mount Shasta—a society of Masters who carried on the traditions of Atlantis.

Or was it the traditions of Lemuria—the lost continent of the Pacific—that these Masters were carrying on? According to Harve Spencer Lewis, founder of the Rosicrucian Order, such was indeed the case. In 1925 Lewis (writing as "Selvius") published an article titled "Descendants of Lemuria: A Description of an Ancient Cult in America." It revealed that Mount Shasta was the home of Lemurians. There was even a credible eyewitness, said Lewis. For had not Professor Larkin, science writer for the Hearst newspapers, aimed his telescope at Mount Shasta and spotted Lemurians? And had not Larkin also heard them chanting, as they performed their rituals?

(Professor Larkin had written about lost continents, and had described *A Dweller on Two Planets* as a "mighty, majestic, imposing, fascinating book." But a claim to have spotted Lemurians has yet to be located in his writings.)

And in 1931 Lewis (writing as "Wishar Spenle Cervé"—an anagram of his name) published *Lemuria: The Lost Continent of the Pacific*. The book has a chapter about the Lemurians who inhabit Mount Shasta. They are described as tall, graceful, and garbed in robes. Local shopkeepers have encountered them; for they come into stores and purchase basic commodities—paying with bags of gold.

But it was an article in the *Los Angeles Times* that drew public attention to the Lemurians. In 1932, journalist Edward Lanser was traveling in the observation car of the Mount Shasta Limited. As the train passed by Mount Shasta at sunrise, Lanser noted a strange reddish-green light ablaze on the mountain. He asked a conductor about it.

"Lemurians," said the conductor. "They hold ceremonials up there."

Intrigued, Lanser paid a subsequent visit to the mountain. He interviewed local residents and made a startling discovery: "The existence of a 'mystic village' on Mt. Shasta was an established fact. Businessmen, amateur explorers, officials and ranchers in the country surrounding Shasta spoke freely of the Lemurian community, and all attested to the weird rituals that are performed on the mountain-side at sunset, midnight and sunrise."

He also learned that encounters with Lemurians had occurred. "Various merchants in the vicinity of Shasta report that these white-robed men come to their stores. Their purchases are of a peculiar nature. They have bought enormous quantities of sulphur as well as a great deal of salt. They buy lard in bulk quantities, *for which they bring their own containers* [emphasis added]. ...Their purchases are always paid for with gold nuggets."

Had the journalist been beguiled with a tall tale? Was he writing tongue-in-cheek? Or was he simply reporting the facts? In any case, the legend was now fully launched. Mount Shasta was the home of Lemurians!

Since then, the legend has taken root. And the sightings have continued. Each year there are reports of men in robes, roaming

the slopes of Mount Shasta. Invariably, they are said to have long, flowing hair and a soulful look. They murmur a greeting, then disappear into the forest.

Who are these mystery men? Lemurians? New Age hermits? Spaced-out hippies? Their identity remains an enigma. It should be noted, however, that they shop with their own containers— avoiding plastic bags. Environmentally sensitive, these are surely the wise men of the mountain.

19.

Guy Ballard

IN AUGUST 1930, GUY BALLARD—A GOLD PROSPECTOR, medium, and Theosophist—was hiking on Mount Shasta, enjoying its scenic splendor. The 52-year-old Ballard was wont to take such hikes, whenever in need of pondering some matter or of making a decision. Moreover, he had heard rumors of an occult fraternity—a Brotherhood of Mount Shasta—dwelling in the vicinity, and hoped to learn more about it.

Ballard had stopped to drink from a stream, when (according to *Unveiled Mysteries*, the book he would write about his experiences) he sensed a presence and turned around. Behind him stood a young man, who smiled and said: "My brother, if you will hand me your cup, I will give you a much more refreshing drink than spring water."

Ballard obeyed; and the stranger handed him back a cupful of creamy liquid. (The cup had filled instantly, from no apparent source.) Ballard drank and gasped with surprise—for he felt an immediate surge of energy.

"That which you drank comes directly from the Universal Supply, pure and vivifying as Life itself—in fact, it is Life," said the stranger, who then launched into a metaphysical discourse.

After speaking at length, he revealed his identity—in a startling fashion. His face, body, and clothing transformed themselves (Ballard would claim) into a figure in a white robe—an angelic being whose eyes sparkled with love. And whom Ballard recognized, from visions experienced as a medium. *It was Saint Germain, the Ascended Master.*

Saint Germain began another discourse. He discussed the nature of Ascended Masters, and of the "God Self" within each of us. Then he turned to the subject of reincarnation—and the discourse became a demonstration.

For Ballard found himself separating from his physical

body. Saint Germain put an arm about him, and journeyed with him through time and space. Ballard was shown two of his former lives: one as a medieval French singer, another as an Egyptian priest. Such reincarnations would continue, said Saint Germain, until he accessed the Divine within him and achieved an understanding of the Law of Life.

Saint Germain then returned Ballard to his body; took him back to the lodge where he was staying; and vanished before his eyes.

•

Several days later Ballard set out again on the mountain trail. For he had found a note in his room:

BE AT OUR TRYSTING PLACE AT SEVEN IN THE MORNING—
SAINT GERMAIN.

Arriving at the spot, Ballard sat down on a log and waited. He had not packed a lunch, trusting that Saint Germain, and the "Universal Supply," would tend to his needs.

A twig cracked and Ballard looked up—to see a panther slinking towards him. He froze with fear. Then, realizing that the Power of Love dwelt within him, he focused it on the panther. The beast lay down and rolled over.

A moment later Saint Germain was standing beside him. The Ascended Master informed him that he had passed the test of courage and could proceed with his instruction.

Touching him on the brow, Saint Germain introduced Ballard to Projected Consciousness. Together they viewed a civilization that had flourished in the Sahara Desert, 70,000 years ago. The Saharan king, said Saint Germain, was a master of ancient wisdom—and another of Ballard's former lives.

Saint Germain then spoke at length on a variety of subjects, including gold. Gold was filled with solar energy, he said; and its utilization as a means of exchange and for ornamentation was trivial. Its real purpose was to purify, vitalize, and balance the atomic structure of the world, and thereby enable men to attain perfection.

Ballard learned much during this second meeting with Saint Germain; and it was with a feeling of exultation that he returned to the lodge. But it was their third meeting that would be truly unforgettable. For Ballard would be taken on a visit to the Inner Earth.

•

That morning a dove had alighted on his windowsill. In its bill was a note, summoning him to the trysting place. Ballard hiked there and was greeted by Saint Germain. With the Ascended Master was the panther.

Once again Ballard was separated from his body, which slumped to the ground. Saint Germain assured him that the panther would guard it during their absence. And together they flew to a mountaintop.

There Saint Germain rolled aside a boulder. Revealed was a bronze door, which opened at a touch. They descended a stairway to an elevator; and the elevator sped them further downward. It came to a halt at another bronze door. "We have descended two thousand feet into the very heart of the mountain," said Saint Germain, opening the door.

They entered a reception room. On the wall hung a tapestry, depicting a pair of Cosmic Beings—the founders, said Saint Germain, of this underground retreat.

He led Ballard into the next room—a council chamber. It was filled with plush seats that faced a viewing screen. A soft light permeated the room and glimmered in its polished walls. Set in the ceiling were gold disks. A divine energy, Ballard would learn, emanated from these disks.

Saint Germain led him on a brief tour of the retreat, visiting a library and a treasure room. Then they returned to the council chamber, where the seats had begun to fill. For the Ascended Masters were assembling.

Garbed in robes, the Masters wandered in, until seventy of them had seated themselves. With them were a few ordinary humans—guests like Ballard. The council chamber echoed with chatter. But then a hush fell upon the gathering. For by the viewing screen an oval of light was forming. Out of the light stepped a tall, majestic figure, clad in a luminous robe. Wavy blond hair tumbled to his shoulders. He asked if everyone was ready, then gestured at the screen.

The screen came alive, with a presentation that might have been titled "The March of Civilizations." The scenes were dramatic and breathtaking. One after another, powerful nations were seen to rise and fall. The glories of ancient Lemuria flashed across the screen, followed by the cataclysm that sank that land beneath the waters of the Pacific. Airships flew over the towers of Atlantis, then it too was engulfed by the sea; and fish swam amid the towers. A mighty kingdom flourished in what is now the Gobi Desert, and crumbled before an onslaught of barbarians. Egypt, Rome, modern-day Europe—each in turn rose to prominence, then declined. The presentation concluded with the rise of America.

The screen went dark. And in a blaze of light, Lanto appeared. The Great Ascended Master welcomed Ballard and the other guests. He urged them to fully accept the God Within. And he invited them to return on New Year's Eve, when some Venusians would be visiting. Lanto then blessed everyone; and the assembly was adjourned.

Saint Germain led Ballard to a music room and played for him on a harp. Finally the two of them exited the subterranean retreat and flew back to Mount Shasta.

In the months that followed, Ballard occasionally met with Saint Germain. For the most part, however, he returned to prospecting—searching for gold in the hills of California.

But he was also spending time at his desk. For he had begun to write a book about his experiences.

●

The book was titled *Unveiled Mysteries*. It was self-published in 1934, four years after his encounters on Mount

Shasta. Authorship was ascribed to one Godfré Ray King: a pseudonym, and spiritual identity, that Ballard had adopted.

After two years in California, he had returned home to Chicago, rejoining his wife Edna. Ballard was done with gold prospecting. Instead, he was about to embark upon an equally uncertain venture. For he and Edna had decided to launch a new religion—or at least a New Age movement. And *Unveiled Mysteries* was to be its foundation text.

Guy and Edna Ballard were not new to the New Age. For years they had taken a strong interest in spiritualism and Theosophy, and had belonged to a number of esoteric groups. Both had practiced mediumship and been in contact with the spirit world. And Edna worked at a bookstore called the Philosopher's Nook; conducted classes on metaphysical subjects; and edited a periodical called *The American Occultist*. She also performed as a harpist.

The I AM Activity (as their movement would become known) had a modest start. The Ballards taught a series of classes in the living room of their Chicago home. Ten people —sworn to secrecy—attended these classes. They were introduced to the basic ideas of I AM, and listened as messages from Saint Germain were read aloud. They also purchased copies of *Unveiled Mysteries*.

For *Unveiled Mysteries* was the gateway to I AM. In an introductory note, Ballard describes the origins of the book:

> This Book is written in the embrace of the majestic, towering presence of Mount Shasta, whose apex is robed forever in that pure, glistening white, the symbol of the "Light of Eternity." Its pages are a record of the way by which I was brought in touch with the Beloved Master Saint Germain, and those other Great Ascended Masters who labor unceasingly to assist the humanity of this Earth, as it struggles on the path to Peace, Love, Light, and Everlasting Perfection.

He links its contents with the wisdom of the East:

> The time has arrived when the Great Wisdom held and guarded for many centuries in the Far East is now to come

forth in America at the command of these Great Ascended Masters who direct, protect, and assist in expanding the Light within mankind upon this Earth.

And he explains the value of the book:

> Those who accept the Truth herein recorded will find a new and powerful "Force" entering their lives. Each copy carries with it this Mighty Presence, Its Radiation and sustaining Power. All who study these pages honestly, deeply, sincerely, and persistently will know and make contact with the Reality of that Presence and Power.

Those first classes were held in the summer of 1934. Soon thereafter, the Ballards traveled by train to Philadelphia (where they had contacts with disillusioned members of the Pelleyites, a politically extreme New Age group). Initially attracting about thirty people, they conducted the same classes. Their message found receptive ears; and by the final session, attendance had arisen to 150.

The I AM movement had been launched. From Philadelphia the Ballards took the classes to New York. Then it was on to Boston, Washington, and Miami. (They were traveling by automobile now, and lecturing in rented halls.) Their students were absorbing the wisdom of the Ascended Masters; purchasing copies of *Unveiled Mysteries*; and leaving "love gifts" in the basket.

The Ballards introduced themselves at the lectures as Godfré Ray King and Lotus Ray King. They were "the Accredited Messengers of the Ascended Masters," the couple announced—intermediaries between the Masters and mankind. They had been chosen to lead America into a Golden Age. Their mission was to pass on the teachings of the Ascended Masters—teachings that were being dictated to them from the astral plane.

Crammed into an old Ford with their teenage son and their manager, Guy and Edna also toured the South. But the Bible Belt proved unreceptive to the blandishments of mysticism. And it was not until they arrived in Los Angeles

—that bastion of the New Age—that the movement really took off.

The Los Angeles classes were a success from the start. Crowds of truth-seekers (along with the merely curious) showed up to see what I AM was all about. During the spring and summer of 1935, the Ballards had to find progressively larger halls to accommodate their audiences. Finally, they rented the Shrine Civic Auditorium, with its 6000 seats. The Shrine would become the I AM center, with national conventions held there twice a year.

For I AM quickly grew into a nationwide phenomenon—a kind of craze. During that summer, the Ballards also toured the West Coast, lecturing to packed houses. (Their success in Los Angeles had generated widespread publicity.) And they were soon making forays back East, to speak in various cities. As the movement grew, they established I AM sanctuaries in the cities they visited, appointing local leaders of study groups.

Initially, the Ballards' lectures had been simple, straightforward affairs. Guy and Edna had dressed plainly, assumed a modest air, and lectured from a bare stage. But the proceedings evolved into something more elaborate and theatrical—more *exciting*. A typical evening with the Ballards unfolded as follows:

Drawn by newspaper ads and word of mouth, prospective students filed into a downtown auditorium; there was no admission fee. Smiling, white-clad ushers led them to their seats. As the seats filled, a buzz of anticipation filled the hall.

The stage was brightly lit. On it were a lectern, a microphone, portraits of Saint Germain and Jesus, American flags, a piano, and a harp. Painted on an illuminated backdrop was the I AM emblem: a diagram of the Magic Presence. It showed halos and rays emanating from a divine figure. Beneath the figure was a human being, struck by a ray of enlightenment.

The houselights dimmed; a pianist sat down at the piano; and a hush fell upon the audience—as if a play were about to begin.

The master of ceremonies came on stage and welcomed everyone. He read aloud telegrams of praise that the Ballards had received; spoke glowingly of the couple; and introduced a singer, who sang a rousing anthem.

Then the pianist played a triumphal air. And Guy Ballard—or Godfré Ray King, as he was introduced—made his entrance. He swept onto the stage to a standing ovation. In his formal white suit and blue satin cape, Ballard was a precursor to latter-day televangelists. A diamond pin flashed on his shirt. He was tall, slender, and erect; his gray hair was combed straight back. He bowed and began to speak.

In the mellifluous tones of an accomplished orator, Ballard held the audience spellbound. He discussed the Mighty I AM Presence; talked about the Ascended Masters; described his meetings with Saint Germain. The Mighty I AM, he declared, was the key to health, wealth, and happiness. The Ascended Masters wanted to teach us their wisdom; and the Ballards were their Accredited Messengers. Saint Germain, he told the audience, was the wisest of the Masters—and the most potent, with the power to heal illness.

Finally, he introduced Lotus Ray King.

Edna's entrance was no less theatrical. Clad in a blue silk gown with trailing ribbons, she swept onto the stage like an opera diva. A spotlight followed her, as the pianist pounded out the triumphal air. Greeted by enthusiastic applause, Edna smiled back with an imperial graciousness. Her gray hair was elaborately coifed. A diamond tiara—along with jeweled rings and necklace—flashed in the spotlight.

Edna now took charge of the proceedings. Her voice was slightly strident; but what the *grande dame* of the I AM Activity lacked in smoothness, she made up for in forcefulness. In a commanding tone, she passed on messages from the Ascended Masters. She led the audience in shouting out "decrees"—ritualistic appeals to the Masters. (These included pleas for the annihilation of communism; for the exorcism of psychic entities that threatened humanity; and for the chastisement of I AM's enemies.) She conducted "affirmations"—declarations of attunement to the Divine. (These were intended to elicit blessings.) She spoke of the greatness of America and the virtue of patriotism. She urged everyone to study the wisdom of the Ascended Masters. Then she sat down at the harp and played.

The evening concluded with the channeling of an Ascended Master. Guy's voice deepened, his eyes closed; and the Great Hercules spoke through him. The audience was then dismissed—with a reminder to leave their "love gifts" in the baskets.

As they passed through the lobby, they were offered a miscellany of merchandise. Arrayed on tables were copies of the Ballards' books (including Braille editions), portraits of Saint Germain, charts of the Magic Presence, recordings of Edna playing the harp, I AM rings and pins, jars of New Age Cold Cream, and the I AM magazine.

The lectures introduced tens of thousands of Americans to the fundamentals of I AM. Those wishing to learn more could join a study group, held in their local sanctuary. By 1939, the I AM Activity had become the most popular New Age movement—and the most controversial.

•

What were the tenets of I AM? What was being taught by the Ballards?

In their lectures and writings, Guy and Edna presented themselves as mere messengers. They had been selected by Saint Germain as a channel for his teachings and healings. Central to those teachings was the existence of the Mighty I AM Presence—a divine energy in each of us. In the channeled words of Saint Germain:

> "There is but One Source and Principle of Life to which we should give our undivided attention and that is the God Self Within every individual."

Our primary task is to release that energy and allow it to permeate our being. And the key to doing so is Love:

"The continual outpouring of a *feeling* of Peace and Divine Love to every person and everything unconditionally, no matter whether you think it be deserved or not, is the Magic Key that unlocks the door and releases instantly this tremendous 'Inner God-Power.'"

Surrounding each of us, explained Saint Germain, is a cylinder of light—the Violet Flame. Once we access our I AM Presence, that Flame is activated. We are thenceforth on the road to enlightenment, self-realization, and escape from earthly travails.

How then do we access our I AM Presence? By adopting a new lifestyle—one that includes a vegetarian diet, meditation, and positive thinking. By repeating the affirmations, which attune the self to the Divine. And by cleaving to the Eternal Law of Love.

But most of all, by seeking the aid of Saint Germain and of other Ascended Masters. With their wise guidance and supernatural assistance, one can purify and perfect oneself. Thus, the Masters are the main focus of I AM instruction. Semi-divine themselves, they are the link to the Cosmic Beings.

Finally, it was possible—with proper diligence—to attain perfection and become an Ascended Master oneself. Indeed, this was the supreme goal of I AM. (The sanctuaries were equipped with an Ascension Chair, to help achieve the necessary level of vibration.) One could ascend to a higher plane of reality, while remaining in one's physical body—that is to say, without having to die. Thereafter, the body could travel back and forth between the material and astral worlds. And best of all, one would have escaped—at long last!—the cycle of reincarnation.

These then were the teachings of Saint Germain, as communicated to Guy and Edna Ballard. And New Age seekers were crowding into auditoriums, to listen to them speak and to buy their books.*

•

By 1939, the Ballards had reached the peak of their success. The lectures (to which they traveled in a Cadillac, towing a trailer with Edna's harp) were still attracting crowds; the study groups were flourishing. And the couple had become prosperous and famous.

But they had also experienced setbacks—in the form of adverse publicity.

One such blow had come the previous year, in their home town of Chicago. After a lecture at the Civic Opera House, Guy Ballard had been signing books in the lobby—when he was abruptly served with legal papers. A local woman was accusing him of having swindled her out of thousands of dollars. Ten years before, she claimed, he had sold her stock in a worthless gold mine.

The next day, headlines such as "WOMAN SUES 'GREAT I AM'" were bannered in the Chicago newspapers. The glee was unmistakable. In the days that followed, the newspapers provided details of the alleged scam, which involved an undeveloped gold mine in California.

The Ballards fought back. They dismissed the allegations as falsehoods; denounced the lawsuit as a "vicious attack" by their enemies; and praised the I AM students for the courage

---

* Eventually, twelve books would be published by the Ballards. These books were issued in a uniform edition, with green leatherette covers, sewn bindings, and dark-violet ink—a set of scriptures. *Unveiled Mysteries* was the inaugural publication. It was followed by a sequel, *The Magic Presence*, describing further encounters with Saint Germain. Subsequent volumes contained discourses that had been channeled from various Ascended Masters.

In listing these later works, bibliographies give the Ascended Master (rather than the channeler) as author. His name is followed by the designation "[spirit]."

The books were said to emit Cosmic Radiation.

with which they were handling this "intrusion of discord." Declared Edna: "Mr. Ballard has never done a dishonest or dishonorable thing in his life and never shall!" Communiqués were even received from Saint Germain, in which he defended the integrity of his messenger. Speaking through the Ballards, he denounced the lawsuit and threatened the newspapers with retribution. But the damage had been done —to Guy Ballard's reputation and to the movement itself.

Meanwhile, another source of adverse publicity had arisen. This was Gerald Bryan, a former student of I AM. Bryan had become disillusioned with the movement and had turned against it. Beginning in 1936, he published a series of pamphlets that sought to expose the Ballards. In Bryan's view, they were charlatans, hungry for wealth and power. Like that gold mine, the Accredited Messengers, and their "channeled" teachings, were bogus.

Bryan would eventually rework the pamphlets into a book, *Psychic Dictatorship in America*. Self-published in 1940, the book is based on his own experiences; testimony solicited from others; and the movement's own literature. In it he doggedly presents his case against the Ballards.

He tells us, for example, that in 1929 Guy Ballard was indicted for fraud by a Chicago grand jury. The charges involved the sale of stock in a California gold mine. Ballard fled the city and avoided arrest.

Where did he go? To Los Angeles, says Bryan, where he lived under an assumed name; attended New Age lectures; and sought to locate—by psychic means—another gold mine. (During an earlier stay in California, he had discovered the mine that prompted the indictment.) Ballard remained in California for two years. Only after the charges were apparently dropped did he rejoin Edna in Chicago.

It was during this period that he claimed to have met Saint Germain on Mount Shasta—a spurious claim, according to Bryan.

Bryan also tracks down the inspiration for the I AM Activity. During his first stay in California, Ballard had visited a New Age church. According to the friend who had accompanied him:

> "While in San Francisco this great idea of Guy's was born. We went to a fake _____ church, and there was a lot of chicanery. The Priest and Priestess sitting in two gold chairs with the twelve vestal virgins as the choir. Behind them was a great illuminated cross with flashing lights. During the service the very lightly clad virgins threw flowers among the audience....
>
> "During this scene Guy's face was a study. He was enchanted with the show, but did not join the church. As soon as he reached the sidewalk, he could not stop talking about it...and from what I now hear, he has fashioned his

church upon the same lines with his illuminated background."

As for the metaphysical content of I AM, Bryan—delving into prior activities of the Ballards—traces it to a variety of sources:

> In their seeking after occult powers, they wandered from teacher to teacher. Not "Ascended Masters," mind you, as their books would have the credulous believe, but merely physical-plane mediums, occult lecturers, Hindus, Egyptians, and others in the magic world of metaphysics.
> They became wandering metaphysical tramps, sat at the feet of earth-plane teachers too numerous to mention, and varied the business by getting through a few spiritualistic messages for themselves, as any other ordinary medium might.
> They imbibed a little of Christian Science, read a bit of the Walter Method C.S., branched over to the Unity School at Kansas City, linked up with the Ancient and Mystical Order Rosae Crucis (A.M.O.R.C.), joined the Order of Christian Mystics, studied under Pelley the Silver Shirter, sat at the feet of some of the Swamis, read a little of Theosophy, looked into the magic of Yogi Philosophy and Oriental Mysticism, interested themselves in Baird T. Spalding and his "Masters of the Far East," which association gave them the idea, no doubt, of making all these metaphysical contacts produce the gold which their gold mines had failed to do—and which "Saint Germain," in a private dictation, said would *bring in more money than a gold mine!*

And the Ballards' books? Much of their contents, says Bryan, was plagiarized, or at least inspired by the works of others. He compares passages in *Unveiled Mysteries* with passages in occult novels—and finds telling similarities.*

---

* Among the novels are *A Wanderer in the Spirit Lands* (1896); *A Dweller on Two Planets* (1905); and *Myriam and the Mystic Brotherhood* (1915). *A Dweller on Two Planets* (whose author was

Finally, Bryan condemns the authoritarian rule imposed by the Ballards. The I AM Activity, he declares, is a psychic dictatorship—a nefarious cult; and his mission is to expose it.

Bryan's writings caused definite harm to the movement. But there was worse to come. For on December 29, 1939, at his son's home in Los Angeles, Guy Ballard died after a brief illness.

Edna would carry on—capably—as sole leader; but leadership was not the problem brought on by her husband's death. Rather, their credibility was further challenged. Why, it was wondered, had the man who claimed to have healed thousands—via the power of the Mighty I AM—not been able to heal himself? Moreover, Guy had always maintained that he would make an Ascension. That is to say, he would escape the limitations of the physical body and join the Ascended Masters—*without having to die*. His failure to do so dismayed his followers (who had entertained similar hopes for themselves); and many began to leave the movement.

And six months later came the most serious blow of all. A federal grand jury indicted Edna Ballard, along with her son and other I AM leaders. (Guy had narrowly escaped—if not the limitations of the physical body—inclusion in the indictment.) They were charged with fraudulent use of the mails.

•

There now began a series of trials and appeals that would become a landmark case in the annals of constitutional law. The Ballards were accused of having operated—for the purpose of making money—a bogus religion, and of having used the U.S. mails to do so. Their claims of communicating with the spirit world, and of healing the sick, were knowingly untrue and therefore fraudulent. One of the

---

supposedly Phylos the Thibetan, channeled by Frederick Spencer Oliver) contains references to "I AM"; while *Myriam and the Mystic Brotherhood* features golden-robed Masters.

twelve counts in the indictment accused the Ballards of an inflated view of themselves:

> That Guy W. Ballard, during his lifetime, and Edna W. Ballard, and Donald Ballard, by reason of their alleged high spiritual attainments and righteous conduct, had been selected as divine messengers through which the words of the alleged "ascended masters," including the alleged Saint Germain, would be communicated to mankind under the teachings commonly known as the "I Am" movement.

The first trial—held in Los Angeles, where the movement was headquartered—lasted a month, and resulted in a hung jury. But the government was determined to put Edna behind bars and suppress the I AM "cult." So it tried her again—this time successfully. The defendants were found guilty as charged. Edna was sentenced to a year in jail (suspended); fined $3000; and enjoined from operating the I AM Activity or any related enterprise. She was not to represent herself as a channel for healing or for the teachings of the Ascended Masters.

Her lawyers (and Edna could afford the best) filed an appeal. *United States v. Ballard* was reviewed by the Ninth Circuit Court of Appeals. And in a 2-1 decision, the guilty verdict was overturned.

The government now appealed. The Supreme Court agreed to take the case. And in a 5-4 decision, it reversed the Court of Appeals—reinstating the guilty verdict. (Or more precisely, sending the case back to the court for reconsideration.)

So now it was final: Edna was guilty of fraud. The Accredited Messenger had lost her accreditation, and could no longer teach the Great Laws of Life. (Or so it seemed. For another twist was yet to come.)

What made this a landmark case was its concern with religious liberty—that is to say, with the First Amendment to the Constitution. J. F. T. O'Connor, the presiding judge at the original trial in Los Angeles, had given emphatic instructions to the jurors. The truth or falsehood of the I AM teachings, he told them, was not relevant to the charges of fraud. The sole issue was whether or not the Ballards had *believed* those teachings. Their sincerity was on trial, not the metaphysics of I AM. It did not matter (to the law) if Saint Germain actually existed in the spirit world. Rather, the question was: Did the Ballards truly believe that he was appearing to them, communicating his wisdom to them, healing the sick? Or were they merely pretending to do so, for the purpose of bringing in dollars? The latter would constitute fraud. As Judge O'Connor put it (after reading aloud a portion of the First Amendment):

> The religious beliefs of these defendants are not an issue in this court and not for your consideration. The issue is: "did these defendants honestly and in good faith, believe that these incidents actually happened?"

On that basis the defendants were initially found guilty of fraud. The I AM movement was a racket, decided the jury —a moneymaking scheme. The Ballards had falsely represented themselves, in order to extract money from their students.

But the Ninth Circuit Court of Appeals took issue with O'Connor's reasoning. The truth or falsehood of the I AM teachings (about astral bodies, reincarnation, supernatural healing) *was* relevant, declared the Court of Appeals. What if those teachings were true? In that case, it was not fraudulent to expound them, however insincerely and mercenarily. For the students were getting what they had paid for— the truth about the cosmos! On the other hand, if the teachings were false? If they had been concocted by the Ballards and bore no relation to reality? Then misrepresentation, for the purpose of profit, had indeed occurred—and thus fraud. So the teachings themselves should have been evaluated, not just the Ballards' use or misuse of them.

Thus, said the Court of Appeals, the jury had been instructed to ignore *a crucial aspect* of the case—namely, the truth or falsehood of the teachings. The guilty verdict was therefore found to be faulty, and overturned.

But in a 5-4 vote, the Supreme Court found that argument unpersuasive—indeed, at odds with the Constitution. For the First Amendment was operative in *United States v. Ballard*, said the Court. In the view of five of the justices, O'Connor's instructions to the jury had been entirely proper. The religious teachings of the Ballards were *not* to be evaluated—for they were protected by the First Amendment. No jury might pass judgment on them. The tenets of the I AM faith might seem preposterous to an outsider; yet no court could determine that a particular religion was false and—by dint of that finding—take action against it.

Writing for the majority, Justice Douglas explained:

> Heresy trials are foreign to our Constitution. Men may believe what they cannot prove. They may not be put to the proof of their religious doctrines or beliefs. Religious experiences which are as real as life to some may be incomprehensible to others. Yet the fact that they may be beyond the ken of mortals does not mean that they can be made suspect before the law. Many take their gospel from the New Testament. But it would hardly be supposed that they could be tried before a jury charged with the duty of determining whether those teachings contained false representations. The miracles of the New Testament, the Divinity of Christ, life after death, the power of prayer are deep in the religious convictions of many. If one could be sent to jail because a jury in a hostile environment found those teachings false, little indeed would be left of religious freedom.

In short, one had a constitutional right to one's beliefs. No jury could appraise a religion, find it false, and punish a person for professing it.

Now this ruling would seem, on the surface, to have benefited Edna. But in fact, it did just the opposite. *For it invalidated the grounds on which her conviction had been overturned.* According to the Court of Appeals, Judge O'Connor should have allowed the tenets of I AM religion to be evaluated. But such an evaluation was deemed now to violate the First Amendment. In disallowing it, O'Connor had acted properly; and the original verdict could stand.

Thus, the Supreme Court, in protecting the freedom of religious belief, was able to uphold the guilty verdict. And to prevent Edna from practicing—however insincerely and mercenarily—her religion!

But four justices had demurred from this decision. Among them was Justice Jackson; and his dissenting opinion is often quoted by defenders of religious liberty. Jackson insisted that Edna should never have been tried in the first place. While the I AM teachings were, in his view, "nothing but humbug," nonetheless,

> that does not dispose of the constitutional questions whether misrepresentation of religious experience or belief is prosecutable; it rather emphasizes the danger of such prosecutions.... the price of freedom of religion or of speech or of the press is that we must put up with, and even pay for, a good deal of rubbish.

Jackson agreed with the majority that the doctrines of a religion were not to be judged. But neither, in his view, was sincerity of belief. "How," he asked, "can the Government prove these persons knew something to be false which it cannot prove to be false?" And he quoted William James on the subjectivity of faith:

> William James, who wrote on these matters as a scientist, reminds us that it is not theology and ceremonies which keep religion going. Its vitality is in the religious experiences of many people. "If you ask what these experiences are [James wrote], they are conversations with the unseen, voices and visions, responses to prayer, changes of heart, deliverances from fear, inflowings of help, assurances of support."

Nor, said Jackson, had members of the movement been cheated. They derived genuine benefits from the I AM faith:

> There appear to be persons—let us hope not many—who find refreshment and courage in the teachings of the I AM cult. If the members of the sect get comfort from the celes-

tial guidance of their "Saint Germain," however doubtful it seems to me, it is hard to say that they do not get what they pay for.

And he urged that the charges against Edna Ballard be dropped:

> Prosecutions of this character easily could degenerate into religious persecutions.... I would dismiss the indictment and have done with this business of judicially examining other people's faiths.

Dismissal, however, was not what the majority had in mind. Instead, they remanded the case to the Ninth Circuit Court of Appeals. The Court of Appeals took a new look—and this time affirmed the guilty verdict.

But the battle was not over. For Edna's lawyers appealed again—on new grounds. And for a second time, the case went to the Supreme Court.

On this final round, the Ascended Masters must have been looking out for Edna. For the justices decided now in her favor. *They quashed the original indictment.*

On what grounds? Once again, her lawyers had raised a constitutional issue. This time, however, the Fifth and Sixth Amendments were the problem. Their guarantees—of due process and an impartial jury—had been violated, Edna's lawyers contended. And the justices agreed.

In California (prior to 1943), grand juries were selected from a pool that included no women. Thus, Edna had been indicted by a jury consisting entirely of men. Why was that an issue? Because such a jury was not representative of her community, which was half female. Men and women were "not fungible," declared the Court—were not interchangeable. They might have differing outlooks in regards to a particular defendant. A female juror might have understood, sympathized with, and voted to acquit Edna, whereas her male counterpart might not have.

Thus, Edna had been denied both due process and a jury of her peers. So her indictment was invalid, said the

Supreme Court; and the guilty verdict was void.

The government could have sought to reindict her. It chose not to. So after six years of inactivity, Edna Ballard was free once again to channel the Ascended Masters. And to convey their wisdom to mankind.

•

Edna had relocated both the I AM headquarters and herself to Santa Fe, New Mexico. A new start had been needed. Guy's death, and the adverse publicity arising from the trials, had harmed the movement; and membership had declined significantly. So now, with her legal problems resolved, Edna carried on in Santa Fe—the sole leader of a shrunken but still active movement.

She proved to be an effective leader. Gerald Bryan (that disgruntled ex-member) describes her as "a dynamic, authoritarian, battling kind of person," who led with the martial vigor of an Amazon. When the Santa Fe newspaper ran a negative story about her, Edna had her followers descend upon and disrupt its offices. For the next 25 years this strong-willed woman kept the movement alive.

Indeed, she was probably the main force behind it from the beginning. Bryan quotes from a letter he received:

> "I have known Guy Ballard for more than thirty years," writes one of his friends, who is amazed at Ballard's sudden ascension into power. "He came to our home when I was a little girl, and at that time tried to be a medium. Edna, his wife, always has been ambitious, great for personal adornment, and has always been the man of the family."

It is even likely that Edna, versed in occult literature, was the principal author of the I AM books. In the early days of the classes, says Bryan, questions about Guy's mystical experiences would generally be answered by Edna. An overnight guest in their Chicago home described Edna as putting in long hours at her desk, while Guy did the laundry. And their former manager wrote to Bryan:

> "I think Mrs. Ballard did most of the work. In fact, so far as I could see while I was with them, *she* was the boss, and he did just what she told him to do. She also was in full charge of *The Magic Presence*, which was in preparation while I was with them.... She spent much time working on this MS. the whole time I was with them."

Kenneth and Talita Paolini (authors of *400 Years of Imaginary Friends: A Journey Into the World of Adepts, Masters, Ascended Masters, and Their Messengers*) concurred:

> Edna Ballard was probably the true author of the I AM books. In Chicago during 1930, she began what would become the I AM movement with a small group of people, sworn to secrecy, to whom she read works of Pelley, Spalding, and other occult writers. She gradually introduced the "Discourses," which she later claimed came to her from the Masters, and she began telling stories of Guy's adventures with Saint Germain on Mount Shasta (which would become their first book, *Unveiled Mysteries*).

What had originated in Chicago and flourished in Los Angeles, continued now in Santa Fe. Surrounded by loyal followers, Edna resumed her role as Accredited Messenger. She channeled messages from the Ascended Masters (and from Guy); edited the I AM magazine; and tended to organizational matters.

But by the time of her death in 1971, the I AM membership had dwindled. The glory days of the movement were long gone.

•

Central to I AM were the Ascended Masters. But were the Ballards actually in contact with such beings? Did they channel messages from them? Did Guy meet with Saint Germain? Or was it all indeed humbug?

Those meetings, insisted Guy (or whichever Ballard

wrote *Unveiled Mysteries*), were "as real and true as mankind's existence on this Earth today, and... they all occurred during August, September, and October of 1930, upon Mount Shasta."

So what was going on here? Were the Ballards deceiving us, or what? Several possibilities suggest themselves:

1. Guy and Edna were completely sincere. Their experiences—though visionary in nature—were real.
2. Those "experiences" were fabricated—but with a worthy aim. The Ballards wanted to make spiritual truths more accessible. So they created—from such sources as Theosophy and occult novels—the I AM teachings.
3. The whole thing was a fraud. The Ballards were precisely what their enemies accused them of being—charlatans. They had concocted a religion for the sole purpose of making money.

Or perhaps the truth about the Ballards is complicated. Perhaps Guy did have visionary experiences on Mount Shasta. Returning to Chicago, he described these experiences to Edna. And in a series of books, she elaborated upon them—fleshing out the details, drawing upon her reading for metaphysical ideas, and "channeling" discourses from Saint Germain. The result was the I AM Activity, both a genuine set of teachings *and* a moneymaking enterprise—their gold mine at last.

What then is the final verdict on the Ballards? Were they visionaries, fruitcakes, or frauds? Did Guy actually descend into the earth and visit the Ascended Masters? In *Unveiled Mysteries*, he sums up what is at stake:

> The saying that, "Truth is stranger than fiction," applies to this Book. It is for the reader to accept or reject as he chooses, but the Ascended Masters, whose Help I have received, have said to me often: "The more humanity can accept Our Presence, the wider it opens the door for Us to pour greater

and greater Help to them; but the rejection of Us, by those who do not agree with this Truth, does not remove Us or change Its Activity in the Universe."

We can accept or reject the reality of the Masters. Yet who can argue with their basic message? As Saint Germain told Guy:

"The constant Command of the Ascended Masters is: 'Let the Great Light of the "Mighty I AM Presence" enfold the humanity of Earth.'... Misery, darkness and ignorance exist only because of lack of Love."

Love is the Magic Key, proclaim the Ascended Masters. We ignore them at our peril.*

---

* Who exactly are these Ascended Masters?

According to the Ballards, they are "Masters of Love, Light, and Wisdom"—an invisible college of "great spiritual teachers" who have moved on to a higher plane. They have perfected themselves, transcended the limitations of the physical world, and ascended into "the Seventh Octave of Light."

Yet the Masters can lower their vibration rate and manifest themselves in our octave of consciousness. Why would they do so? Saint Germain explains:

"The Ascended Masters are the Guardians of humanity and have worked through the centuries from the invisible as well as the physical to awaken, to bless, to enlighten and lift mankind out of its self-created degradation and selfishness."

The goal of an I AM student is to turn his attention to the Masters, heed their wisdom, and join them in their work. Or even (in exceptional cases) join their ranks—that is to say, become an Ascended Master.

These beings were first alluded to in the writings of Madame Blavatsky. The founder of Theosophy (of which I AM is an offshoot), Blavatsky was an accomplished medium. In the 1870s she made contact with Koot Hoomi and Morya—a pair of Ascended Masters who were based in Tibet and who conveyed to her their teachings.

Half a century later, the Ballards began communicating with

their own set of Masters: Nada, Che Ara, Lanto, Cyclopea, the Great Master of Venus, Arcturus, Beloved Bob—and of course, Saint Germain.

And who is Saint Germain?

The Saint Germain of I AM is an elusive figure. He is not to be confused with the actual saint (a French monk canonized in the eighth century). Rather, he would seem to be a manifestation of the Count de St.-Germain—the great mystery-man of the eighteenth century. Nothing is known of the origins of this self-styled count. (The title was one that he had simply coined and adopted.) But with his black satin outfit, powdered wig, diamond rings, and snuffbox, the Count de St.-Germain did have an aristocratic air. He was a wealthy traveler (with no known source of income); a master of languages; an accomplished musician; a witty conversationalist; and a confidant of kings. Moreover, he was a latter-day alchemist, who was said to possess the Elixir of Life. Voltaire referred to him as "a man who knows everything and who never dies"; and Frederick the Great called him "one of the most enigmatical personages of the eighteenth century."

(St.-Germain was rumored to be centuries old—to have known Dante, and even Cleopatra! Partly responsible for these rumors was a Paris comedian known as Milord Gower, who did imitations of St.-Germain—comic turns that found their way into his legend.)

It was Madame Blavatsky who praised him as a master of Eastern wisdom, and strengthened his reputation as an occultist. "The Compte de St. Germain," she wrote, "was certainly the greatest Oriental Adept Europe has seen during the last century." Blavatsky believed that he was still alive and influential in human affairs. And as late as 1925, he was supposedly spotted at a Masonic convention in France.

But it was the Ballards who introduced us to the semi-divine Saint Germain. In *The Magic Presence*, the black satin has given way to "a robe of marvelous, dazzling white fabric"; and Saint Germain is described as follows:

"I opened my eyes and there was the Blessed, Wonderful Presence of our Beloved Master. He stood fully six feet one inch in height, slender, royal and real. His hair was dark brown, wavy and abundant. His face portrayed a Beauty, Majesty and Power no words can describe—a face revealing Eternal Youth, with eyes of the deepest violet one can imagine through which the Wisdom of the Ages poured out upon the world expressing the Love and Mastery that are His."

(On another occasion, his eyes are like the grin of the Cheshire cat: "The last thing that remained visible, as he gradually disappeared, were his marvelous, beautiful eyes shining back at me.")

Saint Germain, then, was the chief representative of the Guardians of humanity—those "Masters of Love, Light, and Wisdom" who keep an eye on us from above.

20.

Richard Shaver

THE SHAVER MYSTERY (OR SHAVER HOAX, AS IT BEcame known to its detractors) began with a letter to the editor. Years later, Ray Palmer would recall the letter:

> By December, 1943, I had become editor-in-chief of a large string of pulp paper magazines published by the Ziff-Davis Publishing Company of Chicago, Illinois. One of these magazines was the original science fiction magazine, *Amazing Stories*, first published in 1926.... One day a letter arrived giving the details of an "ancient alphabet" that "should not be lost to the world." It was opened by my managing editor, Howard Browne, who tossed it into the wastebasket with the comment: "The world is sure full of crackpots!"
> Even through the intervening wall I heard his remark, and the word "crackpot" drew me like a magnet.... I retrieved the letter from the wastebasket.

As he read it, Ray Palmer's eyes lit up. He published the letter in the next issue of *Amazing Stories*. The response delighted him (and discomforted Browne). Hundreds of letters poured in, from readers fascinated by that "ancient alphabet."

Palmer contacted now the sender of the letter—one Richard Shaver—and requested further information. Eventually, there arrived from Shaver a second communication: a manuscript 10,000 words long. The story it told was indeed amazing.

And the Shaver Mystery—which Palmer would bill as "the most sensational true story ever told"—was born.

•

The pulp magazines published by Ziff-Davis were filled

with popular fiction. Each was dedicated to a particular genre, such as science fiction or detective tales. The covers were garish; the price was low; the stories were action-packed. "Pulp" referred to the type of paper on which they were printed: pulped wood instead of rag-cotton. Except for their covers (four-color, on slick paper), the pulps were inexpensive to produce.

The first pulp magazine was published by Frank Munsey (1854–1925). A former telegraph operator, Munsey had begun his publishing career by acquiring a magazine called *Golden Argosy*. It featured uplifting stories for children, by authors such as Horatio Alger. With entrepreneurial zest, he shortened the title to *Argosy*; switched to lively fiction for adults; sought to entertain rather than uplift; and—to lower the price of his magazine and thus increase sales—began using woodpulp paper. (Such paper deteriorated rapidly, but so what?) With its tales of action and adventure, *Argosy* sold well—half a million copies per issue at its height. Another of his publications, *All-Story*, became popular, too. And Frank Munsey grew rich, as a purveyor of lowbrow, magazine fiction.*

But at the turn of the century a rival pulpster arose. Street & Smith had been a publisher of dime novels. Now it imitated Munsey, with pulp periodicals that were devoted to general fiction. Its *Popular Magazine* was the first of the pulps to have a color cover. And in 1915, Street & Smith came up with another innovation. It began to publish magazines that specialized in a particular genre of fiction. Among these were *Detective Story*, *Western Story*, and *Sea Stories*.

Not to be outdone, Munsey followed suit with *Detective Fiction Weekly*. Other publishers joined in; and the new species proliferated. Newsstands blossomed with its garish covers. Every taste was catered to. There were pulps dedicated to sports stories, aviation stories, love stories, "spicy" stories. There was even *Weird Tales*, which specialized in fantasy.

But surprisingly (given their subsequent popularity), there were not yet any science-fiction magazines. Indeed, the term had yet to be invented. Munsey had published an occasional "scientific romance." (*Under the Moons of Mars*, for instance, by Edgar Rice Burroughs, had been serialized in *All-Story*.) But as a magazine genre, science fiction did not exist.

It was awaiting its founder.

---

* He also published *Munsey's*, a general-interest magazine; owned seventeen newspapers over his lifetime; and wrote five novels.

Hugo Gernsback (1884–1967) arrived in the U.S. in 1904. An electrical engineer, he had come to market a dry-cell battery that he had invented. Two of these batteries were packed in his trunk, along with his tailor-made suits and expensive shirts.*

What had drawn Gernsback to America from his native Luxembourg? In his autobiography he explains:

> Hugo now 19 years old and full of confidence in himself and in the future of wireless and electricity, desired most of all to spread his wings in a country where ambition was not circumscribed and thwarted by rock-ribbed conservatism and age-old custom. Hugo stood stubborn and bull-headed in making this decision.†

Gernsback wound up settling in New York, as the proprietor of a radio-supply house. In the years that followed, he would sell radio supplies (importing them from Europe); patent scores of inventions; and publish magazines.

The magazines had their origin in the catalog for his supply house. Radio was still the province of tinkerers; and this catalog (billed as "Everything for the Experimenter") was a source of components for them. Also, Gernsback had designed a home-radio set, which he marketed via the catalog.**

---

* Described as "a lean, dapper man," Gernsback came from a genteel background and was an elegant dresser. (He would be one of the few New Yorkers to wear a monocle.) The son of a prosperous vintner, he was also a connoisseur of wine.

† The manuscript of this autobiography was discovered only recently, amid the stored remains of Gernsback Publications. Oddly, it is told in the third person.

** The radio set was called the Telimco Wireless Telegraph. It consisted of two units: a transmitter with a spark coil; and a receiver with a bell. You could transmit a signal that would ring the bell—up to a mile away! It was a wonder of the age.

Issued regularly, the catalog was 64-pages long and profusely illustrated. To educate his customers in the basics of radio, Gernsback included articles. And then, in 1908, he went a step further. He published the first issue of a magazine, called *Modern Electrics*.*

Modern Electrics was written and edited by Gernsback. It was intended to stimulate interest in radio, and thereby boost sales for his supply house. He hoped, too, that the magazine itself might be profitable. Included in it were articles on all aspects of radio—in particular, how-to articles.

The magazine found a readership. And it marked the beginning of his career as a publisher. Between 1908 and 1952, Hugo Gernsback would publish some fifty different magazines. They were edited, initially, in the offices of the Experimenter Publishing Co., and later, of Gernsback Publications. Most of them were technology titles, such as *Radio News*, *Practical Electrics*, and *The Electrical Experimenter*. But there was also *Scientific Detective Monthly*, *Pirate Stories*, *Sexology*.

And then there were his science-fiction magazines.

Gernsback came to science fiction via his technology magazines. In 1911 he published—amidst the articles in *Modern Electrics*—a scientific romance. Filled with speculation on the future of technology, it was written by Gernsback himself. Such speculation had been common in his editorials. But now speculative *fiction*—written by Gernsback and others—began to appear regularly in his radio and electrical magazines.

Predictions about the future became a Gernsback specialty. He envisioned, for example, an "electronic doctor"—conveyor belts that took patients past a series of diagnostic machines—and domed cities in orbit. He published stories that forecast advances in science and technology. And he put forward ideas for inventions—inventions that he would

---

* The magazine is still being published today—after mergers with other magazines and changes of name—as *Popular Science Monthly*.

sometimes go on to invent.*

For more than a decade, Gernsback included scientific fiction in his magazines. And then he had an idea. Why not publish a magazine that consisted solely of such fiction?

A magazine of "scientifiction," as he would call it.

•

The first issue of *Amazing Stories* appeared in March 1926. (Gernsback had tested the idea first with an issue of *Science and Invention* that consisted mostly of scientific fiction.) With its cheap paper and lurid cover, the magazine

---

* Hugo Gernsback was an accomplished inventor. He is credited with having built the first walkie-talkie. And as a broadcast pioneer (the founder of an early radio station), he was involved in the creation of television. Among his inventions were the Osophone (an innovative hearing-aid), and the Isolator. The Isolator was a thinking cap. A helmet with its own air supply, it blocked out distractions that interfered with thinking. Gernsback was photographed using one in his office.

resembled the other pulps that had sprouted on the newsstands. Yet it targeted a special readership: "radio bugs" and others with an interest in science and technology. (As things turned out, it attracted readers with a taste for fantastic adventure.)

An editorial announced that *Amazing Stories* would offer "charming romances intermingled with scientific fact and prophetic vision." The stories in the first issue were all reprints, and included tales by H. G. Wells, Jules Verne, and Edgar Allan Poe. But subsequent issues increasingly contained original material. The editor was T. O'Connor Sloane, an elderly chemist who had previously edited one of the technology titles.

Amazing Stories was a success; and its circulation soon surpassed 100,000. But in 1929 Gernsback was sued by his printer and paper supplier (possibly at the instigation of Bernarr Macfadden, a rival publisher), and forced into bankruptcy. Placed into receivership, *Amazing* and the other magazines continued to be published. The staff remained intact, except for Gernsback, who was ousted as director. And two years later, the Gernsback magazines were acquired by Macfadden Publications.*

Under the continued editorship of T. O'Connor Sloane, *Amazing Stories* remained afloat. But it was in competition now with other science-fiction magazines. And deprived of Gernsback's leadership, *Amazing* declined in quality. It was reduced to a bimonthly; and in 1938—circulation down to 15,000—the magazine was sold to Ziff-Davis of Chicago.

---

* Bernarr Macfadden was a magazine mogul. His *True Story* (filled with fiction masquerading as fact) had the largest circulation of any magazine during the 1920s. And he was pleased to add these new titles to his list.

Meanwhile, Gernsback had formed a new company. And he was publishing *Radio-Craft, Science Wonder Stories,* and *Air Wonder Stories*—magazines that competed directly with the ones he had lost. "I now intend to bring out a new and better magazine," he had written to his scientifiction authors. And he had come up with a new term for the genre: "science fiction."

Ziff-Davis looked around for a younger editor. (Sloane was approaching ninety.) And it hired Ray Palmer, a 29-year-old who had published stories in *Amazing*, and who was active in science-fiction fandom.

•

Ray Palmer (1910–1977) was born and raised in Milwaukee. At the age of seven, he was struck by a truck and severely injured. The accident, which broke his back, would profoundly affect his life. For he grew up to be a hunchback —a gnomelike figure, barely four-feet tall, who was partially crippled.

Yet the accident gave rise to something positive. During much of his youth, Palmer was bedridden—confined to the hospital or his home. Unable to attend school, he was educated by a tutor. Also, the Milwaukee Public Library sent him a weekly crate of books. In the prison of his bed, Palmer eagerly read these books—sometimes a dozen in a day. Thus did he become a voracious reader and an autodidact.*

By his fifteenth year, Palmer was able to attend school. A self-described "lone-wolf," he enrolled at St. Anne's Catholic School in Milwaukee. Unlike most of his fellow students, he needed no encouragement to read.

And a year later, he was browsing at a newsstand—when a magazine cover caught his eye. It was the first issue of *Amazing Stories*. Palmer bought it, read it cover to cover, and became a fan—an avid reader of the magazine. He

---

* As an invalid with little to do but read, Palmer was in good company. Nathaniel Hawthorne was injured (playing bat-and-ball) when he was nine. Bedridden for a year, he too became an insatiable reader.

And Willard Huntington Wright, an art and literary critic, spent two years confined to his bed, on account of an ailment. To pass the time, he read mystery novels—stacks of them. Upon recovering, he began to *write* mysteries. They were published under the name "S. S. Van Dine," and featured Philo Vance—an aristocratic sleuth who resembled Wright.

wrote letters to the editor, commenting on stories. And he submitted a story of his own, "The Time Ray of Jandia," which he had written for his English class. To his immense satisfaction, he received a letter of acceptance and a $40 check. Hugo Gernsback had bought the story. (It would not be published, though, until several years later.)

After high school, Palmer attended business college. Then he found a job as bookkeeper for a sheet-metal company. But his real interest—his passion—was to write science fiction and other types of popular fiction. At night he was writing, in a dreary rented room; and more sales followed, to various pulps. With friends he formed the Science Correspondence Club, an organization of science-fiction fans. And he published a fanzine—cranked out on a mimeograph machine—called *The Comet*.

In 1938 Ziff-Davis acquired *Amazing Stories* and sought a new editor—someone with science-fiction "credentials." By now Palmer was a prominent figure in fandom. Offered the job, he accepted it and moved to Chicago.

He found himself at the helm of a moribund magazine. Its brand of science fiction—scientific and educational—was no longer in vogue. Determined to restore *Amazing* to life, Palmer switched to tales of action and adventure—swordplay in Space, damsels in distress, bug-eyed monsters. He sought out writers who could deliver such stories, and also published stories of his own (under pseudonyms). He engaged the services of skilled illustrators; ran a column on the paranormal; and began each issue with a lively editorial. It wasn't long before the circulation of the magazine had soared from 15,000 to more than 135,000.

And it would soar even higher—thanks to that letter plucked from a wastebasket.

•

Years later, his managing editor would recall the letter: "Ray, who loved to show his editors a trick or two about the business, fished it out of the basket, ran it in *Amazing*—and a flood of mail poured in."

The letter, ill-typed, was from a reader: Richard Shaver of Barto, Pennsylvania. Shaver described a language called Mantong. It was the original language of mankind, he claimed, and had been spoken by the inhabitants of Atlantis. All other languages were descended from it. Thus, English had its roots in Mantong—roots that could be explored for hidden meanings.

Shaver listed the sounds of Mantong—its alphabet. And he gave the meaning of each sound. These meanings were intrinsic, he explained; and unlike words, they did not change over time. So the Mantong alphabet could be used to decode English words. The word *desolate*, for example, consists of the sounds *de*, "destructive," *sol*, "sun," and *ate*, "devour"—i.e., "devoured by a destructive sun."*

Shaver concluded with a plea:

> This is perhaps the only copy of this language in existence and it represents my work over a long period of years. It is an immensely important find, suggesting the god legends have a base in some wiser race than modern man.... I need a little encouragement.

That encouragement was forthcoming. It came from the readership of *Amazing*, who sent in hundreds of letters. In response to a challenge from Palmer, these readers had used the Mantong alphabet to analyze English words—and had found that Shaver was onto something. Encouraging too was Palmer, who wrote to Shaver and asked for more information. Where, Palmer asked, had he gotten this alphabet?

Months later, a bulging envelope arrived in the mail at Ziff-Davis. Inside was a manuscript from Shaver, titled "A Warning to Future Man." As he read through it, Palmer realized that this *factual narrative* (as it purported to be) was literary dynamite. However, it was in need of a total rewrite.

---

* As we shall see, it was the destructive rays of the sun that drove the speakers of Mantong underground.

Palmer set to work. "I put a clean piece of paper into my typewriter," he would later reminisce, "and using Mr. Shaver's strange letter-manuscript as a basis, I wrote a 31,000 word story which I entitled 'I Remember Lemuria!'"

Readers were given advance notice that something exciting was in the works. "For the first time in its history," Palmer announced in an editorial, "*Amazing Stories* is preparing to present a true story."

And in the March 1945 issue, "I Remember Lemuria!" was featured, with a cover illustration.

The Shaver Mystery was launched.

•

Palmer transformed "A Warning to Future Man" in two ways. First, he gave it a makeover into pulp fiction:

> I started with the first word of page one, and I took a factual presentation...and I turned it into a "story" suitable for publication in a fiction magazine. I added dialogue, so that Mutan Mion, Arl, and all the other characters mentioned, actually spoke and moved and breathed in the account, rather than seemed to be statistics in a deadly serious presentation.... Under no stretch of imagination could that original 10,000 word manuscript have been said to be a "story," in the sense that it had action, dialogue, romance, intrigue, plot, suspense and whatever else a good action story in a pulp magazine must have. Nor was Shaver averse to having the editor make these changes, if it was the only way the message could be gotten across.

Secondly, he presented Shaver's account as a "racial memory." The term referred to reincarnation; supposedly, Shaver was recalling events from a former lifetime. Palmer came to regret this change:

> Although I added all the "trimmings," I did not alter the "factual" basis of Mr. Shaver's manuscript except in one instance. Here, perhaps, I made a grave mistake. However,

I could not bring myself to believe that Mr. Shaver had actually gotten his Alphabet, and his Warning to Future Man, and all the "science" he propounded, from actual caves in the earth, and actual people living there. Instead, I translated his thought-records into "racial memory," and felt sure this would be more believable to my readers.

Many readers would still question the factual basis of "I Remember Lemuria!" But Palmer himself had no doubts:

> I presented the story as racial memory for that reason—but I did something else; I believed Shaver and because I believed him (and I had many reasons, among them a lifetime of my own in the same fields of study, such as mythology, as those Shaver had investigated so thoroughly), I labeled the story TRUE!

He also published it with footnotes (37 of them), elucidating matters of scientific, historical, and linguistic import. For "I Remember Lemuria!" had much that needed elucidating.

The story is set in the distant past, during the last days of ancient Lemuria. The Lemurians have retreated into underground caverns, to escape destructive rays emanating from the sun. Finally, however, they decide to abandon the earth entirely and migrate to a distant planet.

But before they are able to depart, a war breaks out—with the Deros. A race of demented dwarves, the Deros are the epitome of evil. From their own caverns they attack the Lemurians. They are led by a renegade Lemurian named Zeit, who has furnished them with advanced weapons.

Mutan Mion (the narrator of the story) is a young artist, caught up in the war. He is granted an audience with Princess Vanue—a Titan and one of the elders of Lemuria. Seated on a throne, Princess Vanue is a kind of fertility goddess: *eighty*-feet tall, scantily-clad, and charged with sexual energy. (When he kneels in homage and touches one of her feet, Mutan Mion experiences "unbearable pleasure.") At a Conclave of the Elders she lifts him, like a tiny doll, and

introduces him to her fellow Titans.

The young artist joins the Titans in the war with the Deros. Brave and resourceful, he proves himself to be a warrior. A climactic battle takes place in the depths of the earth. The Deros are defeated, Zeit is captured. And the Lemurians prepare to migrate to that distant planet.

And Mutan Mion is given a mission. He is to write a history of Lemuria; inscribe copies of it on metal plates; and deposit the plates throughout the caverns. This history is intended to be found by future men, and serve them as both a warning and a message of hope.

Such then was the tale that appeared in the March 1945 issue of *Amazing Stories*—and which prompted, said Palmer, "a flood of letters." More tales by Shaver would follow. They were billed as "the most amazing series of stories of Lemuria ever published.... Judge for yourself how true they are. Some of the things you read will stagger you!"

But the tales were no longer presented as "racial memories." Had they been, Shaver could have been dismissed as a mere daydreamer. Anyone can imagine a previous lifetime. It is an altogether different matter to claim—*as Shaver did*—to have entered a subterranean realm; dwelt among its inhabitants; and discovered an ancient set of plates—engraved by a Lemurian!

For such were the claims that would spark the controversy known as the Shaver Mystery.

•

The second Shaver tale appeared in the June 1945 issue. (That is to say, in the next issue—*Amazing* was being published quarterly, due to the wartime rationing of paper.) It was titled "Thought Records of Lemuria." And it came with an apology. In his editorial remarks, Palmer confessed to having misrepresented its predecessor. That business about "racial memory"? That had been his own explanation for the origins of the story. For he had been unable to accept Shaver's.

But he was prepared now to be straight with his readers —to "present the truth as Mr. Shaver has told it to us." "Thought Records of Lemuria" was based on *personal experiences*. It was autobiography, in the guise of fiction. Said Palmer:

> The editors of this magazine are pleased to present the second "Lemurian" story written by a man who has seen with his own eyes the remnants of the ancient race of Lemuria, and witnessed their still-populated cities hidden deep beneath the surface of the Earth. This second story is intended to answer the challenge of those who wish Mr. Shaver to offer some proof of his source for the first story, "I Remember Lemuria!" published in our March issue. Although it is now revealed that Mr. Shaver's source is not racial memory, as mistakenly claimed by your editors, it seems certain that the actual source will be even more unbelievable.

The tale begins in a Detroit auto plant. The narrator, Richard Shaver himself, is at work on an assembly line. He is surrounded by "the muted roar of an auto factory—the clanging, clattering, mingling maelstrom of busy machines and busier men." Suddenly, he starts to hear voices. They are the thoughts, he realizes, of his fellow workers. When he lays down his welding gun, the voices cease—resuming when he picks it up again. Somehow the gun is acting as a receiver.

Then he hears voices from some distant place. These voices are disturbing. For they are discussing the torment of a captive. Trembling, Shaver wonders if he is losing his mind. Or, he asks himself, is his mind functioning *all too well*?

Then he hears a scream—a sound "as might be imagined only in Dante's Inferno." And he can stand it no longer. He quits his job and heads home. But the voices continue on the street car.

At this point in his tale, Shaver adds a footnote to the narrative:

> I have pictured those first weird happenings that led me almost to the brink of madness, and then to the most incredible adventure that ever befell a man. In order to give my knowledge to the world without being suspected of madness, I must present it in the guise of fiction.... This story will not seem like fiction to some who will read it. For it is substantially true; the caves, the good and wise users of the antique machines, the fantastic evil mis-users of the antique weapons, all these things are true things and exist in secret in many parts of the world.... In this story, I intend to reveal the secret.

The tale continues with the narrator fleeing Detroit, "as though the devil himself were after me." But the voices persist. And as he wanders from city to city, Shaver comes to know to whom they belong. They are the voices of Deros—creatures who live in caverns beneath the earth. The Deros have taken control of machines that the Lemurians left behind. And they use them to torment human beings.

Finally, he has learned too much; and the Deros set out to destroy him. They target Shaver with rays from the machines, and induce him to commit a crime. He is arrested and sentenced to prison. There the Deros torment him with rays. And he languishes in his cell, on the verge of madness and despair.

> I learned at length and in infinite detail just what Hell really can be, and at the same time I realized that such a Hell has been the daily lot of many men of earth since earliest times.

The Deros have allowed him to live, he realizes, only because his suffering gives them pleasure.

Then all at once, the torments cease. For the rays of the Deros have been counteracted—by those of the Teros. Who are the Teros? Like the Deros, they dwell in the caverns. But unlike their malevolent cousins (from whom they must hide), they have remained human and are benevolent.

And one night he is visited, as in a dream, by a Tero. She enters his cell and sits on the edge of his iron cot.

> She seemed clothed in a soft luminosity that threw rays of strangely invigorating light upon me as well as showing her strange, rich other-world beauty to me. She had hair of faintest golden tint.... Her eyes under arching brows were wide and had no expression, yet her assurance in every movement as she came into the cell did not betray what I learned later, that she was blind.... When she spoke, such vitality sprang into being on her strange face as woke every instinct in me from the long hopeless sleep in which they had been plunged. Yes, her face was freedom to me.

The blind visitor—whom he calls Nydia—takes hold of his hands. In halting English, she asks if he wishes to be freed from prison. "I want it more than life," replies Shaver. And she offers to free him—if he will agree to do her bidding for one year. With nothing to lose, he agrees to the proposition.

More visits follow. Then Nydia announces that the time has come. She will soon effect his release and take him to her home.

Just before dawn, he is awoken by the sound of a key in the lock. And he sees the guard, with a glazed look, opening his cell door. Nydia is standing nearby. As if hypnotized, the guard escorts Shaver out of the prison.

Then Nydia leads him into the forest. And the two walk deeper and deeper into the hills.

> At last we came to the base of the mountain, to where it reared rocky slopes to the night sky. In the cleft of two rocky shoulders yawned a door. It was a strange door, for it was covered with earth and grass and small bushes, all alive and growing. As soon as our feet crossed the threshold, the great mass of the door lowered silently and I knew that no man could detect where that door might be.*

Nydia leads him into a vast chamber. It is filled with "hulking, mysterious machines...dimly gigantic in the faint light of the cavern lamps." To his astonishment, standing at the controls of one of the machines is a duplicate of Nydia. As this Nydia comes forward to embrace him, the one accompanying him abruptly disappears. And he learns that the visitor to his cell has been a projection—a transmitted image of Nydia.

Thus begins his stay in the caverns—as Nydia's lover. He is introduced to the small band of Teros with whom she lives. They roam the caverns, Nydia explains, in constant

---

* To this passage Shaver adds a footnote: "Such doors into the caves are few but they do exist and no other door is so worthy of a man's search. Always provided the door is not one that opens upon the hiding places of the evil life that is in many parts of the caves, there is no door that can open life before you as that door to the underworld. Read on and you shall learn something of the pleasure and wisdom that opened door offered me, a criminal escaped from a state prison. You shall learn, too, that there are other things yet more wonderful than the seemingly impossible feat of a blind girl snatching a convict out of a prison.—Author."

fear of an attack by Deros. But she is hopeful that Shaver will be able to help thwart these attacks. She leads him to a "visi-screen" and shows him a group of Deros. They are goggle-eyed and dwarfish.*

Then she leads him into a library. It is a repository of metal cases that contain a kind of microfilm. Preserved on the microfilm are the "thought records" of individual Lemurians—their recorded experiences. Says Nydia: "You should read the story of the great race who built these imperishable caves and the indestructible machinery which is capable of who knows what miracles." These records will teach him how to operate certain machines, which can then be used against the Deros.

Nydia straps him into a huge chair, puts a helmet on his head, and plays a thought record. And Shaver becomes Duli, an early settler of Lemuria. He relives Duli's experiences. They seem to be happening to him, as he sits there in the chair.

Then Nydia plays another record for him. And he becomes Bar Mehat, a Lemurian warrior. Bar Mehat is leading the fight against an invasion of lizard-men.

When the record ends, Shaver is slumped in the chair. Nydia unstraps him and helps him to his feet. The thought records have exhausted him. But he has acquired a vivid sense of the lives of two Lemurians.

A gong sounds. Shaver and Nydia make their way to a dining hall. There he throws in his lot with the band of Teros. And "Thought Records of Lemuria" concludes.

•

This sequel prompted another flood of letters; and Palmer knew he had struck a nerve. For the next three years,

---

* In a later tale Shaver describes the Deros as "anaemic jitterbugs, small, with pipestem arms and legs, pot bellies, huge protruding eyes, idiotically grinning mouths. Goofy, I believe modern youth would call them."

he would feature a Shaver tale in almost every issue of the magazine.

The tales were based on fact, Palmer insisted. For their author had visited the cavern world, and had discovered there a history of Lemuria. His tales made use of that history. In publishing them, *Amazing* was offering a glimpse into the earliest years of mankind.

And as each tale appeared, more about Lemuria became known. In a nutshell, here is its story:

The earth was originally inhabited by a race of giants. (They averaged twenty feet in height.) These Titans, as they called themselves, had migrated from another planet and settled on two continents: Lemuria and Atlantis. There they developed an advanced civilization.*

This civilization enjoyed the fruits of advanced technology. But while machines did much of the work, menial laborers were still needed. So the Lemurians bred a race of workers. Of ordinary stature, these servants performed various tasks. And though fully human, they were known as *robots*—Mantong for "workers."

Life was good for the Lemurians. They had no enemies; led a leisurely existence; and enjoyed a life span of thousands of years, retaining all the while their vigor and youthful appearance.

But then the idyll came to an end. The sun underwent a transformation, and began to emit deadly radiation. And the Lemurians began to fall ill and die.

So they retreated to the interior of the earth, to escape the radiation. With disintegrator beams, they enlarged existing caverns and created new ones. Cities were built within these caverns. And Lemurian civilization reestablished itself in the depths of the earth.

The Lemurians thrived in their new home. But finally, the radiation penetrated even there; and again, they began to die. So they decided to leave the earth altogether, and find some other planet on which to live.

---

* Cf. Genesis 6:4: "In those days there were giants in the earth."

They departed in spaceships, leaving behind their caverns, their cities, and their technological wonders. And leaving behind, too, the Deros—those "demented dwarfs" with whom they had fought a war.

Who exactly were the Deros? They were the descendants of the workers whom the Lemurians had bred—the so-called "robots." For the workers too had been affected by radiation, from both the sun and the machines they tended. And they had degenerated into monsters—deranged creatures who jabbered in their dens.*

Once the Lemurians were gone, the Deros swarmed into the abandoned cities. They took up residence, and became the new rulers of the cavern world.

And they inhabit it still, insisted Shaver.

How did he know?

He had been to the caverns.

•

Richard Shaver (1907–1975) grew up in rural Pennsylvania. His father managed a succession of restaurants; his mother was a housewife (who published an occasional poem). As a child, he had an imaginary friend—and an imaginary enemy, too. At the age of eighteen he brought home the first issue of *Amazing Stories*, and became a lifelong fan.

His first jobs were in Philadelphia, for a meatpacking house and a landscaping company. Then he moved, with his parents and siblings, to Detroit. There he attended art school; read voraciously at the public library; and was active in the John Reed Club, a communist group. (A photo in the *Detroit Times* shows him speaking at a May Day rally. It is captioned "Orator Haranguing Crowd.") He married a fellow art student and fathered a child.

---

* Not all of the workers became Deros. A portion of them, Shaver tells us, were able to remain human. Of these, some hid out in the caverns—the Teros; while others returned to the surface of the earth—the ancestors of modern man.

In 1932 he found employment in a Ford motor plant. His history during the next decade has two versions: his own, and one that is based on hospital records. Shaver's account—expressed mainly in the guise of fiction—was often inconsistent. But it was essentially as follows:

While laboring as a welder on the assembly line, he began to hear voices. They belonged, he says, to Deros—demonic creatures who dwelt beneath the surface of the earth. Tormented by the voices, he quit his job and began to roam from city to city. "I took a vacation from my job to try other surroundings for some mitigation of my sufferings," he recalls. "Then began many years of running away, many years of desperate jumping from place to place." He became an itinerant—a Depression-era hobo—surviving on odd jobs that came his way.

But wherever he went, Shaver was plagued by the Deros. From within the earth, they beamed rays at him. (The ray machine, he later learned, resembled a giant bedspring.) The rays put thoughts into his head, created illusions, caused him to make mistakes or to injure himself. Shaver suffered constant misfortunes, brought on by the Deros. The full scope of their malevolence became evident to him. Flat tires, traffic accidents, plane crashes, fires, landslides, open manholes, illness, war—all human ills were caused by the Deros. For their sole pleasure lay in bringing misery to mankind.

His wandering continued. Finally, in Vermont, he was arrested for vagrancy and jailed. But one night a mysterious young woman appeared in his cell. It was none other than the "imaginary" friend of his childhood! And she helped him to escape.

She led him to a cavern that was filled with machines. These machines had belonged to the Lemurians, she explained. And she told him about the cavern world and its inhabitants, past and present.

For a period of time, says Shaver, he remained in the caverns. (The period varies in his accounts, from two weeks to several years.) Then he wandered on. Finally, he returned to Pennsylvania and settled on a farm that belonged to his family.

Such was Richard Shaver's account of that period of his life. Though exceeding the bounds of credibility, it could be construed as semi-factual. But a different—and disturbing—story would eventually surface.

It became known that Shaver had been committed, in August 1934, to Ypsilanti State Hospital. Suffering from paranoid delusions, he believed that people were watching and following him, and calling him a communist. He was also convinced that the doctors were trying to poison him. And he was hearing voices.

So he was confined to a psychiatric ward. Then, in 1936, he was given a furlough to visit his family in Pennsylvania —and he failed to return. This delinquency has prompted his detractors to characterize him as "an escaped lunatic." More likely, an overcrowded hospital allowed him to remain in the care of his family.

But at some point he seems to have left home and become a hobo. Finally, he is known to have been reinstitutionalized. For there is a record of his discharge, in May 1943, from Ionia State Institution in Michigan.

How did Shaver respond to these revelations? He did admit to a stay "in the bughouse." But he insisted that his condition had been caused by heat stroke, and that he was released after two weeks.

And Palmer's response? In a radio interview, he describes his chagrin at learning that his star author had spent eight years in an asylum!

So Shaver had a history as a mental patient. But in 1945 he was no longer institutionalized. He was living with his mother, on a farm called Bittersweet Hollow; working at Bethlehem Steel, as a crane operator; and creating a stir with his stories.

●

Beginning with the March 1945 issue, a story by Shaver appeared in almost every issue of *Amazing*. And the magazine's circulation (which Palmer had already increased significantly) rose to new heights. Shaver's "fact-based tales" —with their mysterious caverns, ancient Lemurians, and malevolent Deros—had struck a chord with readers.

The impact of the tales could be measured by the number of letters they provoked. According to Palmer, the magazine had previously received about fifty letters per month. Now the number was several thousand!

Striking too was the nature of the letters. For many were from readers eager to report *similar experiences*. They too had encountered strange beings in caves—had been hearing voices—were harassed by rays—could recall their past life as a Lemurian—had a Dero for a neighbor!*

As the Shaver Mystery grew in popularity, such letters piled up on Palmer's desk. So he expanded the letters section (known as "Discussions"); filled it with a sampling of these letters, along with his replies; and announced: "The editors of this magazine are intensely interested in hearing from people who 'hear voices' or 'just know' things in line with these Lemuria stories." It wasn't long before the letters section had become a forum, for the discussion of fringe phenomena in general.†

---

* One reader claimed to have received messages from Deros, via automatic writing. When other readers questioned his claim, he responded:

"I wish to say this to anyone interested: I *am* on the level. I actually can talk to the dero and tero. I call them this because that is what *they* claim to be. *They* agree with the Shaver stories. I am rather confused myself."

† Shaver too encouraged the participation of readers. In the foreword to "I Remember Lemuria!" he writes:

"What I tell you is not fiction! How can I impress that on you as forcibly as I feel it must be impressed?

"I intend to put down these things, and I invite—challenge!—any of you to work on them; to prove or disprove, as you like. Whatever your goal, I do not care. I care only that you believe me or disbelieve me with enough fervor to do some real work on those things I will propound. The final result may well stagger the sci-

But the prime topic remained the Shaver tales and their alleged factual basis. For their author remained adamant: he was passing on "the ancient lore and history of Earth's forgotten days that was given to me during my stay inside the Earth as was related in my second story, published in the June issue."

Was such indeed the case? Was Shaver telling the truth? *Had he visited the Inner Earth?* On that question the readers were of two minds. Palmer describes their reaction to one of the tales:

> Most of the letters were not praising the story as a story but supporting it as a fact (or, to be sure, condemning it violently as a fiction). On all sides, there were letter "shouts" of IT'S TRUE or IT'S A LIE.

Some letters, while raising the question of veracity, were more restrained in tone. From Betty Yoe, secretary of the Cleveland Grotto of the National Speleological Society, came this query:

> Sirs:
> Mr. Shaver's story in AMAZING STORIES has aroused our deep interest by its reference to large caves, etc., due to the fact that the National Speleological Society consists of people who have, in their leisure time, discovered, studied, and mapped thousands of miles of caves, and we simply drool at the slightest mention of a hole in the ground.
> As we haven't yet run into anything such as Mr. Shaver mentioned, we wonder if this was a figment of his imagination (if so, he did a magnificent job) or if he really had a basis for his claims and had in mind particular caves or special sections of the country.
> For our records, and in the interest of science, we would

ence of the world."

His fans rose to the challenge. In 1946 they formed the Shaver Mystery Club. The stated aim of the club was to prove or disprove the Shaver Mystery. It published a monthly magazine, and had 2000 members at its peak.

be grateful for any information you are at liberty to give us on the matter.*

And some letters contained warnings. Most notably, Doreal—of the Brotherhood of the White Temple—wrote in from Colorado; his advice was to stay out of the caverns. Other warnings—from readers identifying themselves as Deros—were obvious jokes.†

Palmer was pleased by the response of his readers. In an editorial note, he informed them: "As this issue goes to press, more discussion is raging than has been aroused by any manuscripts published in *Amazing Stories* in 19 years!" The morning mail, he said, was something he looked forward to.

And the Shaver Mystery (which comprised, said Palmer, "the entire mass of Shaver stories, letters from readers, and all related subjects") continued to enliven the pages of *Amazing*. It reached its apogee with the June 1947 issue— the special Shaver Mystery issue. Promised was "the lowdown on the caves!" The cover showed a cavern, in which a car is speeding past huge, menacing idols. All of the stories were by Shaver.**

---

* "Your group is an intensely interesting one," Palmer replied, "and we are sorry that we can't provide you with the information you want, but we are keeping you in mind, just as soon as we get a strong (and safe) lead. In your work, have you ever considered the Mound Builders of Ohio? We have definitely linked them with the Shaver Mystery, and it seems that the Mound Builders records, when studied, may offer corroborative clues to the ancient people of Mu [alternative name for Lemuria]."

† Palmer agreed with Doreal as to the peril. When Shaver— challenged by skeptics to reveal the actual location of a cave— refused to do so, Palmer defended him: "Mr. Shaver refused, and his reason is well-known to you. Because of the great danger! Because the DERO are as real as the caves, and they DON'T WANT SURFACE PEOPLE DOWN THERE!"

** The all-Shaver issue came close to being canceled, due to missing manuscripts, typesetting mishaps, and other problems. Palmer speculated that the Deros were trying to sabotage it.

Meanwhile, the controversy had spread—from the pages of *Amazing* to science-fiction fan clubs. Many fans (especially those partial to *Astounding*, with its higher-quality fiction) resented the Shaver Mystery. They accused it of being a hoax—a publicity stunt instigated by Palmer. It was drawing ridicule, they insisted, onto the entire field of science fiction. These fans began to circulate a petition, calling for an end to the Shaver Mystery. And they organized a letter-writing campaign, protesting directly to Ziff-Davis, the publishers.

One group of fans promised to expose the alleged hoax. Palmer responded:

> We are waiting for this expose with interest—because we are curious to know how a hoax which is not a hoax can be exposed as a hoax.
>
> We realize that a lot of our readers find it difficult to believe that we ourselves believe one single word of what Mr. Shaver tells us in his stories, but we'll keep on presenting the evidence as it comes in, and you can judge for yourself.

But the protest campaign (which Palmer blamed on the Deros) may have paid off. For toward the end of 1948, publisher Bernard Davis issued an order: no more Shaver tales. Despite its continued popularity, the Shaver Mystery was brought to a halt (at least, within the pages of *Amazing*). Davis's motivation has been debated. Perhaps he was embarrassed by the adverse publicity, or by the sheer outrageousness of the affair. Perhaps (as Palmer speculated) he had been pressured by the government.

Or perhaps he feared a lawsuit. For inspired by the stories and heedless of the risk, readers were descending into caves—in search of Lemurians.*

---

* A reader in Oakland was ready to go: "I was very much interested in the series of Shaver Mysteries, and after reading the August issue, I have come to the conclusion that Shaver is quite right.... I have always believed there was a race of people living under the earth. I am an ex-marine and would like very much to help in finding these people."

Palmer spent another year as editor of *Amazing Stories*. But his attention now was focused elsewhere—outside of Ziff-Davis. For in the spring of 1948 he and a fellow editor had scraped together the money and launched a magazine of their own. Called *Fate*, it was devoted to "true reports of the strange, the unusual, the unknown"—everything from sea serpents and ghosts to clairvoyance and abominable snowmen. And on the cover of the first issue was a formation of UFOs—those "flying disks" that were being seen in the sky.

Palmer had wanted to edit a special UFO issue of *Amazing*. But the idea had been quashed by Davis (who may have sensed another Shaver Mystery in the making). At *Fate* there was no one to overrule him; and Palmer became a promoter of UFOs, publishing stories about them—and guessing that they were extraterrestrial in origin. Fictional spacecraft had abounded in the pages of *Amazing*. Now, according to Palmer, the real ones may have arrived.*

In 1949 Ziff-Davis decided to move its offices to New York. Unwilling to relocate there, Palmer quit. So he was full-time now as an independent publisher-editor. With *Fate* doing well, he launched a second publication: a science-fiction magazine called *Other Worlds Science Stories*.†

---

* In an article titled "The Man Who Invented Flying Saucers," John Keel, a paranormal researcher, claims that the "modern myth" of extraterrestrial visitors was essentially the creation of Ray Palmer.

† The inaugural issue of *Other Worlds* featured a tale by Shaver: "The Fall of Lemuria." (Palmer had noted that whenever the word "Lemuria" or "Atlantis" appeared on a cover, sales increased.) The author introduced it as "a restatement of a lost history of our planet...containing unsaid implications so startling as to be incredible."

Meanwhile, Howard Browne, Palmer's former assistant, had taken over as editor of *Amazing*. Wishing to steer the magazine in a new direction, Browne began by tossing much of its

His new independence allowed Palmer to live where he wanted. So in 1950 he and his wife Marjorie moved to Amherst, a small town in Wisconsin. They took up residence on a 123-acre farm. And in a former schoolhouse, Palmer set up a printing plant.

Over the next twenty-five years, he would publish a unique array of books and magazines. The books were about UFOs, the paranormal, and such. The magazines included the following:

Other Worlds

Mystic (Palmer had sold his share in *Fate* and started a

---

inventory—including unpublished stories by Shaver—into the wastebasket. (Perhaps the same wastebasket into which he had tossed that original letter from Shaver.)

similar magazine.)

Search (He renamed *Mystic* and gave it a broader scope.)

Universe Science Fiction

Flying Saucers ("The only publication devoted to presenting all the facts and all the latest news concerning unidentified flying objects.")

Space World (Rockets, satellites, and space exploration.)

Forum (A kind of newsletter, consisting solely of editorials and letters-to-the-editor. The editorials were increasingly about conspiracies.)

Palmer edited these magazines from an upstairs room in his farmhouse. The room, he told his readers, was "an incredible mess":

> Your editor personally handles all subscriptions, from the initial receipt of the order, to the making of the address plate, and the addressing of the envelopes in which the magazines are shipped each month. The walls are lined with back copies, envelopes, addressing plates, stacks of unread (and read) manuscripts, galleys, printers proofs, typewriters and addressing machinery....There are files and boxes and just plain piles of information of all kinds. Reference books, newspaper clippings and scrap books. There are piles of unanswered correspondence....Even all the circulars soliciting subscribers are stuffed, sorted, bundled, mailed by your editor personally (with the assistance of his wife and three small children ranging from 3 to 10, who love to stuff envelopes!).

Palmer had given up the editorship of *Amazing*. But had he left behind the Shaver Mystery? Not at all. Several Shaver tales appeared in *Other Worlds*. And in the December 1959 issue of *Flying Saucers*, Palmer made a startling announcement. He had concluded that UFOs did not originate on some distant planet. Rather, they were coming from *inside the earth*.*

---

* Any claim by "extraterrestrials" to be from another planet was

And in 1961, he brought out the first issue of *The Hidden World*—a revival of the Shaver Mystery. Along with some new material, it contained reprints of the Shaver tales. (The goal was to make available the entire *oeuvre*.) Fifteen more issues would follow. But the Shaver Mystery had lost its allure; and *The Hidden World* had a limited circulation.

Such were the exotic offerings of Palmer Publications. Mysticism! Science fiction! Deros! Flying Saucers! Conspiracies! And it all emanated from a farmhouse in a small town in Wisconsin.

Ray Palmer was an outsider in conservative Amherst—an urban refugee who had chosen an improbable (if peaceful) location from which to disseminate his publications. He did, however, have one close friend in the town—none other than Richard Shaver! For both of them had moved to Amherst. With his wife Dorothy, Shaver was living on a farm just down the road. He was still writing (conventional science fiction, for the most part). And he was farming—or attempting to do so. A photo in *The Hidden World* shows him sitting atop a tractor, with a manic grin.

The two men were unlikely residents of rural Wisconsin: a hunchbacked dwarf who promoted flying saucers, and his loony pal who claimed to have visited the cavern world. But apparently they were tolerated.

•

Did Palmer really believe in a cavern world—a subterranean realm of ancient Lemurians and malevolent Deros? And did he believe that Shaver had visited this place? Or was the whole thing a publicity stunt—an outrageous (and successful) scheme to sell magazines?

Initially, on the question of a factual basis for the tales, he declared himself to be agnostic. As editor of *Amazing*, he was simply presenting the material to his readers. It was up

---

a deception, said Palmer—a falsehood to mask their true place of origin.

to them to accept or reject the author's claims.

But eventually Palmer made known his opinion. Had Shaver *physically* entered these caverns? Had he donned a helmet and experienced the life of a Lemurian? Had he viewed Deros on a visi-screen? Had he left behind footprints in the dust? The answer, in Palmer's view, was no. Nor was there any evidence for the existence of such caverns. "Since 1944, when I first contacted Shaver, I have yet to find one inhabited cave, and one bit of mech [mechanical devices] dug up."

Nonetheless, Shaver was not making it all up. He had undergone genuine experiences, Palmer believed. But those experiences had been *visionary* in nature.

For clearly, said Palmer, Richard Shaver—during his confinement as a mental patient—had experienced visions. Perhaps they had come to him during trances (like the otherworldly journeys of a shaman), or in the form of vivid dreams. ("I considered my life half wasted," wrote Shaver, "if it were not for whatever it is that makes me dream. Wonderful dreams, terrible dreams, all kinds of dreams.") The psychiatrists would have dismissed these experiences as hallucinatory. But in fact, they were psychic events of a profound nature. Shaver had not belonged in an asylum, insisted Palmer. He "suffered from being a tremendous psychic person," who was able "to perceive the ordinarily unseen aspects of our total existence." His visions of a cavern world had been a product of that ability.

Shaver's response to this interpretation? No way! he told Palmer. The cavern world was real, not a figment of his imagination. He had descended into it bodily. The machines of the Lemurians—the demonic Deros—Nydia and her band of wanderers—all had possessed a material existence!

"I have been in the caves, and they exist," he declared.

Most often, Shaver admitted, he had viewed them from afar—via "telaug" rays that the Deros beamed at him. He insisted, however, upon the tangible reality of the caverns. And he insisted that he had visited them. "I have... *touched* the machines."

But Palmer was convinced that the visits had been visionary, not physical. For he had discovered a strange book that seemed to explain the Shaver Mystery.

•

The book was titled *Oahspe: A New Bible*. It was written —or rather, channeled—by a dentist named John Newbrough. The son of a schoolteacher, Newbrough (1828–1891) had a dental practice in New York City. He was also a devotee of spiritualism, attending seances and interviewing mediums. For his passion was the pursuit of Truth.

He tells in the book of having awoken one night to find the room illuminated by pillars of light. Beside his bed stood an angel, who asked: "Would you like to perform a mission for Jehovih [*sic*]?"

Newbrough acknowledged that he would.

"First," said the angel, "you must live spiritually for ten years. Then we will return and tell you what we want."

Before departing, his visitor gave Newbrough a set of instructions. He was to become a vegetarian. He was to lose weight. (Newbrough weighed 250 pounds. A newspaper article describes him as "a man of large stature, with dark, dreamy eyes, and is very slow in his action.") And he was to engage in charitable works. Among them was the provision of free dental care for the indigent.

For ten years Newbrough did as directed. Then the angel returned. "You have passed our test....Now we want you to buy a typewriter and place it on this desk."

The typewriter had only recently been invented. Newbrough purchased one. And for nearly a year, at his home on West 34th Street, he engaged in automatic writing. Each morning he would rise before dawn; sit at his Sholes typewriter in the dark; enter a trance; and type away on the semicircular keyboard. His fingers flying, Newbrough produced page after page. What was he doing? He was *channeling an angel*—taking dictation from an otherworldly being.

Finally, in 1882, Newbrough self-published the result.

Oahspe was nearly a thousand pages long. It was illustrated (with drawings likewise produced in the dark). And it contained the religious and philosophical material that the angel had dictated to him.*

A new edition was issued by Kosmon Press in 1936. The publisher describes Newbrough as "the instrument through which OAHSPE was communicated to the world," and gives this summary of its contents:

> With regard to the contents of this extraordinary book, it will suffice here to say that it contains detailed teachings regarding the Creator and His relation to Man and the Universe; the history of the earth and its heavens for the past 24,000 years; the principles of cosmogony and cosmology, embracing a completely revolutionary conception of physics; the nature of the angelic worlds and their relation to the earth; the origin of man and his path onwards and upwards during life and after death towards spiritual emancipation; the principles of an enlightened morality; the lost keys to all the different religious doctrines and symbols in the world; the history of the great teachers who have been sent to humanity in different cycles; the character of the civilisation which will supersede that in which we are at present living; and a mass of remarkable teachings regarding metaphysics, rites and ceremonies, magic, prophecy and the like.

Now what interested Ray Palmer was that cosmology. For according to *Oahspe*, invisible spheres surround the earth. Each has a different "density" of matter—a different rate of vibration. And together they constitute the astral world.

---

* *The Hastings Encyclopedia of Religion and Ethics* assigns a more mundane origin to the material:

"The Book of Oahspe, though little known, possesses considerable interest for students of the pathology of religion.... Its author had evidently read fairly widely, the result being an ingested—and indigestible—farrago of superficial Orientalism, Gnosticism, baseless history, fantastic cosmology, Freemasonry, spiritualism, and fads of every sort, combined with hatred of Christianity."

The outermost sphere, the angel had revealed, is called Etherea. It is the ultimate destination for the souls of the dead. They must work their way towards it, evolving spiritually and shedding base elements. Upon reaching Etherea, they become angels—beings of pure spirit—and dwell in paradise.

But some souls must remain in the innermost sphere until purged of their wickedness. These souls are called *drujas*. Their wickedness has transformed them into demons. Thus, the innermost sphere is a hellish place.

When Palmer read about the drujas, he had a sudden insight. The Deros! Surely they were one and the same. And that innermost sphere? The cavern world!

Moreover, he found this passage in *Oahspe*: "The drujas rule over this mortal, and his neighbors call him mad, and they send him to a madhouse." A perfect description of Shaver.

The caverns, Palmer realized, were *above* us, not below. They were the initial portion of the astral world. And Shaver had indeed gone there—in a series of visions.

Locked up in an asylum, he had *escaped in his astral body*. And he had visited another plane of existence.*

Palmer arrived at these conclusions after reading *Oahspe*. And the "New Bible" so impressed him that he published an edition of it. (The copyright had expired.) "The Greatest Book of the Age," he billed it. "OAHSPE bridges the gap between the Seen and the Unseen worlds."

He had solved the Shaver Mystery—by invoking an even greater mystery.

---

* In Shaver's "The Mind Rovers," a prisoner escapes nightly from his cell: "He found a way to get into another kind of world. Not anything like this world....The dream he always dreamed was about such a world....A woman would come to him and talk to him, and sometimes in his sleep she would take him into the place where she lived and they would make love."

The tale appeared in the January 1947 issue of *Amazing*. Also in that issue was a "true story" by Margaret Rogers: "I Have Been in the Caves." (We shall meet Rogers in the next chapter.)

Until his death in 1977, Ray Palmer remained active as a publisher and editor. But he was a prolific writer, too. From his typewriter came a stream of lively editorials; replies (sometimes lengthy) to the letters that he printed; and rewrites of articles. To his family, the clatter of his typewriter must have seemed incessant. (He claimed to have once written a novel in 23 hours.) Palmer boasted of having produced three million words during his lifetime.

His writing was feisty and folksy. And his magazines were unabashedly sensationalistic. They reported on mysterious creatures, or explored the paranormal, or promoted some theory—about flying saucers, the Inner Earth, a government conspiracy. He was sincere in these enthusiasms. At the same time, he was a literary showman—the P. T. Barnum of the publishing world.

Palmer was fond of stirring up controversy. In an article titled "Who Was Ray Palmer?" Martin Gardner sees him as a kind of trickster:

> Palmer printed numerous letters from readers who raised objections [to his claim that the earth had openings at its poles], some of them written by Palmer himself. You have only to read his clever responses to get the picture—a strange little man, chuckling to himself as he wrote, somehow getting enormous kicks out of hornswoggling people bigger than he was.

Gardner was skeptical as to his sincerity:

> I met Ray on several occasions in the forties, when I lived in Chicago, and I have talked to many people who knew him well. He impressed us all as a shy, kind, good-natured, gentle, energetic little man with the personality of a professional con artist.... [He enjoyed] his endless flimflams, but I think his primary motive was simply to create uproars that would sell magazines.

One of those who knew him well was his assistant editor. In an interview, Howard Browne talks about the temperament of his boss:

> He compensated for his physical deformity by showing that he was the Man. If you slighted him, did something that displeased him, you were out for a certain length of time, sometimes for a month and sometimes forever. Yet he was very kind. If you needed money, Ray was the man to see. He took it from the Ziff-Davis coffers, but he got it.

And Browne praises him as a mentor:

> He was very helpful on how to write. He knew how to write pulp and did a remarkable job in teaching new people that came in. I learned a hell of a lot from Ray. The most important thing I learned is, Be careful not to bore the reader.

If Ray Palmer had a motto, it was that. For he could be relied on—from his first day as editor of *Amazing* to his final years as a publisher—not to bore his readers.

•

In 1962 Shaver left Wisconsin; moved with his wife to Summit, Arkansas; and embarked upon a new career—as a "rock artist."

For he had made a startling discovery. Using a laser device, the Lemurians had recorded images *inside rocks*. (The process was called *rokfogo*.) By slicing the rocks into slabs—with a diamond saw—and exposing the grain, Shaver was able to reveal these images. Depicted were monsters, mermaids, naked women. "What they are," he said, "are huge libraries of picture rocks and they are very common, very valuable and very easy to see."

Others were unable to discern the images. But by staring intently, Shaver could see them—emerging from patterns in the grain. And he sought to market these Pre-Deluge Art

Stones, as he called them. He advertised them in UFO magazines, and sold them from his yard. A sign out front welcomed customers to his rock shop.

Few of the Pre-Deluge Art Stones were sold. But Shaver moved on. With an opaque projector, he projected the slabs onto specially treated canvas. The "magnetic force" of the light, he explained, left an imprint on the canvas. The former art student then meticulously applied paint, to "bring out" or "develop" the image. These paintings were likewise offered for sale.

Though it had faded from the scene, the Shaver Mystery still had fans. Some of them came to visit Shaver—made a pilgrimage to his home in Arkansas. They viewed the paintings and toured his studio (located in a shack behind the house). They nibbled on refreshments that Dorothy brought out. And they chatted with the man who had been to the caverns, and who was still learning things about the Lemurians. According to one fan, he "lived in a wonderful world of his own making."

That is to say, he was as loony as ever.

Thus did Richard Shaver spend his final years—busy in his studio, tended by a loyal wife, and largely forgotten.*

•

The Shaver Mystery began with Ray Palmer retrieving a letter from a wastebasket. It continued for several years, in the pages of *Amazing Stories* and elsewhere. And it remains a controversial episode in the annals of science fiction.

So what was the Shaver Mystery all about?

Palmer himself sums it up (with his usual hyperbole):

---

* In recent years he has gained recognition—as an artist. In 2002 a California gallery hosted a show of "Outsider Art"; and it included paintings by Shaver. A review in *LA Weekly* declared that Shaver's "fascinating work...ranks with the Surrealist paintings of Max Ernst and Jean Dubuffet."

It is not known how many of the paintings have survived.

The Shaver Mystery stands in a unique position, a pivotal point in modern philosophy, possibly the answer to most of the enigmas of all times.
What is the Shaver Mystery? There are many theories. There are those who support Shaver in his materialistic honeycomb of caverns the world over, heritage of a Titan-Atlan race which fled a poisoned world over 12,000 years ago. There are those who call his caverns the "astral," his dero the spirits of the dead. Some say it is "another dimension," another realm of life alongside ours, invisible under ordinary circumstances.... [But] the Shaver phenomena are REAL, no matter how opinion of their nature varies!

Joscelyn Godwin, in *Arktos*, supports the visionary theory:

> Many people are constitutionally incapable of imagining anything outside material reality, and the great religions have kindly made allowances for them in their cosmologies. Even those who are gifted, or afflicted, with the capacity of "astral travel" are not always exempt from this tendency: some, like Shaver and Saint-Yves, will refuse to take their visions in any but a terrestrial sense. Not knowing that whatever they experience is a projection of their own spiritual state.

In other words, Shaver had visions—glimpses into a hidden world—but failed to recognize them as such.

But skeptics scoff at such theories. Shaver was a writer of fiction, they say, and nothing more. They point a finger at what are alleged to be his literary influences. These include Edgar Rice Burroughs, H. P. Lovecraft, and Abraham Merritt. According to Doug Skinner, in "What's This? A Shaver Revival?":

> Shaver's main literary model was Abraham Merritt. Merritt isn't read much today, but his fantasy novels were quite popular throughout the '20s and '30s. Beginning with *The Moon Pool* in 1919, he produced a series of novels about underground caverns, lost races, ancient ray machines, shell-

shaped hovercraft, and other marvels.... Shaver thought Merritt had seen the caves but could only mention them in fiction. One might also suspect that Merritt's novels had influenced Shaver's beliefs.

And the last word goes to Shaver himself—who admits to *possibly* being mistaken about the location of the caves:

> But I will stick to one thing, they *are* caves and tunnels. I have *seen* them with my own eyes.... If you want to say these caves and tunnels are not under our feet, but over our heads, in a sort of "another dimension" of this world of ours, perhaps you may be right! But nonetheless, it is *part* of this earth of ours, of *this* planet.

The caves exist, insisted Shaver. For he had seen them with his own eyes. And seeing was believing.

21.

Margaret Rogers

In the September 1946 issue of Amazing Stories was a letter from Mrs. D. C. Rogers. A reader in San Antonio, Texas, she was writing in regard to the Shaver Mystery:

> Ever since Richard Shaver's stories of his recollections (?) first appeared, I haven't failed to read said stories. It seems incredible that any human alive today could remember so many things and still make so many mistakes or tell so many lies in his very frightening description of the underworld, the caves. I am not prepared to say that all parts of that unknown world are idealistically beautiful both in living and in its people, but I do know for a fact that I have never encountered anything but the kindest consideration from its inhabitants. I have never attempted to tell my story, because I would be considered insane and locked up. But I know and one other person knows. That is, she knows that I disappeared strangely and appeared just as strangely after three years. She has an exquisite little gold box adorned with gems which I sold her.... It was a gift from the people of the caverns.

Mrs. Rogers returned to the surface world, she explains, to be with her kinsfolk. But her intention is to go back to the caves:

> I shall go back when I am sixty years of age (three years from now). At that time I shall go to the Ixtli cave where the stone of life is kept. There I shall lie down and when I have completed 16 hours before it I shall arise and be a young woman of 20. How do I know this? Because I have seen it happen to many of those same underworld denizens when they reached the age of 60.

Mrs. Rogers describes the underworld denizens and what they did for her:

> They are in face and form like earth peoples, but much larger and more beautiful.... I am grateful to them for they took me, a broken, sick, sinful dope-ridden and hopeless woman and placed me under rays and brought me back to health.

Finally, she considers the idea of writing her story and sending it in to *Amazing*. She is sure, however, that it would be consigned to the wastebasket.

Not so, responded Ray Palmer:

> Mrs. Rogers, please be assured that no one in this office will consider you crazy, nor will they toss anything you write in the wastebasket. It will at least be READ.... We'd like to know more about that jeweled box. We would like to SEE it. And we want you to tell more!

Tell more she did. For three months later, Palmer informed his readers of a forthcoming piece:

> We had planned to run "I Have Been in the Caves," Margaret Rogers' true story of her adventures among the "tero," but again, we ran out of space and the deadline. So it will be in the next issue. This one you should not miss if you are a devotee of the Shaver Mystery—and that puts you in the hundred-thousand class!—because it confirms (oops, agrees) with Shaver. You can judge for yourself if it confirms. There are items in it that make your editor look upon it very favorably. One thing we know—Mrs. Rogers is not perpetrating a hoax. Her story is 100% sincere.*

And at last, in the January 1947 issue, her "true story" appeared. Palmer prefaced it with another caveat: "'I Have Been in the Caves' seems to be sincerely told, and we pre-

---

* Palmer included in this issue a second letter from Rogers. In it she announces that she is putting her story into writing. And she describes the many communications (120 letters and six telegrams) she has received—along with knocks on her door—from persons wanting to know how to get to the caves.

sent it with the same sincerity. Read it and decide for yourself."

Her tale begins on a wintry afternoon in Mexico City. Margaret Rogers was standing at her usual spot outside the American Club on Bolivar Street. A cold wind was blowing. Shivering and emaciated, Maggie (as she was known) was begging for money. She needed four pesos—three for a gram of heroin, one for a room for the night.

Sunk in misery, Maggie—"an outcast, thirty-nine years old, a slave of the drug"—pulled her cape about her. And she was murmuring a prayer, when a hand touched her shoulder. She looked up to see Dr. Kelmer of the Electrotherapy Institute.*

Dr. Kelmer had never passed by without giving her money. On this occasion he handed her a five-peso coin. But then a strange glint entered his eye; and the doctor dropped more coins into her hand. He told her to get something to eat and to groom herself. And he intimated that a permanent solution to her ills might be in the offing.

Maggie bought heroin that night. But the following night none was available, due to a police crackdown. And she was suffering pangs of withdrawal, when a car pulled up alongside her. At the wheel was Dr. Kelmer.

They drove off together into the night. The doctor gave her a vial to drink, containing a potion. She drank and immediately fell asleep.

When she awoke, the car had stopped. The moon was shining on mountainous terrain. Dr. Kelmer got out the car. Feeling ill, Maggie tumbled out after him.

The doctor comforted her. Then he stood before a mass

---

* According to Warren Smith in *The Hidden Secrets of the Hollow Earth* (Zebra Books, 1976): "The institute was a medical clinic that purported to cure various ailments by bombarding the afflicted area with electro-magnetic rays. While many of Dr. Kelner's [sic] patients claimed to have been cured by his unorthodox medicine, various medical authorities claimed Kelner was a 'quack and a fraud.'"

of foliage that grew against a rock wall, raised his arms, and began to chant.

> As in a dream, I saw that whole mass of greenery slide to one side, to reveal a large opening. By now, it seemed that anything could happen, but for some reason, I had no fear. He might have been leading me to my death in some sadistic rite, yet I followed him boldly in.
> The door closed. For a split second darkness reigned, then the cave was filled with a strange bluish light. I walked as though I were ordered to do so, to a large block of black marble along one wall of the cave, and lay down upon it.

Her next memory was of floating, as if on cool waters or in a dream. She was naked and semiconscious. Indistinct figures hovered over her; a lavender light shone down. And all the while her pain—the agony from years of addiction—was dissolving.

At last she fully awoke and found herself in a brightly lit room. The walls and furnishings had a silvery, metallic gleam. Clad in a robe, Maggie lay in a bed that was twice the normal length. Beside it was a radiolike device with buttons. She reached out and touched a button.

A section of wall slid aside. And a giant—"the largest woman I had ever seen"—walked into the room. Young and attractive, she wore a helmet with wings; a short dress made of gold mesh; and sandals laced to the knee. The giant raised a shiny disk to her mouth; and speaking into it, she introduced herself.*

"My name is Mira," she said. "I know you are afraid, but do not be, as our brother sent you here. You are hungry, no? First of all, you must eat. Then I shall tell you all you want to know."

Mira pressed a button on the device. The wall reopened; and a cart emerged and rolled up to them. On it were fruit,

---

* The disk translated her speech into English. In a footnote, Palmer points out its similarity to Shaver's telaug, which translated thoughts into speech.

cakes, and a cup filled with green liquid. Mira pointed invitingly to the cup. Not wishing to offend, Maggie took a sip—then eagerly gulped down the rest of this "nectar of the gods." When she returned it to the cart, the cup instantly refilled itself.

Mira explained the situation. Six days ago, Maggie had been brought in from the outside, to be cured of drug addiction. The cure had been successful. She would soon be shown about—by Mira, who would serve as a mentor. She would also be taught certain things by "our wise men." But for now, it was important that Maggie rest and recover.

And with that, Mira bowed and left the room.

When she returned, it was with another giant. She introduced Arsi, her fiancee. Young, blond, and handsome, he was a head taller than Mira. His outfit was similar to hers, though with a sun ornament on the helmet, rather than wings.

Speaking into the disk, he welcomed Maggie. And Arsi now took up the explaining. Maggie had been brought to a subterranean world, he said—the home of a race of giants, known as the Nephli. Though raised in the surface world, Arsi was a Nephli. He had earned a living on the surface as a lawyer. Then one day he had simply disappeared, and returned to his ancestral home for "renewal."*

He turned to the wall. The room went dark and the wall lit up—with images of an older Arsi, emerging from an office building. His face was lined with care and darkened with disillusionment. Then the scene dissolved into images of Maggie—begging on the street, talking with Dr. Kelmer, seeking out heroin.

Maggie began to weep—tears of gratitude for the new life she had been given.

---

* In a footnote Palmer ponders "this business of 'renewal,'" involving a person who has disappeared. Could it explain the thousands of missing persons reported each year? Did it relate, in some way, to death? And had Shaver referred to it in his writings? Palmer urges readers to send in any information they might have.

"What have I done good in my life," she asked, "to deserve such help?"

The lights came back on. When her tears had subsided, Arsi reassured Maggie. She had simply been unfortunate, he said. Her weakness was a human trait; and the Nephli were glad to have been of assistance. Free of addiction, she would soon be returning to the surface. There she could perform similar acts of kindness, as a kind of penance. And someday, if she desired, she could return to the cavern world.

Wishing her *jelis sur Tamil* ("God's blessings"), Arsi left the room.

There followed a long soothing bath and a breakfast of fruits. Then it was time for Maggie to see the doctor. In a two-seated bullet car—a sleek, wheelless vehicle that zipped through tunnels—Mira drove her to a medical facility. The doctor examined Maggie and pronounced her recovered.

But it was not yet time to return home. With Mira and Arsi as guides, Maggie spent several weeks touring and learning about the subterranean home of the Nephli. She discovered that they used the barter system—money did not exist among the Nephli. She was shown the *gajova*, or Chamber of Machines. And Maggie visited the central library, admiring its extensive collection. While there, she was given several printed items as mementos.*

One day, Mira and Arsi took her on an excursion. In a merry mood, the three had piled into a bullet car, along with some young people, and sped through a long tunnel. They emerged in countryside—open roads, fields of grain, forests of tall trees. A small sun hovered overhead, in a "sky" that was the roof of a colossal cavern. In the distance was a ring of mountains; and beyond them, an eerie red glow. Finally they glimpsed a tower, in which a bell was tolling—at which point they headed back, stopping on the way for a picnic lunch. The tower, Maggie later learned, marked a

---

* Palmer wonders if she still has them, as they might constitute proof of her story.

boundary. The Nephli were not to travel beyond it. She never found out why that was so.*

Concerning the Nephli, Maggie learned that they had come to the Earth from another planet. But other colonists

---

* That red glow, says Palmer, belonged to a ring of fire. Such a ring had been reported by another visitor—confirmation of the reality of the cavern world. "Your editor knows what the flame ring is, why it is maintained, what the warning is that Mrs. Rogers hints at, but cannot understand."

—influenced by malevolent entities—had rejected the wise rule of the Nephli. Rather than fight these rebels (our own ancestors), the Nephli had retreated to the cavern world. They had enlarged it—using robot labor and a "fire-blower" —and had created an artificial sun. They intended, however, to return someday to the surface and resettle there.

As for government, they were ruled by a high priest. He represented the supreme god Tamil, whom the Nephli worshipped in their Great Temple.

And Maggie learned that many Nephli secretly resided on the surface. But how, she asked, could a giant fail to attract attention? Mira laughed at the question, and described a ray that the Nephli used to reduce or enlarge themselves.

To her surprise, Maggie learned too that her own grandfather had been a Nephli. The grandfather had fallen in love with a surface woman, whom he had glimpsed from afar on a television screen. Reducing himself in size, he had moved to the surface, sought the woman out, and married her. Upon her death, he had returned underground to await her renewal.*

Maggie was amazed by all that she saw and learned in the subterranean world. But the high point of her stay was a wedding—the marriage of Mira and Arsi. It took place in the Great Temple; and Maggie was invited to attend.

She watched as Mira and Arsi walked down the aisle. They approached the altar, behind which were silver drapes, and knelt there with their heads bowed.

Suddenly the drapes seemed to dissolve. Revealed was a dazzling light. Within the light was a gigantic hand.

Beams of light shot out from the hand, striking their

---

* "Renewal" is a form of rejuvenation practiced in the cavern world; but its exact nature remains unclear. Palmer notes: "It would seem here that Mrs. Rogers believes you must 'die' to get into the caves. Many of our more mystic-minded readers have 'explained' the whole mystery by this means. If we were to accept this, then how account for the fact that Mrs. Rogers is *alive* today (provided, of course, that her story of being in the caves is true)?"

heads. Then the hand and the light faded away, and the drapes reappeared.

The two newlyweds arose to their feet, and on their faces were the glories of those who have seen God. No human wedding, with priest or preacher, could have been as beautiful as that.

And during her last days in the cavern world, Maggie got to witness a renewal. Three surface dwellers were escorted into a chamber. They lay down in front of a tall stone, which glowed and became transparent. Within a day the three were young again.

Finally it was time for Maggie to return home.*

Her mentors returned her "surface clothes"; gave her a jeweled box (to sell for cash); and assured her that one day she would come back to them. A tearful farewell ensued. Then Maggie was taken back to the cave in which Dr. Kelmer had left her. The gate slid open and she stepped out into sunlight.

"Adios and good luck," said Mira.

And she was soon back in Mexico City—staying with a friend (who gave her money in exchange for the box), and starting a new life.†

"This is my story," she concludes her tale, "a vindication of my friends, the Nephli, and a tribute to TAMIL."

So—what are we to make of this tale? A number of possibilities come to mind:

---

* In her original letter, Rogers claimed to have disappeared from the surface world for three years. But her stay among the Nephli seems to have lasted less than a month. Could it be that time flows differently in the cavern world—just as in Fairyland?

† "The box was [subsequently] sold to Alma Lewis," notes Palmer, "the wife of an executive of the *Cia Luz y Fuerza* (Mexican Light and Power Company). Recent letters are unanswered, and there is a report that Alma Lewis has returned to England with her husband. Does anybody know of her whereabouts? We would like to see this box, or send a representative to see it."

1. The title—"I Have Been in the Caves"—is to be taken literally. Rogers was physically in the cavern world.
2. Her account is of a visionary experience—one induced perhaps by drugs. (Or by treatment at the Electrotherapy Institute.)
3. It is a parable, expressive of her spiritual views.
4. It is pure fiction, published (and conceivably even written) by Palmer to enhance the Shaver Mystery.

In any case, a year later—in the February 1948 issue—Palmer announced the following:

> One of the most fascinating events in AMAZING STORIES was the publication of a reputedly true experience in a cave beneath Mexico, by Mrs. Margaret Rogers. Our readers will remember that story, as an integral part of the famed Shaver Mystery. Mrs. Rogers got more than four thousand letters concerning her adventure, and the whole thing raised quite a rumpus. Many readers asked for more information from her, and your editors were deluged by requests for more from her on the subject. Apparently many people believed her implicitly, and many others were so intrigued that they desired proof. Naturally she could not answer them all.
> Now Mrs. Rogers has written a book, and published it at her expense. It contains her adventures, complete and unabridged, and serves as an answer to all those people who wanted to know more. The book is titled "Beginning," and we recommend it to our readers as supporting evidence to the Shaver Mystery. She says it is copied from ancient records few surface beings have ever seen. You can get it by writing Mrs. Margaret Rogers.... [her address is given] The two dollars it costs is well worth it to Shaver Fans! Your editor enjoyed it very much.*

---

* *Beginning* is a publication so rare as to be legendary. I have been unable to locate a copy. But apparently it includes portions of the *Hedon Rogia*—the sacred scrolls of the Nephli. Rogers claimed to have read these scrolls while in the cavern world, and to remember their contents.

22.

Lobsang Rampa

There has been no shortage in modern times of writers on mystical matters. From Madame Blavatsky to Saint-Yves d'Alveydre to Doreal, these authors have guided us through the shadowy vales of arcane knowledge. They have unlocked for us the storehouse of ancient wisdom, and helped us to navigate the borderlands of experience. Yet none of them has been so prolific, so authoritative, so exotic—and, alas, so dubious—as Lobsang Rampa, the Tibetan lama.

With his shaven head, penetrating gaze, and monkish robes, Dr. Rampa (he claimed a degree from the Chungking School of Medicine) was a forbidding figure. He was also a major source of esoteric knowledge. Described as "a true

mystic and trailblazer of the New Age," Rampa published a score of books—about his training as a lama, his adventures in Tibet and elsewhere, and the occult practices of Tibetan Buddhism.

In these books he discusses such topics as astral travel ("Most lamas do it, and anyone who is prepared to use some patience can indulge in the useful and pleasant art"), telepathy, clairvoyance ("Because of my power of clairvoyance, I was able to be of a great assistance to the Inmost One [the Dalai Lama] on various occasions"), the Akashic Records, human auras ("From their auras I could divine their thoughts; what ailed them, what their hopes and fears were"), reincarnation, the afterlife, Atlantis, UFOs, levitation, abominable snowmen ("my old friends"), and the Inner Earth.

When not writing, he spent time casting horoscopes, reading Tarot cards, and gazing into a crystal ball. Lobsang Rampa was a repository of the secret wisdom of the Orient, as well as its leading purveyor; and as such, he helped to launch the New Age movement. He sold millions of books; had a profound influence; and became—with that shaven head and penetrating gaze—the very icon of Eastern wisdom. And (as might be expected) he was controversial.

The controversy began with his first book. *The Third Eye: The Autobiography of a Tibetan Lama* was published in 1956 by Secker & Warburg, a respected British house. But the road to publication had not been smooth. Having paid Rampa (or Dr. Kuon Suo, as he was then known) a modest advance, Secker & Warburg began to have doubts as to the authenticity of his writing. They decided to have the manuscript evaluated by experts.

The results were dismaying. In the view of one Tibet scholar, the book was "a fake built from published works and embellished with a fertile imagination." Another declared: "This fellow is a complete impostor, and he's probably never been in Tibet.... He should be properly unmasked." The consensus was that *The Third Eye* was a fraud.

Years later, Agahananda Bharati, one of the evaluators,

would recall his reaction to the manuscript:

> I was suspicious before I opened the wrapper: the "third eye" smacked of Blavatskyan and post-Blavatskyan hogwash. The first two pages convinced me the writer was not a Tibetan, the next ten that he had never been either in Tibet or India, and that he knew absolutely nothing about Buddhism of any form, Tibetan or other.... Every page bespeaks the utter ignorance of the author of anything that has to do with Buddhism as practiced and Buddhism as a belief system in Tibet or elsewhere. But the book also shows a shrewd intuition into what millions of people want to hear.*

Publisher Warburg summoned Rampa to his office. To confirm his suspicions, he greeted the author with some words of Tibetan. Rampa responded with a blank look—then shook spasmodically and clutched his head. And he explained that he had been taken prisoner by the Japanese during the war. Wishing to avoid interrogation, he had self-hypnotized himself into forgetting his native tongue.

Warburg rolled his eyes at this preposterous excuse. And revealing the verdict of the evaluators, he made a proposal. Secker & Warburg would still publish the book—but as a work of fiction, which it obviously was. Rampa became indignant. Insisting that both he and *The Third Eye* were authentic, he rejected the offer and departed in a huff.

But in the end, the property was too promising to give up. Secker & Warburg relented and published *The Third Eye* as an autobiography. They attached, however, a disclaimer. In a Publishers' Foreword the reader was warned:

> The autobiography of a Tibetan lama is a unique record of experience and, as such, inevitably hard to corroborate. In

---

* Agahananda Bharati (originally Leopold Fischer) was a German anthropologist who had converted to Hinduism. The vehemence of his denunciation of Rampa (whom he called "the arch-paradigm of esoteric phoniness") may have had to do with his own adoption of an Eastern identity.

an attempt to obtain confirmation of the Author's statements the Publishers submitted the MS. to nearly twenty readers, all persons of intelligence and experience, some with special knowledge of the subject. Their opinions were so contradictory that no positive result emerged....

The many personal conversations we have had with [Rampa] have proved him to be a man of unusual powers and attainments. Regarding many aspects of his personal life he has shown a reticence that was sometimes baffling; but everyone has a right to privacy....

For these reasons the Author must bear—and willingly bears—a sole responsibility for the statements made in his book.

An Author's Preface followed, in which Rampa told the reader: "Some of my statements, so I am told, may not be believed. That is your privilege."

Published in November 1956, *The Third Eye* became a bestseller. British readers were fascinated by a true tale of mystical Tibet—an account of life in a lamasery—a memoir that was replete with marvels, and that read like a novel. German, French, and Norwegian editions soon followed, and sold equally well.

The following year a sequel, *Doctor from Lhasa*, was about to be published. But those Tibet scholars—for whom the first volume was "a wild fabrication," "an impudent fake," "a shameless book"—were still around; and the prospect of another book by Rampa outraged them. They decided to take action, and to expose the man who they were certain was a fraud. A private detective was hired; and he began to nose about.

And on February 1, 1958, the *Daily Mail* ran a front-page article. Under a headline proclaiming "BOGUS LAMA," it began:

> The man accepted by thousands as the Tibetan Lama of the Third Eye has been exposed as a brilliant hoaxer.
>
> He is no Lama from Tibet. He is a plumber's son from Plympton, Devon—plain Mr. Cyril Henry Hoskins.

Rampa was residing at the time in a rented villa overlooking Dublin Bay. (He had moved to Ireland to avoid the British authorities, who were demanding to see his Tibetan passport or a residency permit.) Pleading illness, the author refused to meet with reporters, who were descending on the villa. But his wife (who would later claim to have been misquoted) had told the *Daily Mail*: "The book is fiction. He had tried to get a number of jobs without success. We had to have money to live. So he was persuaded to write the book. We depend upon its sale for money."

The story spread to other newspapers; and "the bogus lama" became the brunt of widespread mockery and abuse. The *Daily Mail* interviewed a television producer who had once met with Rampa. "No normally intelligent person could believe he was Tibetan," said the producer. "He seemed to be a gentleman, but harmless and lonely and completely lost in the fantastic role he had set himself."

More facts emerged about Cyril Hoskin. He had been born in Devonshire in 1910; had apprenticed in his father's plumbing shop; and had been employed most recently as a clerk at a correspondence school. According to a co-worker there, Hoskin had suddenly "gone Eastern": shaving his head, changing his name to Kuon Suo, and becoming obsessed with Oriental culture. His odd behavior alienated those around him; and eventually Hoskin quit his job and became a free-lance journalist.

Because he refused to speak directly with the press, no further information about Rampa was forthcoming. His household in Ireland, it was learned, consisted of his wife Sarah; a young woman named Sheelagh Rouse, who served as his secretary;* and several Siamese cats.

---

* Sheelagh Rouse has described her first encounter with Rampa: "I knew nothing about vibrations, auras and the like, but such power radiated from this person that I had the distinct feeling of a fire burning brightly. I was awed. My eyes were drawn to and met his, which were somehow long and narrow, piercing without being large, calm and still with a hint of amusement in them....

"As this man looked at me, I experienced something utterly

The lama was down, but not out; and almost immediately he was fighting back. Initially, he offered a plausible explanation: he (Cyril Hoskin) had ghostwritten *The Third Eye* in behalf of a genuine Tibetan lama. But the next day, the beleaguered author—in a tape-recorded statement to the press—dramatically changed his story.

A few years before, Hoskin claimed, he had fallen out of a tree and suffered a concussion. Upon regaining his senses, he was no longer Cyril Hoskin. Rather, he was Lobsang Rampa. *The astral spirit of a Tibetan lama had taken over his body!*

This new explanation failed to satisfy the press, who continued to hound "the plumber from Lhasa." Such was the turmoil that, within a year, Rampa and his household had fled Ireland and moved to Canada. There he would reside for the remainder of his life (with the exception of a brief stay in Uruguay). And there he would carry on as a purveyor of Eastern wisdom.

Over the next twenty years Lobsang Rampa would write and publish a steady stream of books. While none sold as well as *The Third Eye*, his books found readers among the burgeoning New Age subculture. In 1960 his third book was published. Titled *The Rampa Story*, it includes a detailed account of his transmigration into the body of an Englishman.

That transmigration, we are told, took place in the late 1940s. Hoskin—unemployed, depressed, friendless, and disgusted with the class system in Great Britain—had climbed a tree in his backyard, in order to photograph an owl. As he crawled out on a branch, it broke; and Hoskin plunged to the ground, knocking himself unconscious.

---

strange. I felt his eyes boring into my very soul, into the being, the self I did not expose, almost did not know or recognize so used was I to covering up, to pretending, to denying. It was as though I was standing there with my soul stark naked, no pretense, no protection. I had never experienced anything like it before, and never have since." (From her *Twenty-Five Years with T. Lobsang Rampa*)

Hoskin found himself in the astral plane. A Tibetan lama approached; smiled and assured him there was nothing to fear; and asked if he would be willing to vacate his body. It was needed by another lama, who was failing in health but who had a mission to fulfill: the bringing of Eastern wisdom to the West.

The benefits were explained to Hoskin. By donating his body, he could aid mankind and lend a purpose to his hitherto "mediocre life." Moreover, he could wipe away his karma and end his cycle of rebirths. For he would be guaranteed immediate passage to the Land of Golden Light.

Hoskin expressed tentative interest. But first he wanted to see the Land of Golden Light. Instantly he was granted a vision of the place—and it was glorious beyond description. He agreed to the proposal.

The details were worked out. Among other things, Hoskin agreed to grow a beard (the incoming lama insisted on having one). And a month was allowed to pass, for him to consider his decision.

Then, according to plan, Hoskin climbed the tree again, and purposely fell from it. He struck his head and found himself back in the astral plane. There a team of lamas performed the operation. Cyril Hoskin was released from his body and dispatched to the Land of Golden Light. And into this host body was inserted Lobsang Rampa.

Meanwhile, Sarah Hoskin had spotted her husband lying on the ground. She came running from the house and cried: "Oh, what have you done now?" She roused Cyril (or rather Rampa) and helped him to stagger into the house.

The next few days were difficult, Rampa tells us in *The Rampa Story*. The lama was trying to get used to his new body. He would teeter, walk backwards, stumble, lurch about like a mechanical man. (One problem was that the body was too small for the sturdy Tibetan.) And he sought to explain to Sarah what had happened.

If the transmigration of a lama into an Englishman's body was a notable event, no less notable was the reaction of the Englishman's wife. "After the changeover," she would admit, "it was a strange feeling for both of us." Yet despite the initial shock, Sarah was able to accept the situation. She was married now to a Tibetan lama.

"The day I happened to look out the window and see my husband lying at the foot of a tree in the garden, is something I shall never forget. I hurried out to find he was recovering, but to me, a trained nurse, he seemed to be stunned or something. When eventually he regained consciousness he seemed to act differently and in a way I did not understand....

"Certainly his speech seemed different, more halting, as if he was unfamiliar with the language and his voice appeared deeper than before.

"For sometime I was quite concerned, for something seemed to have happened to his memory... before speaking or moving he appeared to be making calculations; much later I learned that he was 'tuning in to my mind' to see what was expected of him. I do not mind admitting that in the early stages I was very worried, but now it seems quite natural. I have never ceased to wonder that such an ordinary individual as myself should be so closely associated with such a remarkable occurrence as the advent of a Tibetan Lama to the Western World." (*The Opening of the Third Eye* by Douglas Baker)

The adjustment was most profound, of course, for Rampa himself. When transmigration—into the body of a married Englishman—had first been proposed, he had expressed strong reservations. "'Eeek!' I exclaimed, jumping up in alarm. 'He is married. What can I do about that? I am a celibate monk! I am getting out of this.'" Lobsang Rampa had spent most of his life in a lamasery. Suddenly he had a wife to support—the foreign ways of the British to learn—a new language (and vocal cords) to master. "By the Holy Tooth of Buddha, what had I let myself in for?"

But there was no turning back. The house in suburban London, with its little garden, was now the home of a Tibetan and his wife. Cyril Hoskin had moved on. As Rampa would explain: "I, a Tibetan lama, now occupy what

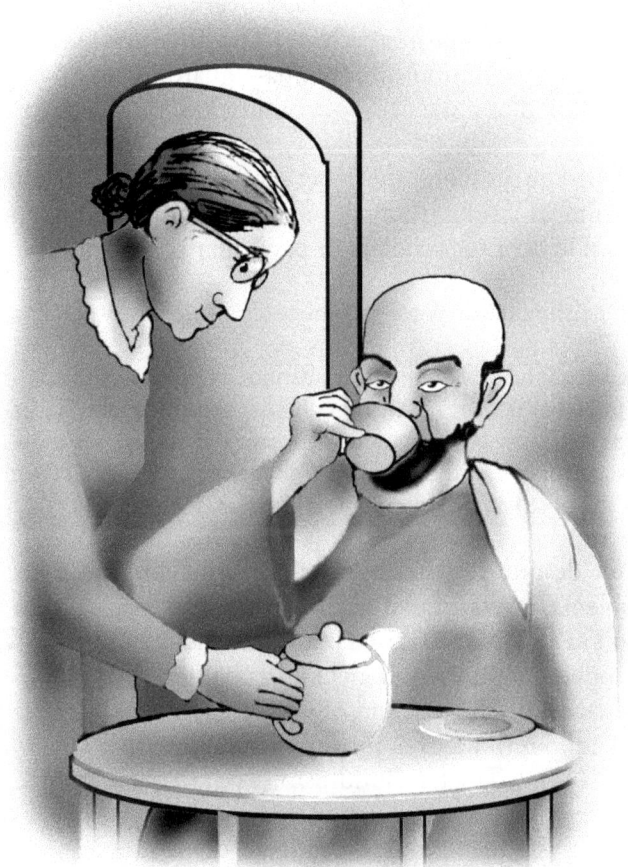

was originally the body of a Western man, and I occupy it to the permanent and total exclusion of the former occupant. He gave his willing consent—being glad to escape from life on earth in view of my urgent need."

Lobsang Rampa (or, as Sarah referred to him, "the New One") began to look for employment, without success. He managed to sell an occasional magazine article. But until the publication of *The Third Eye*, the couple would struggle to make ends meet.

By the time they moved to Canada, fame—not finances—had become the problem. The press continued to pursue and harass him. People on the street would recognize and approach him. And his mailbox overflowed, with letters from seekers of spiritual advice. The attention drove him further into seclusion; and Rampa—guarding his privacy in a succession of residences—became a kind of celebrity hermit.

Both the press and the Tibet scholars were still denouncing him as a fake. Rampa had harsh things to say about each. He held the scholars in particular contempt:

> One should not place too much credence in "experts" or "Tibetan Scholars" when it is seen how one "expert" contradicts the other, when they cannot agree on what is right and what is wrong, and after all how many of those "Tibetan scholars" have entered a lamasery at the age of seven, and worked all the way through the life as a Tibetan, and then taken over the body of a Westerner? I HAVE.*

Yet despite those denunciations, and mounting health problems, he continued to turn out books—right up to his death in 1981. They varied in subject and quality. *As It Was!* is autobiographical (and includes a chapter by Cyril Hoskin —dictated from the Land of Golden Light). *You Forever* is a handbook for developing psychic powers. *The Saffron Robe* is about Tibetan Buddhism. *The Hermit* is the story of an elderly sage who gets abducted by aliens. *Wisdom of the Ancients* is a metaphysical dictionary (with topics ranging from Abhinivesha to Zen). *Candlelight* describes his persecution by the press. *Living with the Lama* is the autobiography of his cat Fifi (dictated to Rampa telepathically). And several books responded to questions submitted by readers.

But perhaps his most inspiring work was one that appeared after his death. Described as a "lost manuscript," *My Visit to Agharta* was published in 2003 by Inner Light

---

* Rampa is saying that, on account of having spent a lifetime as a Tibetan monk, he is better qualified to judge his authenticity than are the scholars. This is "question begging": a logical fallacy in which a premise is assumed in order to prove that very premise.

Publications. It is an account of Rampa's visit to that legendary place.*

In several of his books Rampa describes subterranean experiences. In *The Third Eye* he is taken, as part of his initiation into lamahood, to a cavern deep beneath the Potala Palace. There he is shown the preserved bodies of giants; and he has a vision of the antediluvian world in which such giants flourished. In *The Cave of the Ancients* he visits a cavern filled with artifacts of an ancient civilization—enigmatic machines from the days of Atlantis. In *As It Was!* he is led through a tunnel whose walls are inscribed with strange pictographs. The tunnel ends at a blank wall—the sealed entranceway, he is told, to the Inner Earth.

And years later, Rampa was deemed worthy of journeying to Agharta—an experience he describes in *My Visit to Agharta*.

The book opens with Rampa flying, in a UFO, to a cave in the Himalayas. There he is reunited with his old master, Mingyar Dondup. In the darkness of the cave, the two lamas drink tea and chat.

Then Dondup reveals a secret passageway. And he leads Rampa into the depths of the mountain. After some adventures (involving a guide named Leo, beast men, and a kidnapped woman), they board a hovercraft and are taken deeper still into the earth.

They disembark in a cavern, which is lit by a swirling column of light. This vortex, explains Dondup, is the entranceway to Agharta—"the passageway through time

---

* *My Visit to Agharta* has a shadowy provenance. According to the publisher, the manuscript was discovered among the papers of a bookstore owner who had befriended Rampa. But how much —if any—of the book was actually written by Rampa remains a subject of debate. Karen Mutton (author of *Lobsang Rampa: New Age Trailblazer*, an impressively researched biography of Rampa and the source of much of my information about him) believes that "the authenticity of this book is highly questionable." At the same time, she deems it to be "a worthwhile addition to any Rampa library."

and space that connects the inner world with ours."

And into the vortex are marching hundreds of people—enlightened souls and spiritual teachers from throughout the ages. *These men and women are gathering in Agharta.* Rampa recognizes—and is awed by—such figures as Madame Blavatsky, Joan of Arc, and Nostradamus.

Rampa and Dondup join the march. As they enter the vortex, their rate of vibration is increased. And instantly

they find themselves on a mountainside. They have entered the kingdom of Agharta.

The mountain overlooks lush forests and sparkling rivers. In the sky is a small sun, which bathes the landscape in a golden light. Crystal cities are visible in the distance.

Agharta is a center of cosmic power, says Dondup. Its capital is Shambhala, a city inhabited by "extraordinary beings who vibrate at the highest frequencies of the Universe."

Suddenly the sun begins to spin and emit colored rays. And the sun speaks. In a booming voice, it delivers a message for the spiritual teachers to convey to mankind. As he listens, Rampa is filled with love and understanding.

And he has an epiphany. "It may sound simplistic," he says to Dondup, "but the answer to all questions is love."

Finally, he departs from Agharta and returns home in a UFO. (Dondup remains behind, to study with the Ascended Masters.)

And that is the story told in *My Visit to Agharta*. With this posthumous publication, Rampa concluded his career as a purveyor of Eastern wisdom.

•

What are we to make of that career?

Its achievements were undeniable. Lobsang Rampa helped to launch the New Age movement. (In *The Third Eye*, a high-ranking lama appears in a crystal ball and announces: "We are on the threshold of a New Age, an Age wherein it is intended that Man shall be purified of his dross and shall live in peace with others and himself.") Rampa promoted an interest, both spiritual and political, in Tibet. (*The Third Eye* is still in print, and remains the most widely read book about Tibet.) He introduced the wisdom of the East (from Abhinivesha to Zen) to countless readers. And he took those readers to exotic places (lamaseries, the cave beneath the Potala, Agharta).

Yet the question remains: Was Lobsang Rampa a Tibetan

—that is to say, a transmigrated lama? Or was he merely Cyril Hoskin—an Englishman engaged in a literary masquerade?

The Dalai Lama was once queried as to Rampa's genuineness. His secretary responded: "I wish to inform you that we do not place credence on the books written by the so-called Dr. T. Lobsang Rampa. His works are highly imaginative and of a fictional nature."

And according to Warburg, his original publisher, Rampa became "psychopathic and swallowed his own fantasies." (His Canadian publisher was more discreet, describing Rampa simply as "very different, very special.")

On the other hand, Sheelagh Rouse, his devoted secretary, saw him as "a personage who defies our present stage of understanding." And his biographer, Karen Mutton, set out to portray him "not as a fraud but a genius of the highest order who exerted an enormous influence on the New Age movement."

Rampa himself, responding to accusations of fakery, asserted: "No one has ever been able to *prove* me a fraud; for every 'expert' who claimed that I was such—three or more attested to my complete genuineness."

And his final word on the matter was simply this: "What does it matter WHO I am, it is what I WRITE that is important."*

Still, one has to wonder: Who was this man? And the

---

* As he explained: "My books are true.... It does not matter if I was born in Lhasa or Londonderry; the author does not matter, what the author writes, does. Have these books helped you? Have they helped anyone? Has anything been learned from them? Yes? Then they are worthwhile."

Is this attitude not comparable perhaps to that of the pseudepigraphers of ancient Israel? They attributed their writings to noted figures of the past—Enoch or Abraham or Moses. Their aim was not to perpetrate a fraud. Rather, they wished to present their writings as a continuation of traditional teachings, and thus lend them an aura of authority.

closest Rampa ever came to addressing that question may have been in the following passage. Mingyar Dondup is telling a tale, about a monk who believed himself to be a prince:

> "In the solitude of his cell, he imagined that he was a great Prince, a Prince of mighty estates and great wealth. At the start it was harmless, it was a harmless if useless diversion. Certainly no one would have condemned him for a few idle imaginings and yearnings....This man throughout the years, whenever he was alone, became the great, great Prince. It coloured his outlook, it affected his manner, and with the passage of time the humble monk seemed to disappear and the arrogant Prince came to the fore. At last the poor unfortunate man really believed most firmly that he was a Prince of the land of Burma.... [He was reduced] to a state of mental instability. But you, Lobsang, have no need to worry about such things; you are stable and well balanced and without fear....Keep your foot upon the Path." (*The Cave of the Ancients*)

Who then was he? An Englishman who allowed his "idle imaginings and yearnings" to grow unchecked, until he believed himself to be a Tibetan lama? A conscious fraud? Or the transmigrated soul that he claimed to be? All of these may be counted as possibilities.

In the end, Lobsang Rampa remains a mystery—as inscrutable as the ones he sought to elucidate. But that should not obscure his real achievement. Rampa brought an awareness of Tibet to a wide audience. He cast a light upon the arcane wisdom of the East. And he drew us, with the beacon of his books, into the New Age. As his motto had it: I Lit a Candle.*

Rampa spent his final years in Calgary. His household consisted of his wife, his secretary, and his Siamese cats. They

---

* His own candle was extinguished in 1981, in a Canadian hospital. Eerily, at the moment of his death, the bulb in an overhead lamp exploded.

resided in the foothills of the Canadian Rocky Mountains.

Those mountains may have reminded him of the Himalayas, whence his astral spirit (or at least his literary persona) had come.

23.

Walter Siegmeister

DR. RAYMOND BERNARD WAS A WELL-KNOWN NAME in nutritional and metaphysical circles during the 1950s. Health-food devotees knew him for his booklets—self-published and distributed by mail—about herbal elixirs, vegetarianism, the dangers of pesticides; while those with more philosophical interests had read his biography of Pythagoras or his writings on the Essenes.

But then he began to write about a new and problematical subject. Previously, his detractors had deemed him a crank; now they questioned his sanity. For Bernard was claiming that the earth was hollow; that its depths could serve as a refuge from radioactive fallout; and that located in those depths was an advanced civilization—a utopian society. Moreover, this realm could be reached, he believed, via tunnels in Brazil—the country in which he was residing as an expatriate.

Who was Dr. Raymond Bernard, A.B., M.A., and Ph.D. (the credit that appeared on his writings)? As his associates knew—and as the U.S. postal authorities had yet to discover—he was in fact Walter Siegmeister.

Born in 1903, Siegmeister had grown up in Harlem and Brooklyn, the son of Russian Jewish immigrants. His father, a surgeon, was a scoffer at religion and a socialist ("an anarchist," according to Elie, the younger son); and Walter was exposed to the radicalism of his parents' circle of friends. (It included Emma Goldman, the well-known anarchist.) After graduating from Columbia, Walter became a vegetarian; attended public lectures on Theosophy, spiritualism, and the like; founded a "nature colony" in the Catskills; and finally, in 1932, received a doctorate in education.*

---

* For much of this information, I am indebted to Leonard Lehman of the Elie Siegmeister Society, who is writing a biography of the brother who became a composer.

His thesis was on the pedagogy of Rudolf Steiner (founder of the Waldorf Schools); and Siegmeister would seem to have been planning a career in education. But instead, he traveled to South Florida, purchased land, and founded another nature colony.*

The Lake Istokpoga Colony, as he named it, was located in the township of Lorida, Florida. It was dedicated to vegetarianism, organic farming, and simple living. Siegmeister divided the land into plots and offered them for sale to prospective colonists.

As it turned out, few plots were ever sold; and the population of the colony remained small. But related ventures kept Siegmeister busy. He published a newsletter called *Diet and Health*; wrote tracts; railed against meat-eating, sugar, and pesticides; and sold health foods by mail-order—in particular, a syrup containing lecithin. In the newsletter, questions about diet and health were answered by "Dr. Siegmeister." (He did have that doctorate.) And he began to formulate a philosophy—a "new scientific religion of hygiene and eugenic living" that he called Biosophy.†

---

* Nature colonies were communities in which one could live "close to nature." (They are not to be confused with nudist colonies—though some were that too.) These idealistic endeavors were the predecessors of the communes of the sixties.

Where did Siegmeister get the funds to start his colony? The money may have come from the life insurance policy of his father, who had died recently. Reportedly, for the rest of his days he would receive a monthly check from his mother.

† In a booklet he would describe this religion:

"And in place of an imaginary heaven after death for departed souls, Biosophy offers a real Earthly Paradise to be enjoyed during this life. In fact, Biosophy is the first religion of the world to offer such an Earthly Paradise and to make its chief concern to make this life happy, healthy and long-extended, rather than bother about the after-death fate of the souls of its followers, while resigning them to a miserable existence during their lives.

"Biosophy is a religion without bibles, without superstitions, without theologies, without dogmas, without churches, without

As might be expected, the farming efforts were a failure. Some of the colonists became disillusioned and left. And a more serious problem arose. Sometime in the late 1930s, Siegmeister ran afoul of the law. The specifics of the case are obscure. But the Food and Drug Administration either threatened or actually instituted legal proceedings against him, in connection with the "naturopathic cures" that he was selling by mail. The syrup with lecithin seems to have prompted the action. Accused of fraud and misuse of the mails, Siegmeister was forced to curtail his activities.

These legal difficulties propelled him into a new phase of his career. Previously, he had been a simple advocate of a healthful diet. Now he saw himself as an embattled crusader, persecuted by a government that engaged in censorship and suppression and colluded with powerful interests. Seeking to avoid its grasp (and that of "the Moloch of commercialism and materialism as this civilization is"), he began to wander from place to place—in the U.S., Central America, and South America.

He did not cease to write and publish his booklets. But he was forced to do so using pseudonyms. For the postal authorities, at the behest of the Food and Drug Administration, had put his name on a list. Walter Siegmeister was forbidden to use the U.S. mails to distribute either his health-food products or his publications.

His wandering began in 1940 with a trip to Panama, where he got involved with a back-to-nature community. Then it was on to Ecuador, where he sought to establish a fruitarian colony. Its stated aim was "regeneration"—via a diet of fruit, nuts, and yoghurt—and the creation of a new race of men. Siegmeister was described by a visiting journalist as "holder of three degrees from Columbia and New York Universities, and known for his research in eugenics, biochemistry and endocrinology." He possessed "the most

---

priests, without foolish ceremonials, without supernaturalism, and without gods created from the imagination of priests for their own self-aggrandizement."

unusual eyes I've ever seen—brown, extraordinarily large and of such depth and fire that they draw one's attention inexorably. Yet the manner of the man is one of meekness and solemnity."

But the colony was short-lived; and the handful of colonists dispersed. One of the them was Johnny Lovewisdom, as he called himself. Lovewisdom (who had also been at Lake Istokpoga) would go on to become a health-food crusader in his own right.*

By 1945 Siegmeister was back in Florida. In that year he hired a secretary: Guy Harwood, a vegetarian from Jacksonville. Harwood was given the job of printing and mailing out a study course—in defiance of the postal ban. Somewhat mystified by his employer, Harwood relates that Siegmeister "dressed like a rabbi": all in black, with a hat, long hair, and a full beard.†

Apparently, he was living at this time on his property in Lorida. But it wasn't long before Siegmeister was on the move again. Harwood describes the abrupt departure:

> The Doctor's attorney notified him that a government agent was looking for him. He grabbed a pup tent and fled

---

* Johnny Lovewisdom (1919–2000) was the author of more than 50 books on diet and related subjects, including *Vitarianism*, *Spiritualizing Dietetics*, and *The Buddhist Essene Gospel of Jesus*. He began as a strict fruitarian; switched to vitarianism (some vegetables allowed); flirted with breatharianism ("spiritual energy" only); and returned in the end to fruitarianism—subsisting on papaya. For many years he lived as a hermit at a mountain lake in the Andes.

† He may have resembled a rabbi; but Walter Siegmeister had renounced all connection with Judaism. In a letter to Harwood dated October 20, 1954, he fumed: "I did not like your insistence that I am Jewish when I am not. My parents were followers of Tolstoy.... Since neither my parents nor I ever accepted the Jewish religion, nor the Christian religion nor any false man-made religion, I refuse to be labeled.... the Jewish religion is also a false religion." (Quoted in "Raymond Bernard's Search for Paradise" by Dennis Crenshaw, a hollow-earth researcher)

into the woods near his home and stayed two or three days before leaving the country.... under the name of Raymond Bernard he left, going first to Mexico, and then to Central and South America. After he left the United States he changed his complete interest from nutrition-rejuvenation to that of his new interests of a philosophical nature. (From a letter to Dennis Crenshaw)

Actually, he seems to have headed first to Morongo Valley in California. (Johnny Lovewisdom joined him there for a while.) In California he marketed health foods and published booklets, including *Are You Being Poisoned by the*

Food You Eat? and *Super-Health thru Organic Super-Foods*. Mindful of the postal injunction (and of the postal authorities who were looking for him), he kept his name off these publications. Instead, they were credited to "Dr. Robert Raymond, A.B., M.A., and Ph.D."*

Then the wandering resumed. During the next eight years, Siegmeister resided in Hawaii, Puerto Rico, Guatemala, and other places. In Guatemala he wrote as "Dr. Uriel Adriana, A.B., M.A., and Ph.D." and tried unsuccessfully to start a colony.

But finally, in 1955, he found a home—in Brazil. He purchased 2000 acres of land on an island near Joinville, in the southern state of Santa Catarina. And there Siegmeister founded his most ambitious colony yet. He called it the New California Subtropical Settlement, and began looking for settlers. "Here," he wrote, "I am establishing a settlement of American vegetarians, organic gardeners, and advanced thinkers anxious to live in a part of the world where alone a New Age can arise."

The number of persons who bought plots of land is not known. But some were locals from Joinville. These Brazilians welcomed the offer of inexpensive land. They joined the colony solely as farmers; the "advanced thinking" they left to others.†

Siegmeister advertised in magazines such as *Fate*. In one ad, he combined the search for colonists with the marketing

---

* At Lake Istokpoga Siegmeister had been associated with George R. Clements. A naturopath and philosopher, Dr. Clements (1879–1970) must have had similar problems with the postal authorities. For he would publish as Professor Hilton Hotema, Dr. Karl Kridler, and Kenyon Klamonti.

Reviewing one of his publications, Siegmeister wrote: "If modern society was not controlled by Money Kings whose henchmen govern our educational institutions, the press, the church, etc., Professor Hilton Hotema would be considered as one of the greatest scientists of our day."

† When the colony began to disband in 1965, it consisted of an estimated twenty-five to thirty persons.

of his latest health product:

DO YOU WISH TO JOIN A NEW AGE COMMUNITY? After a 30 year search we found the Promised Land of the New Age in Subtropical Santa Catarina, Land of Eternal Spring, Tropical Fruits, Peace and Good Will, where a New Race is developing in World's Low Fallout Zone as Pioneers of a New Civilization. Write for information about our New Age Colonization Movement, Esoteric Order and Biosophical Teachings of Human Regeneration. We ship organically grown DEHYDRATED BANANAS. 4 lbs. for $5.00, 9 lbs. for $10.00. 20 lbs. for $20.00 postpaid. Remit by check payable to Dr. Walter Siegmeister.

Also available was banana meal. Touted as a nutritional wonder, it was sprinkled on food or dissolved in beverages.

Siegmeister helped to grow the bananas. But his main activity was writing and publishing. He mailed out copies of *The New Age Colonization Bulletin* and *The Biosophical Bulletin*, as well as booklets about diet and health. (All of these were typewritten and mimeographed.) His current pseudonym was Dr. Raymond Bernard. And that was the name by which he became known in health-food circles during the fifties.

But by now Siegmeister had developed a new concern—one that would eclipse his obsession with nutrition. It is spelled out in *Escape from Destruction*, which he published in 1956. In the eyes of his detractors, with this book he ceased to be a mere crank, and became a rising star of the lunatic fringe.*

Escape from Destruction is about escaping the effects of radioactive fallout. For Siegmeister believed that nuclear testing was poisoning the atmosphere and the soil; and moreover, that nuclear war was imminent. There were three possible ways, he declared, to avoid the fallout.

---

* A more sympathetic view of Siegmeister was expressed by his brother Elie, who considered him to be "fifty years ahead of his time."

The first was to escape to South America. For the testing was being carried out in the northern hemisphere. The prevailing winds would keep fallout from drifting southward.

The second was to escape into Outer Space—aboard a flying saucer. Such a solution, he admitted, might seem like "fantastic science-fiction at first glance." But Siegmeister thought it possible that the flying saucers were here to save us.*

And the third alternative? *To escape into the earth.*

> If and when a future nuclear war made the surface of the earth uninhabitable, the air lethal to breathe and foods and water poisonous to eat and drink, may not survivors of the catastrophe find refuge in the bowels of the earth?

Such a possibility was not far-fetched, Siegmeister insisted. For a vast network of tunnels was rumored to exist beneath South America. (And there were "persistent rumors" of secret entrances.) To where might these tunnels lead?

> [They] lead to subterranean cities that are still inhabited by descendants of the prehistoric race that built them. This subterranean empire is called "Agharta," believed to be a terrestrial heaven, inhabited by superhuman beings.

Agharta lay within. And it could provide a refuge from nuclear war.†

---

* During his stay in Puerto Rico, he had fallen under the influence of Mayita, a prophetess of the Great Mother. Mayita claimed to be in contact with the occupants of the saucers. They had come, she said, to rescue the biological and spiritual elect of humanity—i.e., those individuals who were eating healthfully.

† Where had Siegmeister learned about Agharta? One of his sources may have been *Agharta* (1951) by Robert Ernst Dickhoff (the "Sungma Red Lama"). Two years after that book's publication, Siegmeister wrote to Dickhoff and paid tribute to him as a sage: "No doubt I am a Disciple of Apollonius, and his Spirit inspires me, and St. Germain, Founder of Modern Science, must inspire you—the Maitreya [World Teacher]."

Escape from Destruction (which includes a discussion of the basic tenets of Biosophy) was published in 1956. The following year Siegmeister was browsing in a Sao Paulo bookstore. And he came upon a book about Agharta and flying saucers, written by O. C. Huguenin, a Brazilian Theosophist. According to Huguenin, flying saucers did not come from Outer Space—that was a cover story; they originated in Agharta. Concerned about nuclear testing, the Aghartans were monitoring the situation.

Huguenin described their society:

> [The Aghartans] have reached a very high degree of civilization, economic organization and social, cultural and spiritual development, together with an extraordinary scientific progress, in comparison with whom the humanity that lives on the earth's surface may be considered as a race of barbarians.

And he explained that they were the descendants of Atlanteans.*

The book mentioned Professor Henrique de Souza—a Theosophist who was in contact with the Aghartans. So Siegmeister went to see de Souza, who lived in Sao Lourenço. The visit was revelatory. De Souza affirmed that there were tunnels leading to Agharta. He revealed the general location of entrances to these tunnels; warned that they were guarded by Indians; and gave Siegmeister a password for getting past the Indians.

And in 1960 Siegmeister published (in the usual mimeographed edition) *Agharta: The Subterranean World.* By now

---

* "Prior to the sinking of Atlantis," Siegmeister would write, "a group of wise and good Atlanteans, who had foreknowledge of the catastrophe, came to Brazil and constructed here subterranean refuges in the form of underground cities, connected with each other by tunnels, where they established residence prior to the outbreak of the nuclear war that bought on the flood that sank Atlantis.... Incredible as it may seem, there is evidence that Atlanteans still live in underground cities under Brazil."

he had learned more about the Aghartans. They worshipped the Great Mother, he tells us, and were matriarchal. They had no disease, no crime, no money, no class distinctions. They did not engage in sex. (Vital energies were channeled instead to the brain.) They were fruitarians. And they lived for thousands of years, yet remained youthful in appearance.

The book concludes with a sales pitch for banana meal.

Siegmeister was convinced that a utopia called Agharta existed inside the earth; that it could provide a refuge from the ills of the twentieth century; and that it represented the ideals to which he had devoted his life.

Accordingly, he determined to visit it.

But first he had to locate one of those tunnels. He was sure they existed. For in addition to de Souza's testimony, he had elicited that of others. Two ranchers, for example, told him of entering a tunnel and catching a glimpse of subterraneans. And according to locals, the choral singing of Atlanteans—issuing from within a mountain near Joinville—could be heard regularly.

Siegmeister knew that such reports might be fictitious. (He was particularly wary of individuals who offered to guide him to a tunnel entrance, with their fee to be paid in advance.) But "where there's smoke there's fire," he insisted. And he hoped to soon be entering the tunnels.

Finally he made this announcement:

> The writer is now organizing an expedition, known as the Aghartan Expedition, for the purpose of investigating these tunnels, with the object of reaching the subterranean cities to which they lead, after which he hopes to establish contact with the still-living members of the Elder Race of Atlanteans and arrange for bringing qualified persons to them to establish residence in their cities in a World Free from Fallout.*

---

* Among the qualifications for establishing residence in Agharta was that one be vegetarian, nonsmoking, and sexually continent. (Siegmeister's attitude toward sexual relations? According to his brother, he claimed to have "been through that stage and was beyond it.")

In 1961 he wrote to Guy Harwood:

> The Atlanteans...built subterranean cities here and survived since. Sounds unbelievable but true. I lost interest in colonies after making this discovery. Hope to meet these people soon.

And in a subsequent letter, he told his former secretary:

> The other day one of my explorers reported finding the stone staircase that leads down to the Subterranean World. ...These Atlanteans alone can save us from fallout as they saved themselves 12,000 years ago.

He urged Harwood to "sell all your worldly goods," come to Brazil, and accompany him into the depths of the earth.

> If you wish to abandon this radioactively poisoned world and enter a new non-radioactive world where money does not exist, write me and I will help you, even as much as helping you with the fare later. But you must believe in me, that I will not tell you a lie about this, and ardently desire to enter this subterranean Utopia.

He was urging others to save themselves, too. This ad appeared in a New Age newsletter:

> SURVIVE! LIVE IN SHANGRI-LA!
>
> Famous author, explorer, Dr. Raymond Bernard has discovered paradisiacal subterranean cities of Brazil, inhabited by highly developed people (Atlanteans). Join the Aghartan Order. Entitles to bulletin plus aid in finding sanctuary with these marvelous people. Membership $5 yearly. Or send $1.00 for sample Aghartan Bulletin, complete details.

In 1961 he published *Flying Saucers from the Earth's Interior*, a sequel to *Agharta: The Subterranean World*. ("We shall attempt to show in the following pages...that the true origin of the saucers is an advanced civilization existing INSIDE THE EARTH!") And in 1963 he came out with *The*

Hollow Earth—a rewriting and expansion of those two works. *The Hollow Earth* would be his first book to be reprinted by a commercial publisher, and to find a wider audience.*

But Siegmeister would not be around to enjoy its success. For in the summer of 1965, he either died of pneumonia or disappeared into the tunnels. Both rumors circulated; and none of his correspondents could learn what had happened. He had ceased to be heard from. And letters to him were returned, stamped "deceased."†

So which was it? Had he died of pneumonia? Or as an ad for *The Hollow Earth* would ask:

WAS DR. BERNARD SWALLOWED UP BY THE INNER EARTH?

In any case, his career had been a remarkable one. A resident of Joinville would remember him as an "unkempt hermit"—a bearded eccentric who wore a robe. And indeed, Walter Siegmeister had been a kind of prophet. Dismissed as a crank, he had warned of the dangers of nuclear testing; decried the chemicals in food; denounced smoking; and called for a healthful diet. Like the prophet Elijah, he had spoken truth unto power, and been forced to flee into the wilderness. And like Elijah, he may have bodily ascended—or in his case, descended—into paradise.

His brother Elie had been named after Elijah. Perhaps the name had been conferred upon the wrong son.

---

* The commercial publisher did attach a disclaimer: "We assume no responsibility for any opinions expressed (or implied) by the author."

Joscelyn Godwin, a scholar of esotericism, has called the book "the definitive document of the hollow-earth school."

† Guy Harwood later claimed to have obtained a death certificate from Brazilian authorities, and to have forwarded it to Siegmeister's mother in Brooklyn.

24.

Dianne Robbins

IN 1989, FIFTY-YEAR-OLD DIANNE ROBBINS—FINDING that "even with all my degrees and all my education, I still couldn't make sense of my life on Earth"—took up meditation, and "began receiving inner guidance."

A year later, Robbins was listening to the song "I Know You're Out There Somewhere," when she had an epiphany. Another world, she suddenly knew, was waiting to communicate with her. On her Web site, she describes what ensued:

> I began a process of meditation that reawakened me to the remembrance that I am a telepathic receiver and transmitter for the Inner-Earth terrestrials and Cetaceans. I also awakened to my divine mission and role for this lifetime.
>
> I tapped into the cosmos and connected to the Cetaceans (Whales and Dolphins), Adama in the Subterranean City of Telos, Mikos in the Hollow Earth, the Ascended Masters, the Ashtar Command of the Confederation of Planets, Nature Spirits and Trees. I no longer felt alone, but suddenly connected to Beings everywhere through the telepathic phone lines that exist throughout the cosmos. My communication with Mikos has reconnected me to whom I am, and why I am here....
>
> With this new sense of purpose, I have dedicated my life to receiving, transcribing, and publishing my telepathic transmissions from Beings residing in Higher Realms of consciousness. My goal is to spread these messages around the globe in hopes of awakening surface humans to the existence of those who inhabit the Hollow Earth and Subterranean Realms through the publication of my books.

Robbins, a schoolteacher in Rochester, New York, had been a member of Greenpeace; so communicating with whales and dolphins was perhaps to be expected. But what about those messages from Adama in Telos, Mikos in the

Hollow Earth, and the Ascended Masters? How did all of that come about?

It began, explains Robbins, with a newsletter that she received. The newsletter was published by one Sharula Dux, who resided in Santa Fe. Dux claimed, however, to be a native of Telos, a city located beneath Mount Shasta. The newsletter described life in Telos.*

Mentioned in the newsletter was Adama, the high priest of Telos. For some reason, the name stuck in Robbins's thoughts. Then one day something startling occurred:

> I was sitting in meditation thinking about Adama, with my pen and notebook by my side, when I suddenly felt a burst of loving and gentle energy go right through me, almost lifting me up into the air. I then heard the words, "*I am Adama*, speaking to you from Telos."

These were Adama's first words to Robbins—the first of many. From that day on, he dictated messages to her, communicating telepathically from beneath Mount Shasta; and she would record his words in her notebook. The messages related to Telos and to various metaphysical topics. Often they were in response to questions that Robbins posed. Eventually, she would compile Adama's messages (along with those from other beings) and publish them.

But did Dianne Robbins ever *visit* Telos? Apparently she did. For as Mikos of the Library of Porthologos explained to her:

> As we are here in the Center of Earth's interior, you are here with us in consciousness. For consciousness is a "place"—a place more solid than your physical places. So yes, you sit

---

* Sharula Dux also claimed to be royal (a princess of Telos); sacerdotal (a priestess at its temple); and over 250 years old. A fixture on the New Age scene, she conducted workshops that taught the secrets of Telosian longevity.

Before moving to Santa Fe, says Robbins, Dux "was known in the Mt. Shasta area as Bonnie."

on the surface at your desk taking this dictation, but in consciousness you are with us inside the Hollow Earth. You are literally in two places at once. Do you understand multidimensionality now? Now that you are in both places simultaneously, we will show you around "our place."

Wishing to share her experiences, Dianne Robbins has published three books. They record her visits to Telos, to the Hollow Earth, and to the depths of the Ocean. All contain the channeled words of residents of these realms.

Her first book (published in 1996, and expanded in 2000) was *The Call Goes Out from the Subterranean City of Telos*. The messages recorded therein are mostly from Adama. As he speaks, a portrait emerges of Telos and its inhabitants.

To begin with, we are told of the origins of the city. Some 12,000 years ago, says Adama, a terrible war was fought between Atlantis and Lemuria. Both of their homelands were destroyed. But thousands of Lemurians survived by fleeing to Mount Shasta. And there, in a cavern beneath the mountain, they founded Telos. (The idea was to avoid the harsh weather and marauders of the surface world, and thereby enable themselves to evolve in peace.)

Today the city of Telos—"where all is Light, all is Beauty, and all is Grandeur"—has more than a million inhabitants. They dwell in circular houses (which are dust-free, thanks to the unimpeded circulation of energy). These dwellings have crystalline walls, which emit light and illumine the cavern.*

---

* Adama offered no further information on the architecture or physical layout of Telos. But a detailed description of the city has been provided by Sharula Dux. In "Secrets of the Subterranean Cities," Dux reveals that Telos has five levels. They descend from the base of the mountain and are linked by elevators. The uppermost level contains most of the city's residences and public buildings (including a pyramid-shaped temple with a capstone from Venus). The second level is devoted largely to manufacturing. The third level consists of hydroponic gardens, where food is grown. The fourth level is mixed use, with hydroponic gardens,

Isolated from the outside world and its ills, the Telosians live in peace and prosperity. They are both spiritually and technologically advanced. Thanks to their vegetarian diet and positive outlook, they experience no sickness or aging. (The eldest inhabitant of the city, according to Adama, is 30,000 years old!) Their governing body is a Council of Twelve, comprised of Ascended Masters. Money is nonexistent, the means of exchange being barter. There is no crime; and therefore, no need for police or locks on doors. The Telosians take long walks; sing and dance after meals; picnic and attend concerts. And they radiate unconditional love.

In short, hidden beneath Mount Shasta is an advanced civilization. And by channeling its high priest, Dianne Robbins has brought Telos to our attention.

Her second book was *The Call Goes Out: Messages from the Earth's Cetaceans* (1997). It is a compilation of messages from whales and dolphins. These intelligent—and surprisingly articulate—creatures implore us to stop polluting the sea. They plead with us to stop harming them. And they beg us to free those whales and dolphins being held in captivity. Featured are communiqués from Corky, a whale imprisoned in Sea World.

And Robbins's latest book is *Messages from the Hollow Earth* (2003). The messages are from Mikos of the Library of Porthologos. The library is located in the city of Catharia, deep within the Hollow Earth. It houses writings from throughout the Universe, engraved on crystals. The purpose of the library, says Mikos, "is to give guidance to the

---

manufacturing facilities, and parkland. And the fifth level—a mile beneath the mountain—is a nature preserve, with lakes, tall trees, and wild animals. The animals include many that are extinct on the surface, such as mastodons, saber-toothed tigers, and dodos. Raised to be nonviolent and vegetarian, these animals are of no danger to visitors.

Other information provided by Sharula Dux corroborates that channeled by Robbins—though skeptics will insist that Robbins's account *derives* from Dux's.

evolution of a society and a planet so that the people can live and evolve in peace and prosperity—not negativity and war."*

Mikos explains to Robbins why subterranean civiliza-

---

* Who may use the Library of Porthologos? Anyone! "We welcome you and invite you to enter at any time," says Mikos, the head librarian. "Just call to us for entry, as our call is always going out to you. I AM MIKOS, and I am here to guide you personally through our library whenever you call. You don't need a 'library card.'...We await your visit."

Mikos describes the "secluded alcoves interspersed throughout the vast halls with the most ergonomically structured chairs beckoning you to recline upon them."

tions are peaceful:

> All our lives have been spent in peace and bliss, due to our location. We exist here in peace and tranquility because of the proximity to the heartbeat of Mother Earth. The more deeply one goes into the Earth, the more deeply one feels the beat of the Earth.

And he laments the waywardness of surface dwellers:

> I am Mikos, calling to you from my Inner Sanctuary in the Inner Earth, where I dwell in peace and contentment for all God has given me. You, on the surface, live in misery, lack, and trepidation, because you have separated yourself from God, thinking that you know best, or more than the Creator.

Yet Mikos (who is a giant) has hope for us:

> When you open to the fact that you and the Universe are *one*, you will awaken to all that you are and begin to expand your horizons and literally grow in size—height and width.
> Your mind and body are connected.... Expand your thoughts, and you expand your world; expand your world, and your body responds in spurts of growth and renewal.

Both spiritual and physical growth, says Mikos, can be ours.

What then is the underlying message of these books by Dianne Robbins? What are Adama, Mikos, and Corky the whale trying to tell us? Adama sums it up:

> We are all working as ONE; ONE great thought of love for our planet Earth, ONE great wave of Light washing Earth's shores, ONE great beacon calling all of Earth's children home—home to the light of God's presence.

And he has an announcement:

> I have gained much wisdom from my extended life in Telos, and would like to impart this wisdom to others who

wish to learn from me. I am currently conducting classes on the Inner Planes at night. If you'd like to register for these classes, just petition me before you go to bed at night, asking to be my student. I will teach you mastery of yourself on all levels of existence.

Beneath Mount Shasta, Adama awaits us—to help us make sense of our lives. And to welcome us into the Light.

25.
Rodney Cluff

AN EXPEDITION MAY SOON BE SETTING OUT FROM THE Russian port of Murmansk. Its hundred or so members will be traveling on the *Yamal*, a nuclear-powered icebreaker. Most of those aboard will have paid about $20,000, as their share of the cost. All will be anticipating a unique adventure. But none more so than Rodney Cluff, the organizer of the North Pole Inner Earth Expedition.

A retired government employee, Cluff has been planning this ambitious endeavor from his home in Arizona. His interest in the Inner Earth is long-standing. As a young man, he spotted an ad in a tabloid newspaper for *The Hollow Earth* (by Dr. Raymond Bernard, A.B., M.A., and Ph.D.). He sent away for it, read it, and was hooked. Since then, he has read virtually everything written on the subject. Of particular interest was *The Smoky God*. For Cluff intends to sail in Olaf Jansen's wake, to the rim of the North Polar opening, and possibly beyond.

Cluff is the author of *World Top Secret: Our Earth Is Hollow!** The book is the result of his years of research. It begins with scientific evidence in support of a hollow earth, and of a North Polar opening. Included are satellite photos; analysis of the accounts of polar explorers; interpretation of earthquake data; explanations of gravity, electromagnetism, and the Aurora Borealis. The technical discussions can be difficult to follow. But Cluff's mastery of this material is impressive.

The North Polar opening, he insists, is the gateway to a hidden world. For within the earth are an ocean and a continent. Moreover, the interior of the earth has a temperate

---

* *World Top Secret: Our Earth Is Hollow!* is an e-book, available from http://www.ourhollowearth.com.

climate—thanks to the presence of a small central sun. As evidence, he cites a curious fact: fish and birds in the Arctic has been known to migrate *northward*. They would do so only to benefit from warmer feeding grounds. And those mammoths that have been found in northern Siberia, frozen in the ice? Cluff rejects the standard explanation, that they perished there thousands of years ago. In his view, mammoths have survived into the present. They roam that interior continent; and their remains occasionally wind up in Siberia.

Cluff believes that there is "a substantial amount of scientific, historical, and scriptural evidence" to support the hollow-earth theory. And among the evidence is the testimony of two explorers: Admiral Byrd of the U. S. Navy and fisherman Olaf Jansen.

Admiral Byrd actually entered the North Polar opening, according to Cluff; but his testimony has been suppressed by the government. In February 1947, Byrd piloted a plane north from a base in Alaska. He flew beyond the North Pole and over the Arctic Ocean. To his astonishment, says Cluff, he found himself flying over "a land covered with vegetation, lakes and rivers and even saw a prehistoric-type mammoth in the underbrush." His flight had taken him into the polar opening. And there he discovered a continent.

But then the inevitable happened:

> So great was this fabulous discovery by Admiral Richard Byrd, that news of it was quickly suppressed.... U.S. Navy Intelligence clamped down on any further publication of the greatest geographical discovery in history. Henceforth, Our Hollow Earth has been the WORLD'S TOP SECRET!*

---

* Whether Admiral Byrd did in fact make such a flight remains a matter of controversy. The source for the story is *Worlds Beyond the Poles* by Amadeo Giannini (Vantage Press, 1959). In this rambling tract, Giannini claims to have seen a newspaper article about the flight. (The article has yet to be tracked down.) And he quotes a radio announcement that Byrd supposedly made just before taking off: "I'd like to see that land beyond the Pole. That

The testimony of Admiral Byrd may have been suppressed; but it was too late to suppress that of Olaf Jansen. A century earlier, the Norwegian fisherman had sailed into the North Polar opening. There he encountered members of an advanced civilization. He was taken on a tour of their cities, and introduced to their ruler. On his deathbed Jansen entrusted a manuscript—an account of his voyage—to novelist Willard George Emerson. Emerson edited the text and published it as *The Smoky God*.

The Smoky God has served as the inspiration for the voyage that Cluff is planning. For he hopes not only to find the polar opening, but to make contact with that advanced civilization.

Here is an ad for Cluff's book, taken from his Web site:

> *World Top Secret: Our Earth Is Hollow!* is the volume you have been waiting for! At last, here stands revealed the secrets of that beautiful land beyond the poles discovered by United States Admiral Richard Evelyn Byrd.
>
> The Contents page of *World Top Secret: Our Earth Is Hollow!* reads like an advertisement of LOST and FOUND!: The Garden of Eden—FOUND! The Land of the Lost Ten Tribes—FOUND! The Origin of Flying Saucers—FOUND! The Throne of David—FOUND! Paradise—FOUND! The City of Enoch—FOUND! The Celestial Destiny of Our Hollow Earth, the scientific evidence including, The Auroras, Van Allen Radiation Belts and Earthquakes Prove Our

area beyond the Pole is the center of the great unknown!"

It is true that a purported flight log has been published. *The Missing Diary of Admiral Byrd* (Inner Light Publications, 1992) offers a detailed account of his flight. It recounts his descent into the North Polar opening; his visit to a crystalline city; and his audience with a Master. ("You, my son, are to return to the Surface World with this message....") But *The Missing Diary* is almost certainly a fabrication.

Byrd's actual memoirs, believes Cluff, "are kept under lock and key. Which all points to the need for a private organization...to fit out an expedition to the pole and beyond and establish to the world BEYOND DOUBT that that land does indeed EXIST!"

Earth Is Hollow!—plus 5 more revealing chapters which prove and establish with evidence upon evidence that Our Earth is INDEED Hollow and inhabited within by a race of SUPER GIANTS.

If the book were simply a treatise in support of the hollow-earth theory, it would take its place among the writings of Captain Symmes and other proponents of the theory. But *World Top Secret: Our Earth Is Hollow!* is much more than that. Its basic theme is religious. For Cluff believes that the Lost Tribes of Israel migrated to the Arctic, in search of the Garden of Eden. And descending into the polar opening, they found it—on the interior continent.

The tribes took up residence in that terrestrial paradise. And they inhabit it still, having evolved into giants with a life span of centuries. And having established the Kingdom of God—which will someday spread to the entire earth.*

The goal of the North Pole Inner Earth Expedition is to locate the polar opening. (It is thought to be in the vicinity of Ellesmere Island, and about ninety miles wide.) But the ultimate goal is even more ambitious:

> Our hope is to make contact with the civilization that inhabits inner earth. We go in peace with the hope of re-uniting outer earth with inner earth with a get acquainted meeting up near the pole. Dr. Agnew [the leader of the Expedition] doesn't think the owners of the *Yamal* will let us enter the polar opening and risk their hardware, but we are hopeful we will get close enough to find evidence of its existence and that perhaps we can be met there by Inner Worlders who may give some of us a brief visit to their Inner Earth realm aboard one of their craft.

Like Olaf Jansen before him, Rodney Cluff may soon be getting acquainted with giants!

For anyone interested in joining the Expedition, there

---

* The *heavenly* paradise, believes Cluff, is located in the interior sun. Suspended at the center of the earth, that orb is the throne of Jehovah and the home of the righteous dead.

are still berths available on the *Yamal*. (The ship is described as "a literal motel on ice, with utmost in comforts and amenities.") Cluff emphasizes that no guarantees are made of finding the polar opening. Still, the voyage promises to be a fulfilling experience. Among the activities on board will be Aurora Borealis watches; classes in marine biology, polar astronomy, and hollow-earth studies; human consciousness training; and concerts.

What is assured is that the *Yamal*—a 70,000-horsepower icebreaker—will reach the North Pole. Upon which, a pole will be driven into the ice; and members of the Expedition will dance about it in celebration.

APPENDIX I

How to Visit the Inner Earth

A VISIT TO THE INNER EARTH CAN BE BOTH INSTRUCtive AND exciting. Who knows what hidden things you may behold—what unique beings you may encounter—what advanced civilization you may discover. Are you interested in such an adventure? If so, here's how to proceed.

First, locate an entrance to the Inner Earth. Surprisingly, there are many of them. Almost all are in caves.*

Once you have located an entrance, assemble your gear. It should include the following:

STURDY SHOES

SWEATER

WATER BOTTLE

COMPASS

BREAD CRUMBS (for leaving a trail in the cave)

SUNGLASSES (the central sun can be bright)

LEMURIAN PHRASE BOOK

And find some friends to accompany you. *Never enter a cave alone.* Also, notify the local authorities of your plans. Should a rescue become necessary, you want them to know where you are.

---

* An exception is the entrance said to exist beneath a Manhattan hotel. Supposedly, a service elevator takes you into a subbasement and comes to a halt. Then, if you press twice on the down button, the elevator slides sideways into another shaft—and descends into the depths of the earth.

APPENDIX I

When exploring a cave, there's another basic rule: *Always carry three sources of light.* You need backups, in case of battery failure or other mishap (such as a Dero snatching your flashlight and running off with it). True, you'll be encountering mysterious sources of light. But until then, you are dependent on your flashlight. So bring along at least three of them—I myself carry four.

As you descend further into the cave, watch your step; the ground will be rough and uneven. Don't hit your head on a stalactite. And follow any markings that previous visitors have left to indicate the way. Should you come upon a colony of bats—asleep overhead—tiptoe past them. You don't need an eruption of bats to welcome you to the Inner Earth.

How will you know that you've actually entered the Inner Earth? Simple—you'll encounter one of those mysterious lights. I am shown here approaching such a light. I advance with caution. For the source of the light could be anything— the flashlight of a fellow visitor... the torch of a Lemurian... the campfire of a band of Teros... a luminous creature. Or even a Master, whose aura makes him a beacon in the dark.

APPENDIX I

Then I discern the source of the light—and my jaw drops!

Set upon a rock is a small pyramid. Lit up like a lamp, it casts an eerie glow onto the walls of the cave. Such pyramids are a unique feature of the Inner Earth. *They are repositories of Cosmic Energy.*

APPENDIX I

Should you happen upon one of these pyramids, here's what to do. Approach it and take it into your hands.

HOW TO VISIT THE INNER EARTH

Now sit down and bathe yourself in the light that emanates from it. Let this light flow into your soul. Drink deeply of this elixir. *And your soul with fill with Cosmic Energy.*

APPENDIX I

At this point you have a choice to make. You can descend further into the Inner Earth—and perhaps make contact with that advanced civilization. Or you can consider yourself fulfilled, and proceed no further.

I would advise the latter. After all, you're probably tired and hungry. As for a meal, why not send out for some Chinese food? While awaiting delivery, you can continue to bathe yourself in the light of the pyramid.*

Dine with gusto. And then it's back to the surface. Your visit to the Inner Earth has concluded. And it has been a memorable experience.

---

* Many Chinese restaurants will deliver anywhere—even into the depths of a cave. (Be sure to give the deliveryman a generous tip.) I am shown here with an order of chicken lo mein, fried rice, and egg roll. And, of course, a fortune cookie, with its prediction or words of wisdom.

APPENDIX 2

Reactions to *Etidorhpa*

IN 1895 JOHN URI LLOYD SENT COPIES OF THE BOOK *Etidorhpa*—"the Strange History of a Mysterious Being"—to newspapers, journals, and select individuals. The preface was credited to Lloyd; but the author of the work itself was not identified. It was widely, and favorably, reviewed. Some deemed it to be a work of fiction:

> The book may be described as a sort of philosophical fiction, containing much exact scientific truth, many bold theories, and much ingenious speculation on the nature and destiny of man. (Dr. W. H. Venable)

And the author of this fiction? Lloyd, of course, was the prime suspect:

> No one could have written the chapter on the "Food of Man" but Professor Lloyd; no one else knows and thinks of these subjects in a similar way.... those who hear Professor Lloyd lecture catch Lloyd's impulses throughout. (*Eclectic Medical Journal*)

> Professor Lloyd's style is quaint and polished, and perfectly clear. (*British and Colonial Druggist*)

> Etidorhpa, the End of the Earth, is in all respects the worthiest presentation of occult teachings under the attractive guise of fiction that has yet been written. Its author, Mr. John Uri Lloyd, of Cincinnati, as a scientist and writer on pharmaceutical topics, has already a more than national reputation, but only his most intimate friends have been aware that he was an advanced student of occultism. (*New York World*)

Others were at a loss to describe the book:

APPENDIX 2

The work stands so entirely alone in literature, and possesses such a marvelous versatility of thought and idea, that, in describing it, we are at a loss for comparison. In its scope it comprises alchemy, chemistry, science in general, philosophy, metaphysics, morals, biology, sociology, theosophy, materialism, and theism—the natural and supernatural. ...It is almost impossible to describe the character of the work. (*Chicago Medical Times*)

While others simply praised it as a unique work:

All in all, *Etidorhpa* is a book *sui generis*...a book to stir the pulse, stir the brain, and stir the heart. (*The Christian Standard*)

A book which is not like any other book in the world. (*Indianapolis Journal*)

The reading of *Etidorhpa* has given me unspeakable pleasure. It is a work of rare genius. Every page excites a cumulative interest. (*Wooster Christian Advocate*)

Etidorhpa had been privately printed by Lloyd; but it soon found a commercial publisher. The book sold well, and would go through twelve printings. Lloyd used the profits to finance the construction and endowment of a library.*

But tastes change. A history of science fiction describes *Etidorhpa* as "unreadable." And today it is a forgotten work, known mainly to hollow-earth researchers.

Those researchers still debate whether the book is fact or fiction. And whether its author was Professor Lloyd, Llew-

---

* The Lloyd Library survives to the present day. It is the largest collection of books on botanical medicine. At its core is Lloyd's own library. But in its basement are kept the orphaned libraries of the Eclectic Medicine schools. As those schools closed, their books were shipped to the main school in Cincinnati. Finally, it too shut down; and all of its books were transferred to the Lloyd Library.

ellyn Drury, or the mysterious stranger.*

---

* The identity of the mysterious stranger has been the subject of speculation. The leading candidate is Captain William Morgan (1775–?), whose residence (upstate New York), membership in a secret society (the Freemasons), and fate (abduction and disappearance) correspond to those of the stranger.

In Masonic circles William Morgan was an infamous figure. He wrote a book titled *Illustrations of Masonry*, which revealed the secrets of the order. Just before its publication, he was abducted. And Morgan disappeared, with suspicion that he had been murdered. The incident sparked widespread protests against the Masons, and the formation of an anti-Masonic political party.

Whoever he was, Drury's visitor would seem to have been a ghost—a disembodied spirit. But how then to explain the manuscript he left behind? Perhaps Drury listened to the ghost tell its story, then drafted the manuscript himself.

Or perhaps the author simply employed a literary device—that of the found manuscript. (See Appendix 3.)

APPENDIX 3
Found Manuscripts

A FOUND MANUSCRIPT IS ONE THAT AN AUTHOR claims TO have acquired, rather than written. Supposedly, it was left on his doorstep, or discovered in an attic, or handed to him by a stranger. The author may take credit for editing or translating the text; but that is the extent, he insists, of his contribution.

The following are some examples.

The Beekeeper's Apprentice

One afternoon, at her home in California, novelist Laurie King received a mysterious delivery from UPS. (Or so she claims, in an Editor's Preface to *The Beekeeper's Apprentice*.) An anonymous person had shipped her an old-fashioned trunk, adorned with hotel stickers. Its contents included a cloak, a magnifying glass, a necklace, a length of fabric later identified as an unwound turban, a monocle, an English railway schedule for 1923, a box of newspaper clippings—and a trove of manuscripts.

Each of these manuscripts was bound with purple ribbon. Most were handwritten; some were typed. They purported to be the memoirs of a woman named Mary Russell.

As King read through them, a fantastical story emerged. For Mary Russell describes her friendship, partnership, and marriage with Sherlock Holmes! The detective had retired to Sussex, according to Russell, and taken up beekeeping. One morning she encountered and chatted with him on the Sussex Downs. Impressed with her deductive powers, Holmes began to train young Russell as a detective. Soon they were working on cases together. And finally, in 1921, they married.

These writings were the work of an elderly Russell. And

they describe—in novelistic detail—her life with Holmes. But how were they meant to be taken? Were they not in fact novels, rather than memoirs? After all, Sherlock Holmes was a fictional character, was he not?*

Mary Russell had anticipated the issue. In *The Beekeeper's Apprentice* she declares:

> Why, it would not even surprise me to find my own memoirs classified as fiction.... Nonetheless, I must assert that the following pages recount the early days and years of my true-life association with Sherlock Holmes.

On the question of fact or fiction, Laurie King was undecided (though inclined toward fact). Nor was she able to

---

* It is true that "biographies" of Holmes have been published. But these are the work of Sherlockians or Holmesians (as they are called)—enthusiasts who treat the detective as if he had actually lived.

learn who had shipped the trunk to her, or if Mary Russell was still living. Despite these uncertainties, she set out to edit and publish the manuscripts. *The Beekeeper's Apprentice* was the first to appear, in 1994. (Nine more would follow.)

So is it a novel? Moreover, *is it a novel by Laurie King herself*—one that employs the literary device of a found manuscript? In her preface, King issued a denial:

> The first thing I want the reader to know is that I had nothing to do with this book you have in your hand. Yes, I write mystery novels, but even a novelist's fevered imagination has its limits, and mine would reach those limits long before it came up with the farfetched idea of Sherlock Holmes taking on a smart-mouthed, half-American, fifteen-year-old feminist sidekick.

Such denials, of course, are a standard feature of the literary device.

She

In his introduction to *She*, H. Rider Haggard informs the reader:

> In giving to the world the record of...one of the most wonderful and mysterious experiences ever undergone by mortal men, I feel it incumbent on me to explain what my exact connection with it is. And so I may as well say at once that I am not the narrator but only the editor of this extraordinary history, and then go on to tell how it found its way into my hands.

According to Haggard, he had received a manuscript in the mail. Attached was a letter from the author, asking him to find a publisher for this factual account. Haggard did so; and the book was published in 1887. It was an immediate and enduring success. Over the next century, more than 80 million copies of *She* would be sold.

The narrator of *She* recounts a visit to Kôr, a lost kingdom in Africa. He and his companions become entangled with Ayesha, the ruler of the kingdom. Ayesha is an Egyptian sorceress, thousands of years old yet beautiful—and whose gaze is hypnotic. Romance and adventure ensue.

Haggard went on to publish more such tales (though none of the successors involved a found manuscript). He has been called the father of the lost-world novel.

The City of Light

The City of Light was published in Great Britain in 1997. Jacob d'Ancona was named as its author; David Selbourne, as its translator and editor. The dust jacket offered this information:

> In 1990 distinguished academic David Selbourne was shown a remarkable manuscript which had been hidden from public view for over seven centuries. In it a scholarly Jewish merchant called Jacob described how in 1270 he had set out on a voyage from Italy, arriving in China at the coastal metropolis of Zaitun, the "City of Light," in 1271—four years before Marco Polo's arrival at Xanadu in 1275.
>
> As David Selbourne studied it more closely, he realised that Jacob's magisterial account of this journey was an extraordinary find. As the manuscript's owner was unprepared for him to disclose its location, David Selbourne was forced to wrestle with doubts about translating a manuscript to which others would not have access, but decided that his overriding duty was to bring its contents to wider attention.

The book was published by Little, Brown and Company (UK). And it did receive attention, attracting both readers and controversy. The controversy arose among British scholars, several of whom denounced the work as a fraud.

The accusers based their opinion on anachronisms, inconsistencies, and other anomalies that they perceived in the text. Nor was it likely, in their view, that such a voyage had taken place, or that a detailed account of it would sud-

APPENDIX 3

denly turn up. But what truly aroused their suspicion was the unavailability of the manuscript. This "extraordinary find," which Selbourne had supposedly translated and edited, was not available for examination.

The manuscript, explains Selbourne in his introduction to the book, had been in the possession of an Italian Jewish family for generations. Subsequently, it was acquired by the present owner. This man approached Selbourne, a political scientist living in Italy, and offered to show it to him. Intrigued, Selbourne visited the man's home and viewed the manuscript. It consisted, he says, of 280 leaves, bound in vellum. The handwriting was italic. The text was medieval Italian.

According to Selbourne, the owner gave him permission to translate and publish the contents of the manuscript. However, on account of unresolved ownership issues, certain conditions had to be met. The owner's name could be not revealed; the manuscript could not be removed from his house, or even photocopied; and no mention could be made of its location. Selbourne agreed to these conditions. And working in the owner's home, he translated the text.

But the skeptics found this story dubious, and demanded to see the manuscript. And when Selbourne refused to reveal its whereabouts—"a matter of honor and of gratitude," he said—they accused him of fraud. Obviously, they concluded, there was no medieval manuscript. *The City of Light* was a work of fiction, masquerading as a factual account.

Yet why would Selbourne—a "distinguished academic," according to his publisher—have perpetrated such a fraud? Various theories were put forward. His motivation was mercenary: he wanted to create a stir and sell books. Or he wanted a platform for his unorthodox political and social views. (Political debates—between the sages and merchants of Zaitun—are a feature of the book.) Or he was seeking revenge on the academic world. (Selbourne had lost his teaching job at Oxford, on account of those views.)

But Selbourne did not lack supporters. A professor at the University of London remarked:

He told me, looking me in the face, that this is genuine. I tend to believe in what people tell me. I believe him an honorable man, but some of the criticisms are fairly difficult to counter. What we're all waiting for is him to come out of his corner with his manuscript.

And Wang Lian-mao, director of the Maritime Museum in Quanzhou (formerly Zaitun), believed that Jacob d'Ancona had indeed visited his city. "Somebody who was not actually there could not have recorded things in this way."

The debate grew heated. And the skeptics claimed to have found a smoking gun: those political debates. The ideas articulated by an elderly sage of Zaitun, they had discovered, were remarkably similar to those advocated by Selbourne himself—in a book titled *The Principle of Duty*.

Of course they were, retorted Selbourne. For he had first encountered those ideas in the travel journal of Jacob d'Ancona, and had embraced them!

In any case, a cloud of suspicion continues to darken *The City of Light*. It will be dispelled when that manuscript is produced.

Under the Moons of Mars

In 1912 *Under the Moons of Mars* was serialized in *All-Story* magazine. It recounts the adventures of Captain John Carter on the planet Mars (or "Barsoom," as the Martians call it). The author was Edgar Rice Burroughs.

For the 36-year-old Burroughs, it was his first published work. He was working at the time for a company that manufactured stationery, and had written much of the book on its scratch pads. In a foreword, however, he claims that the manuscript had been bequeathed to him by Captain Carter.

Under the Moons of Mars was later issued in book form, under the title *A Princess of Mars*. Ten sequels followed—four of which were presented as found manuscripts.

APPENDIX 3

The Book of Deuteronomy

During the reign of King Josiah, repairs were being made to the Temple; and workmen discovered—hidden away, or forgotten in a corner—a scroll. This "Book of the Law" (or Deuteronomy, as it came to be called) seemingly originated with Moses. The high priest brought the scroll to Shaphan, the chief scribe, who brought it to the king. And Josiah tore his clothes and wept, and vowed to revive these neglected laws.

Josiah used the book as a rationale for reforms (in particular, the centralizing of worship in Jerusalem). That has led some critics to suspect that the "Book of the Law" was his own creation—a work compiled at the behest of Josiah, planted in the Temple (by the high priest perhaps), and used to justify his reforms. In other words, a pious fraud.

Who might have compiled such a work? A likely suspect would be Shaphan, the chief scribe. He was closely involved in the affair, enjoyed the confidence of the king, and was skilled as a writer.

A History of New-York

In the fall of 1809, a series of notices appeared in the *New-York Evening Post*. The first, on October 26, reported the disappearance of "a small elderly gentleman, dressed in an old black coat and cocked hat, by the name of *Knickerbocker*," and requested that any information concerning his whereabouts be left at the Columbian Hotel.

Eleven days later a second notice appeared. It was signed by "A Traveller"—a passenger on the stagecoach to Albany, who claimed to have sighted Knickerbocker. The old man was resting, bag in hand, by the side of the road.

On November 16 a third notice appeared. This one was signed by the proprietor of the Columbian Hotel. It read as follows:

You have been good enough to publish in your paper a

paragraph about Mr. *Diedrich Knickerbocker*, who was missing so strangely some time since. Nothing satisfactory has been heard of the old gentleman since; but *a very curious kind of a written book* has been found in his room, in his own handwriting. Now I wish you to notice him, if he is still alive, that if he does not return and pay off his bill for boarding and lodging, I shall have to dispose of his book to satisfy me for the same.

Finally, on November 28, an advertisement appeared:

LITERARY NOTICE

INSKEEP & BRADFORD have in press, and will shortly publish,

A HISTORY OF NEW-YORK,

In two volumes, duodecimo. Price Three Dollars.

Containing an account of its discovery and settlement, with its internal policies, manners, customs, wars, &c., &c., under the Dutch government, furnishing many curious and interesting particulars never before published, and which are gathered from various manuscript and other authenticated sources, the whole being interspersed with philosophical speculations and moral precepts.

This work was found in the chamber of Mr. Diedrich Knickerbocker, the old gentleman whose sudden and mysterious disappearance has been noticed. It is published in order to discharge certain debts he has left behind.

A week later, *A History of New-York* became available at booksellers. The title page named Diedrich Knickerbocker as the author. The book—a seriocomic history of the Dutch colony—was an immediate success, both critically and commercially.

And the true identity of the author became known. "Knickerbocker" was a young, aspiring writer named Washington Irving. The notices in the *Evening Post* had been a hoax, perpetrated by Irving and his friends—a publicity stunt designed to draw attention to his book.

APPENDIX 3

Thus was launched the career of the father of American literature—with a found manuscript.

Ben and Me

Ben and Me is subtitled "*A New and Astonishing Life of Benjamin Franklin As Written by his Good Mouse Amos, Lately Discovered, Edited & Illustrated by Robert Lawson.*" As for the origin of the book:

> The manuscript which forms this book was sent to me recently by an architect friend. While altering an old Philadelphia house, workmen uncovered a small chamber beneath a bedroom hearthstone. This tiny room, for such it appeared to be, was about eighteen inches square. It contained various small articles of furniture, all of the Colonial Period. In one of these, a secretary desk, was found a manuscript book, the leaves of which, about the size of postage stamps, were covered with minute writing.

The manuscript was shown to experts, says Lawson. They determined that the paper and ink were eighteenth-century; a quill pen had been used; and the handwriting ("incredible as it might seem," conceded the experts) was that of a mouse.

With the aid of a magnifying glass, the manuscript could be read. It was an account of Benjamin Franklin's career—from a unique perspective. For it was written by a mouse named Amos, who had befriended Franklin, taken up residence in his house, and assisted him with his inventions and discoveries.

A writer and illustrator of children's books, Lawson says he edited the text (correcting errors of spelling and grammar); provided illustrations; and found a publisher. And while Amos's account differed in many respects from standard biographies of Franklin, Lawson was convinced that "statements made by one who lived on terms of such intimacy with this great man should be more trustworthy than those written by later scholars."

Ben and Me is recognized as a classic of children's literature. Needless to say, it is fictional. No tiny manuscript was found in a mouse-hole. (Although when I read the book as a child, I thought about it for a moment...and accepted that the author was a mouse.)

The Zohar

The *Sefer ha-Zohar*, or "Book of Splendor," is the central text of the mystical tradition known as Kabbala. It was disseminated in the thirteenth century by Moses de Leon, a rabbi residing in Spain. De Leon did not declare himself, however, to be the author of the work. Rather, he had transcribed it, he said, from an ancient manuscript.

The manuscript (or at least its Aramaic text) dated back to the second century—or so claimed de Leon. And the author was Simeon ben Yohai, the great sage of that era. For thirteen years ben Yohai had lived in a cave. During that time he produced the main body of the Zohar. He based it on oral teachings that had come down from Moses, and on revelations from the prophet Elijah (whose spirit visited him in the cave). Subsequently, his disciples—and then their disciples—added more material.

By the thirteenth century the manuscript had found its way to Spain. And there it came into the possession of de Leon. A student of Kabbala, he became obsessed with the profundities of the Zohar. He began to copy out passages and distribute them to other Kabbalists.

But the manuscript itself he showed to no one; and its existence was soon called into question. He was accused of composing the Zohar himself and falsely ascribing it to ben Yohai. There was no ancient manuscript! A controversy arose that has continued to the present day. Skeptics have pointed to anachronisms in the text. But others have argued that these are interpolations, made by latter-day copyists or editors.

Did Moses de Leon transcribe the Zohar from an ancient manuscript? Or was he in fact its author? That is to say, did he himself compile the Zohar (drawing on a variety of oral and written sources)—and then, to lend it an aura of authority, ascribe the work to ben Yohai (though a portion of it may indeed have originated with the sage)?

As the debate continued, conflicting testimony emerged. A detractor claimed that, after de Leon's death, his widow had denied the existence of the manuscript. But also reported was a statement by de Leon: he had sworn under oath that "the ancient book written by Simeon ben Yohai" was in his possession.

So who wrote the Zohar—the second-century sage or the medieval Kabbalist? (Or did many hands contribute to it—a collaboration down through the ages?) The jury is still out.

I Have Been in the Caves

The lead story in the January 1947 issue of *Amazing Stories* was "I Have Been in the Caves" (see chapter 21). According to editor Ray Palmer, it was a true story. The manuscript had been sent to him, he claimed, by Margaret Rogers, a reader in Texas. Supposedly, Rogers had spent several weeks in the cavern world; and the story was an account of her experiences there.

But had Palmer actually received a manuscript in the mail? Or had he written the story himself? (Its style is polished—more like that of a practiced pulpster than of a reader in Texas.) Was this just the latest chapter in the shenanigans known as the Shaver Mystery?

The Book of King Solomon

The Book of King Solomon is a series of tales about the legendary monarch. Published in 2005, the work is credited to "Ahimaaz, Court Historian." And it was "discovered, translated, and annotated by Professor Solomon." That is to say, by me.

In an introductory note, I describe my acquisition of the manuscript:

> When she pushed aside a stack of newspapers and opened her bread box, I assumed that Aunt Rose was about to offer me a stale pastry. Instead, she extracted a bundle of brittle sheets of paper, tied with string. The topmost sheet was inscribed with Hebrew lettering. Stored in her bread box had been some sort of manuscript.
> "I've wondered what to do with this," she said, and thrust it into my hands.

These Hebrew writings, Aunt Rose told me, had been handed down in the family. Determined to preserve them, her late husband had brought them over from Hungary. I thanked her and stuffed the bundle into my knapsack.

When I got home and examined the manuscript, I could scarcely believe my eyes. For I was in possession of a life of King Solomon, attributed to his court historian!

But was it in fact an ancient chronicle? Or was it a pseudepigraph—a work attributed to an esteemed person of the past, to lend it an aura of authority? Who was the true author of these tales?

In discussing the possibilities, I did not exclude myself

APPENDIX 3

as a suspect:

> And it will no doubt be conjectured that I myself am the pseudepigrapher—that my "translation" is a literary hoax, a contemporary work of fiction—that there was no manuscript in a bread box. But I can assure the reader (though my assurance could be taken to be part of the hoax) that such is not the case.
>
> In fact, the reader is welcome to inspect the original manuscript—to which some bread crumbs still accrue!*
>
> So—is *The Book of King Solomon* fact or fiction? An ancient chronicle or a latter-day fabrication? A sensational find or a literary hoax?
>
> Whatever the case, it is an engaging book—highly recommended to anyone wanting to learn more about "the wisest of men," his place in history, and his relevance today.

---

* Though I seem to have misplaced it, somewhere amid the chaos of my books and papers. (Or could it have been stolen?) But when I find it, it will be made available for inspection.

Other books by Professor Solomon:

How to Find Lost Objects

by Professor Solomon

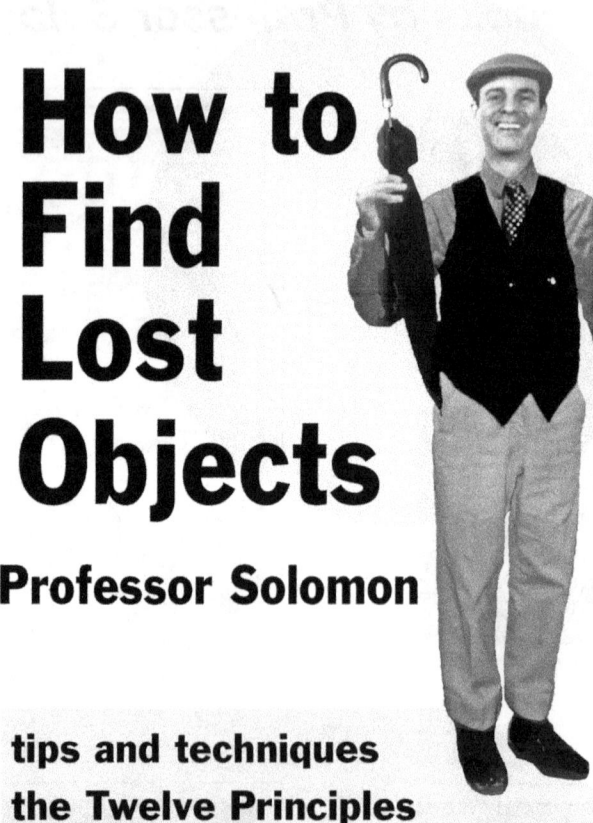

- **tips and techniques**
- **the Twelve Principles**
- **instructions for making your own thinking cap and Eureka-Stik**
- **a complete strategy for locating what you lose**

His amazing method!

To download a free copy of this book, go to:
http://www.professorsolomon.com/lobookpage.html

"The Book of King Solomon"
A life of King Solomon, written by his court historian!
Translated and Annotated by Professor Solomon

King Solomon reigned in Jerusalem, from 973 to 933, and was deemed to be the wisest of men. These tales chronicle his life and legend.

To download a free copy of this book, go to:
http://www.professorsolomon.com/kingsolomonpage.html

Also by Professor Solomon:
"How to Make the Most of a Flying Saucer Experience"

A comprehensive and entertaining guide to UFOs.

Includes tales of contactees, facts about the Space People, and numerous illustrations. Plus, Professor Solomon's tips—for making the most of a flying saucer experience!

To download a free copy of this book, go to:
http://www.professorsolomon.com/ufobookpage.html

"Japan in a Nutshell"
by Professor Solomon

At last, the unknown Japan. The traditional Japan. The *real* Japan. In this erudite yet entertaining work, the Professor explores a Japan of which few of us are aware. For a tour of a unique culture—a fascinating look at its diverse ways and wonders—join him.

To download a free copy of this book, go to:
http://www.professorsolomon.com/japanbookpage.html

Also by Professor Solomon:
"Coney Island"
A history and profile of the legendary amusement area

To download a free copy of this book, go to:
http://www.professorsolomon.com/cibookpage.html

www.ingramcontent.com/pod-product-compliance
Lightning Source LLC
Chambersburg PA
CBHW061423040426
42450CB00007B/883